Lights and Shadows

of

Army Life:

or,

Pen Pictures from the Battlefield, the Camp, and the Hospital.

By REV. W. W. LYLE, A. M.,
CHAPLAIN ELEVENTH REGIMENT, O. V. I., U. S. A.

THIRD EDITION.

CINCINNATI:
R. W. CARROLL & CO., Publishers,
73 WEST FOURTH STREET,
OPERA-HOUSE BUILDING.
1865.

STEREOTYPED AT THE
FRANKLIN TYPE FOUNDRY,
CINCINNATI, O.

TO

COLONEL P. P. LANE,

ELEVENTH REGIMENT OHIO VOLUNTEERS,

This Volume

IS DEDICATED,

AS AN HUMBLE TRIBUTE OF RESPECT FOR HIS PURE PATRIOTISM; HIS ARDENT DEVOTION TO THE CAUSE OF HUMAN LIBERTY; HIS BRAVERY AS A SOLDIER; HIS RESPECT FOR AND INTEREST IN OUR UNION DEFENDERS;

AND AS AN HUMBLE BUT SINCERE ACKNOWLEDGMENT OF THE INTEREST HE EVER MANIFESTED IN THE MORAL AND RELIGIOUS WELFARE OF HIS COMMAND.

THE AUTHOR.

CONTENTS.

CHAPTER VIII.

CHAPTER IX.

CHAPTER X.

CHAPTER XI.

CHAPTER XII.

CHAPTER XIII.

CHAPTER XIV.

CHAPTER XV.

CHAPTER XVI.

CHAPTER XVII.

CHAPTER XXVII.

CHAPTER XXVIII.

CHAPTER XXIX.

PREFACE.

It is said that a preface is seldom read. From this it has been inferred that it is unnecessary to write one. Some literary oracles have even gone further, and asserted that it is a violation of good taste to detain the reader at the threshold of a book, and compel him to endure several pages of prefatory explanations, which, at the best, are but covert egotisms, when, it is to be presumed, he is desirous of entering at once upon the work of examining the book itself. Others, with equal authority, declare that a proper regard for the claims of etiquette demands that strangers be introduced to each other by a third party, and that the same rule holds good in the literary world. Whatever opinion may be adopted on this not very important question, the general practice seems to be in favor of the time-honored custom of making at least a bow to the reader before thrusting upon his attention the full contents of a volume. It is generally safe, in matters of mere etiquette, to follow established customs. In the present instance it is considered not only safe, but necessary.

A few sentences will comprise all that need be said in this prefatory note.

And, first, the book is not a history of the war; it makes no such pretensions. Even in the brief sketches given of several severe battles, such as South Mountain, Antietam, Chickamauga, etc., no attempt is made at elaborate details. The sketches themselves are merely outline pictures, with here and there some scene of touching pathos, a bright beam of sunshine, perhaps, against a dark background, or some humorous incident reproduced, and thrown in, by way of relief, to some somber shadows. It is believed that, however rough the outlines may be, they are faithfully and correctly sketched. More accomplished artists may glance at such outlines, drawn, as they have been, amid the excitements and dangers of the camp and field, and which have been traced by those who mingled in the scenes described; they may correct all the erratic lines of the humble sketchers, fill in where there were only unmeaning blanks, finish what was unfinished and imperfect, and leave, for the admiration and safe-keeping of future generations, critically correct and elaborately finished pictures, that will live and be admired ages after such humble sketches as the following will have been buried beneath the waves of oblivion.

However imperfectly the work of tracing the LIGHTS AND SHADOWS OF ARMY LIFE may have been done, it has been a labor of love. Undertaken at the repeated and urgent solicitation of friends, both in and out of the army, it has been prosecuted with a twofold purpose, namely, to pay an humble tribute to the bravery, integrity, and moral worth of our patriot heroes, and bring before the Christian public facts connected with the religious experiences of our soldiers in the field, and place upon record facts and incidents which testify to the saving power of the Gospel. Other and abler pens have given thrilling narratives of the devotion, zeal, unflinching courage, and heroic endurance of our brave defenders, and others will yet be employed in the same noble work. While the author has by no means ignored such a worthy theme, but has recorded, in the following pages, numerous incidents of bravery and endurance, he has sought, at the same time, to bring out, in bold relief, the less imposing, but not less important and interesting, facts connected with the living and dying of our patriot heroes. Nearly three years' service in the army, both East and West, afforded ample opportunities to notice the fruits of religious culture and effort upon the soldier, whether he was resting in camp, or was on the long, weary march; amid the dread scenes of the battlefield, or in the wards of the hospital. While the author, therefore, has grouped together incidents of the camp, or sketched tragic scenes and heroic deeds on the battlefield, given here or there some humorous occurrences, or traced some army movements, he has endeavored to keep steadily in view the moral and religious elements connected with the army. The saving power of the Gospel of the Son of God, the strength which is imparted to the heart of man, through faith in our Lord Jesus Christ, and which buoys him up amid the most trying and terrific earthly scenes—the cheering influences of religious hope and trust in the hour of sickness, and amid heart longings and loneliness, together with the glorious triumphs of the believing soul in the hour of death, have all been exemplified in the army; and the following pages have been primarily devoted to the recording of such facts and incidents as illustrate these truths.

To all who love our Lord Jesus Christ, and who labor and pray for the salvation of the world; to all whose hearts thrill with patriotic ardor and devotion at the sight of that dear old flag—dearer now than ever, because stained with the life-blood of Freedom's martyrs—and which is the emblem of peace to "men of good will," and the emblem of liberty to the oppressed of all nations; to all who love and honor the memories of our fallen heroes, and who treat with respect and honor our living defenders; to all who labor, by word and deed, in behalf of our beloved country; to all who are willing to make every sacrifice in order to hand down to coming generations an unbroken, unimpaired, and untarnished heritage of freedom; to the weeping fathers and mothers and wives and children of those who have fallen in battle, and to the noble women of the land, who have labored so heroically and perseveringly to sustain the thrice-blessed Sanitary and Christian Commissions—to all such does the author humbly commend this unpretending volume, with the prayer that it may not only interest, but instruct and comfort, every reader.

Note.—A word, by way of explanation, relative to some features of a local character connected with the volume. In order to relieve the book from any undue prominence of merely local, or rather, regimental interest, and yet weave into the general narrative outline sketches of regimental history, the author, at the suggestion of friends in whose wisdom he could trust, has simply noted matters of general interest connected with the history and movements of the Eleventh Ohio Regiment, of which he had the honor of being chaplain, and thrown into an appendix items of interest to those who had friends in the regiment. To the friends of those connected with the Eleventh it will be an interesting feature of this work. The intention was to give an abridged history of the regiment proper, but this was found to be impracticable. A list of those killed in battle or who died of wounds or disease is given. The author has spared no pains to make it as reliable and interesting as possible.

Lights and Shadows of Army Life.

CHAPTER I.

O Star-spangled Banner! the Flag of our pride!
Though trampled by traitors and basely defied,
Fling out to the glad winds your Red, White, and Blue,
For the heart of the Northland is beating for you!
And her strong arm is nerving to strike with a will,
Till the foe and his boastings are humbled and still!
Here's welcome to wounding and combat and scars,
And the glory of death—for the Stripes and the Stars!

From prairie, O plowman! speed boldly away—
There's seed to be sown in God's furrows to-day!
Row landward, lone fisher! stout woodman, come home!
Let smith leave his anvil, and weaver his loom,
And hamlet and city ring loud with the cry,
"For God and our country we'll fight till we die!
Here's welcome to wounding and combat and scars,
And the glory of death—for the Stripes and the Stars!"

E. D. Proctor.

Introductory.

In all ages of the world the military hero has been applauded, his name recorded in history, and his deeds celebrated in song. The chisel of the sculptor, the pencil of the painter, the harp of the minstrel, and the pen of the historian have vied with each other in paying honors to his genius and in eulogizing his bravery. While the more prominent or more fortunate of those who have hewed with their swords a pathway to fame have been thus immortalized by history and art, the humble ballad literature of various nations, distinguished more for its chivalrous spirit and adaptation to the necessities of a rude age, than for its elegance of diction or literary taste, has embalmed, in rustic song or simple melody, the memories of less noted, but no less honorable, heroes of humbler name.

Many of those thus honored, however, although brave in personal daring, and great in military genius, neither drew their swords in defense of human rights, nor lived nor labored for the benefit of their fellow-men. While they cut their way to a niche in the temple of fame, or to the crown and scepter of imperial honor and power, it was over the prostrate forms of those whom they had robbed of their rights; and they drove their chariot-wheels over the mangled bodies of unnumbered slain, and amid the smouldering ruins of peaceful homes, while the music to which they kept step in their career of conquest were the groans of anguished hearts, and the agonizing cries of the wounded and the dying. A selfish ambition—a cruel, devouring lust for power and dominion—governed them in all the plans they formed and in all the battles they fought; and they considered no destruction of human life or happiness too costly a sacrifice to make in order to secure the coveted prize. Thus they lived and planned and fought, not to bless, but to curse mankind. Around their names and deeds have been thrown those seductive charms which unhallowed Genius so frequently creates, and with which she seeks to conceal the profligacy and tyranny of wicked men; but Time has lifted the gorgeous drapery, and revealed the so-called heroes of ancient and modern times in all their moral leprosy and deformity.

But there have been true heroes, nevertheless. There have been pure-hearted patriots, who have toiled nobly for their country—brave defenders of human liberty, who have bared their bosoms to the tyrant's sword, rather than permit his chains to be placed on their own or their children's limbs—noble, devoted adherents of righteousness and truth, who, with the Bible in one hand and the sword in the other, have at once sought to maintain inviolate the sacred principles of civil and religious liberty, and to strike down, if need be, the assailants of either the one or the other. True, their names and noble deeds have not always been recorded in history, or celebrated in song. Yea, rather, many of the bravest and best of such heroes have been stigmatized as the basest of men; their motives have been impugned, and their noblest deeds denounced, while their memories have been loaded down with reproach, and their names pronounced with scorn and derision. But the same hand that has torn away the gilded, gaudy drapery with which kingly tyrants and imperial robbers have been invested, has also removed the stigma and reproach that the foul hand of Wrong had sought to fasten upon the memories of the truly good and great; and to-day, more than at any previous era of the world's history, are the noble deeds, the patient endurance, the spotless integrity, and the deathless devotion to principle of such heroes better understood and more fully appreciated. The efforts which we, as a people, have put forth, as well as the sacrifices we have made in order to subdue a rebellion, the foulest in spirit and design the world has ever seen, have led us to a clearer understanding and appreciation of the worth of the world's unhonored heroes. We have learned, in a most practical and impressive manner, that a nation's safety or the interests of humanity rest not in the hands of a favored few, whose claims for superiority are constantly urged, but in the pure, brave hearts and strong hands of the toiling many.

The history of the war for the preservation of the Union is a record of personal bravery and self-sacrificing devotion, on the part of the loyal men and women of the nation, to which history furnishes no parallel. During these years of bloodshed and strife, our cities and hamlets and rural abodes—the luxurious dwellings of the city merchants, and the log-cabins of our frontier farmers—have sent forth as heroic men as ever drew sword; and they have furnished as illustrious examples of womanly tenderness, affection, and love, blended with the truly heroic in self-sacrificing devotion and patient endurance, as the world has ever seen. No monumental brass or marble will ever receive for safe-keeping the names of all the heroes and heroines of this mighty struggle for freedom; neither will the historian's stately periods nor the poet's touching lyrics hand down to posterity the records of their noble deeds, or the requiems sung over their honored graves. The richly carved, storied urn may be costly and beautiful, but it will be broken in pieces and buried in the dust. The "ever-during brass" may be elaborately finished, and the names of the illustrious dead deeply engraven upon it, but it will corrode and waste away. The stately monumental marble may be solid in structure and imposing in appearance, but it, too, will crumble and decay. The historian's records may be just, and the poet's songs may be sweet, but they will all be marred by the fingers of hoary Time. But good thoughts and noble deeds never die. Like their authors, they are immortal. They go marching down the ages with stately, steady tread, elevating and ennobling successive, generations, and moving forward the shadows on the dial-plate of human destiny, long after the bosoms that gave them birth are buried beneath Oblivion's wave. The noblest monument that will ever be reared to the honor of our heroes in the field and our heroines at home, who have acted so nobly and endured so patiently, will be a free, happy, redeemed country; and the sweetest songs that will be sung in their praise will be the jubilee anthems of earth's disenthralled sons and daughters—anthems which will yet be heard on every shore; for every nation under heaven will be brought under the influence, and share in the benefits of the present struggle for Liberty, Righteousness, and Truth.

The simple sketches which follow will show the reader how some of our noble heroes live, and they will also show how some of them have died on the battlefield and in the hospital.

God and our Country.

On a bright, beautiful Sabbath in April, 1861, there met in the Franklin Street Presbyterian Church, Troy, Ohio, as sad and yet as brave and hopeful a congregation as perhaps ever met, or ever will again meet, within those walls. Fathers and mothers, wives and children, had come together to join in farewell religious services with loved ones who had promptly answered to their country's call, and who, on the morrow, were to depart for that dark field of strife on which were marshaled the armed legions of a wicked and causeless rebellion. The Star-spangled Banner was unfurled, and hung in graceful folds from the pulpit; and that flag, always beautiful in the eyes of every true American, and ever dear to his heart, never seemed so beautiful nor so precious as at that moment. During the previous night, and the greater part of this sacred day, the rooms attached to the church had been filled with ladies, busy at work preparing lint and bandages, and other articles considered necessary for the soldier; and it will ever be remembered as one of the strange yet significant facts connected with the history of this war, that the click of busy sewing-machines, and the hum of voices that tell of earnest labor, mingled on that hallowed day with the sacred songs of the sanctuary. The electric wires had flashed the news all over the land that the Star of the West had been fired into, Fort Sumter bombarded, and the national flag trailed in the dust by traitor hands. The blood of Massachusetts' freemen had stained the streets of Baltimore, and it had been declared by rebel mobs and by traitorous legislators that troops rushing to the defense of the National Capital would not be permitted to tread the soil of Maryland. The whole country was excited. Conflicting emotions swayed the public mind. Some were in fear and sadness, and could only ask, What next? Others were bitterly indignant, and called only for speedy and condign vengeance on the heads of traitors, while all the truly loyal and brave breathed but one determination—that, with the blessing of God, the foul rebellion must be quelled, and the Union be preserved, at whatever cost of treasure and blood.

The meeting on this peaceful Sabbath, in the sanctuary of God, was but one of thousands such held all over the land, and was significant as showing the elements of religious hope and trust that, from the commencement of the war, have entered so largely, and marked so distinctly, the patriotism of the loyal North. Addresses of thrilling earnestness and lofty patriotism were delivered by the Rev. W. M. Cheever, of the Franklin Street Presbyterian Church, the Rev. J. J. Thompson, of the M. E. Church, and others, after which a copy of the New Testament was presented to each volunteer, in the name of the Troy Female Bible Society. As the sacred volumes were being distributed, and words of cheer spoken to each recipient, a feeling of deep solemnity pervaded the entire assembly, and the language of every one seemed to be, "OUR TRUST IS IN GOD!" The entire services were of such a deeply interesting character, while the surrounding circumstances were so thrillingly impressive, that no one could possibly be an indifferent spectator. That meeting will never be forgotten, especially by those for whose special comfort and encouragement it was held.

The volunteers present at this meeting were two companies raised by Captain A. Coleman and Captain J. C. Drury, subsequently known as Companies D and H of the Eleventh Regiment Ohio Volunteer Infantry. Little did the writer of these pages think, as he gazed upon those brave, patriotic men, and joined with others in speaking words of cheer to them, that in a few short months he would be with them on the tented field, and sharing with them their perils and privations. Still less did he think that three years and three months would roll round ere they would return to their homes; and that, even then, war's fierce tumults would still be raging in the land, and the wicked pro-slavery rebellion still be showing its defiant front. But, so it is. In peace as well as in war—with nations as well as with individuals—we know not what the future may develop; neither can we tell what strange positions we may occupy, nor by what unexpected and unwonted circumstances we may be surrounded.

I have mentioned this little incident as a fitting introduction to the pen-pictures of the following pages, thinking that no apology is needed for bringing before the reader the fact that the noble Eleventh Ohio, as well as other regiments, went forth to fight for home and country, for liberty and truth, with the dearest and holiest remembrances and associations of the sanctuary of God, and with the prayers and blessings of Christian patriots.

A few months rolled past. The three-months' service had been finished, the regiment reorganized and mustered in for three years. The first Kanawha campaign had been accomplished, and Floyd and Wise driven from the Valley, and the Eleventh had come down the Kanawha River to Point Pleasant, and were in winter quarters, when the author of these pages was surprised by the announcement that he had been appointed chaplain of the regiment. A week or so thereafter found him, for the first time, on the sacred soil—or, rather, *in* the sacred *mud*—of Virginia, and, for the first time, within the army lines.

After reporting for duty, the first official work I performed was visiting the hospital. The immediate result of the first visit was the entire change of preconceived opinions relative to military hospitals in general, and of regimental hospitals in particular. I had pictured to myself dreary, hopeless, repulsive scenes, such as I had read of in the published correspondence from the French and English armies in the Crimea, and imagined that, even at the very best, our sick and wounded soldiers must necessarily be partially neglected, and their wants unsupplied. War, too, it had been stated, had an indurating effect on the human heart, and that the camp was only a school of vice and immorality, and that, therefore, an indifference to the sufferings and necessities of others would be the inevitable result of such influences as surround the soldier. But although not adopting the whole of such gloomy views of army life and experiences, I was not prepared for a scene so entirely the reverse of what I had anticipated. Every ward in the hospital was scrupulously clean, every cot was neatly arranged, the patients looked quite comfortable and cheerful, and I noticed that the hospital attendants were kind and attentive. Dr. Hartman, as brave and generous a man as ever entered a hospital, and who, during the three years he was in the army, did more for the comfort of the soldier than many surgeons in shoulder-straps, and that, too, while drawing only the pay of a private soldier, was acting as warden.

Although the exigencies and necessities of several active campaigns have shown me some hospital scenes very different from this, I have never had occasion to change the opinions then formed of the general manner in which our brave soldiers were cared for when sick or wounded. That blessed institution, the Christian Commission, with its noble band of laborers, and its generous supplies of good things for soul and body, was not then in existence. The Sanitary Commission, too, was but in its infancy, and Government supplies alone were depended upon in attending to the wants of our sick and wounded soldiers. If at that time, and under such circumstances, they were comparatively so comfortable, any one can form an idea of their improved condition under the auspices of these twin institutions of patriotism and Christian beneficence. If the writer had a hundred voices, he would employ them in urging upon the attention and fostering care of every man and woman in the land the claims of the Christian Commission, knowing, as he does, from experience in the field and in the hospital, how much good it has accomplished and is still accomplishing in the army.

FIRST IMPRESSIONS.

The sight of a large multitude is always interesting and impressive. This is true, whether in civil or military life. The spectator, however, is often swayed by very different and even conflicting emotions; for the opinions he may form concerning such a spectacle, as well as the impulses or feelings it may awaken in his heart, will be in accordance with the views he entertains, exalted or otherwise, concerning human duty and destiny. The motives by which he is actuated in mingling with his fellow-men, and especially with those who are brought into close and important relationships, will also have a decided influence upon his opinions of their individual or aggregate value, as well as upon the manner in which he acts toward them.

The politician, for example, looks upon them as so many of "The People," who must be reasoned with, cajoled, hoodwinked, flattered, or bullied into some political scheme. The political economist looks upon them as so many consumers as well as producers of the necessaries of life, and who will increase or diminish the resources of government according to their individual and aggregate intelligence and industry. The patient plodder in dry, matter-of-fact statistics looks upon them as so many breathing numerals, increasing in a certain ratio not very clearly defined, and which are to be considered valuable only as supporting some scientific theories. He delights not so much in the individual or aggregate value of the living numerals as their dumb representatives on the census returns; for he can exultantly refer to the figures on the tables in support of his theories, for figures, like facts, are stubborn things, and will not lie. The man of busy wheels, spindles, looms, cranks, and levers, looks upon them as so many living "hands" with brains to think, and whose principal responsibilities during one-half of their time is to work with or control the movements of brainless hands of brass and steel. The professional warrior, like an Alexander or a Napoleon, looks upon a multitude of men as so many individual forces which may be combined—so many nerves and muscles that may be equipped, drilled, and disciplined, and whom, for his own glory, he will lead forth and dash upon similar battalions of living, thinking beings, or hurl in impetuous storms upon yawning embrasure or bristling earth-work. The Christian, on the other hand, not forgetful of man's earthly relations, duties or necessities, but with feelings of deep interest and Christ-like love, looks upon them as so many precious immortals, for whom the Savior suffered and died, and who have to work out the great problem of human duty and destiny. He looks upon them as heirs of immortality, who will never scale the hights or fathom the depths of their own spiritual capacities, nor reach the boundary line of their own existence; as so many individuals, around each of whom are clustering responsibilities and duties, sympathies and emotions, that will seal and settle forever the destiny of each, and raise to the high position and glorious enjoyment of heaven, or sink to the dishonor and despair of hell.

On many occasions, I have seen immense armies, either in camp, where the white tents, gleaming in the summer's sun, looked like a dream of fairy-land, or on the march, when it seemed as if a nation were on a pilgrimage. And I have seen the same armies as they rushed on to battle, when the ground shook with the tramp of armed men, the roar of cannon, and the sharp rattle of musketry, and when it seemed as if the very heavens were filled with shrieking demons of death and destruction, in the shape of shot and shell. And, whether reposing quietly in camp, on the weary march, or amid the perils and excitements of battle, I always experienced solemn and even sad emotions when contemplating such masses of men. Not that I ever had a doubt in regard to the righteousness of the cause in which we were engaged—not that I entertained any fear regarding the final result of the struggle—but because of the all-important questions pertaining to the eternal interests of each individual soul. There is something fearfully solemn connected with such questions when applied to one human being; but when thousands and tens of thousands of deathless spirits are placed before us, and we try to grasp as it were the infinite aggregate of hope and fear, pleasure and pain, glory and despair, life and death, undying energies, immortal appetites and capacities, and unsatisfied longings, we sink beneath the rushing tide-wave of our own aroused emotions, and can only exclaim, "Who is sufficient for these things!"

Add to all these the peculiar circumstances connected with army life, and it will soon be apparent that the responsibility attaching to those who go forth to labor for the moral and spiritual welfare of the soldier are of the most solemn and important character. It is no trifling matter to preach Christ and salvation anywhere, and under any circumstances; but to do so in the army, among those who are not only away from the temporal comforts and the social and religious privileges of home, and who are always exposed to danger and death, the sacred responsibilities connected with such work are seen to be vastly increased. These, and other matters that might be named, are what make a chaplain's position at once honorable and responsible. It is but anticipating what may be referred to in the following pages to state, that on addressing the regiment, for the first time, as it was drawn up in line, I felt that if the Grace of God, the Wisdom that cometh down from above, were needed for weak man to guide him in efforts to do good, especially among those who had nobly laid their all upon their country's altar, that was the hour, and those were the circumstances when such was specially needed.

As an evidence of the kind interest felt in the spiritual welfare of the soldiers in the field, as well as a record of the encouragement given to laborers in the army, the following incident is recorded.

A large meeting of the Sabbath-school children and their friends was held in Troy, to participate with the Band of Hope, in a Bible presentation. Mrs. Lizzie James, in behalf of the children, presented a beautiful Bible, on which was a suitable inscription. The following was the address she made on the occasion:

"No fact more strongly marks the fearful war which is now upon us than the unity of purpose on the part of our soldiers in the field, and of friends at home. Very many and varied are the good things prepared by loving hands at home, for the comfort of dear ones far away in the camp, or in the field, and we all take an interest in the good work which our mothers and sisters are engaged in, for the benefit of our dear fathers and brothers in the army. In token of our love for the soldier, the Band of Hope have directed me, to-day, to present their offering for the noble Eleventh Regiment. Though onr offering is of but little pecuniary value, yet it is a priceless treasure—the richest ever presented to man. We rejoice to know that many of the Eleventh Regiment are Christians; and we feel assured, therefore, of the appropriateness of our offering.

"Chaplain Lyle, in placing this volume in your hands, we are more than glad that you are chaplain of our own Eleventh. Take this Blessed Volume—this Chart of Life—and present from it to your soldier Christians things both new and old. May its lessons, as you shall dispense them, from time to time, comfort and sustain the tried and tempted, encourage the penitent, awaken the careless; and, with the attendant blessing of the Divine Spirit, may every member of your regiment be presented perfect in Christ Jesus. Our most fervent prayers shall rise before God that your ministrations may be abundantly blessed—that the dying soldier taught therefrom, whether breathing out his life in the hospital or on the battle-field, may triumphantly say: 'But thanks be to God, who giveth the victory through our Lord Jesus Christ!' and, at last, greet you, their chaplain, where men learn war no more. Take this Book, this Word of the Lord, and bear it to your gallant men from the Troy Band of Hope."

CHAPTER II.

SLAVERY AND THE REBELLION—A SOLDIER'S OPINION OF THE ISSUE—ORGANIZATION OF A REGIMENTAL CHURCH, ETC.

What gives the wheat field blades of steel?
What points the rebel cannon?
What sets the roaring rabble's heel
On the old star-spangled pennon?
What breaks the oath of the men of the South?
What whets the knife for the Union's life?
Hark to the answer—Slavery! WHITTIER.

It is a well-known fact that, when the rebellion first threatened the overthrow of the country, and it was distinctly affirmed by rebel leaders that slavery was to be the corner-stone of the Southern Confederacy, and, indeed, was the prime moving cause of the foul conspiracy, the masses of the loyal people were slow to believe that the institution of slavery was, in any important respect, connected with the rebellion. They were equally oblivious to the fact that to deal death-blows upon the one, was to insure the destruction of the other. And so very anxious were many of the political and military leaders to convince slaveholding rebels that the Government had no intention of interfering with the institution of slavery, that declarations were made, officially and otherwise, that any such interference would not be tolerated; and that, in the event of any uprising of the slaves against their masters, the whole strength of the Federal army would be brought to bear upon such demonstrations so as to crush them; and further, that fugitive slaves from the rebel lines would invariably be sent back. In strict accordance with such a policy, books or tracts sent to the soldiers by private parties, or by public societies, known as reformatory, were carefully examined, lest any anti-slavery sentiments should be propagated in the army, and sectional feelings or issues introduced into military circles. Many chaplains, in their religious exercises, carefully ignored the existence of the agitating subject, or gave it a wide berth, when they accidentally drifted in that direction; while every conceivable plan was adopted to cool down the Southern heart, which had been so frequently and so terribly "fired up." As an evidence of the extent to which this spirit prevailed at the commencement of the war, it may just be stated that when the American Reform Tract and Book Society of Cincinnati sent packages of reading matter into the army, addressing them to the care of regimental chaplains, some of them thought that they had been grossly insulted, and their respectability and good standing in the army greatly endangered by such high-handed impertinence. One chaplain we heard of, culled out all the tracts that contained the slightest symptoms of Abolitionism, and deliberately burned them; and another, after asking the advice of his colonel, a godless pro-slavery scoffer, disposed of his packages in a somewhat similar manner. Others of these clerical compromisers were careful to procure tracts and papers from the American Tract Society alone. In doing so, there was not the slightest danger of meeting with any sentiment likely to disturb the most sensitive of pro-slavery consciences; for, at that time, any reference to the "sum of all villainies," by way of condemnation, would not have received the "approbation of all evangelical Christians;" and hence, any such references were carefully excluded. It is, perhaps, but just to say, in this connection, that in this year of grace, Eighteen hundred and sixty-five, after the lessons taught by four years of relentless effort on the part of slaveholding traitors to overthrow the institutions of liberty in our beloved country, and to roll back the advancing tide-wave of liberty throughout the world, the position of the Tract Society at New York has been considerably modified. When the last link of Oppression's chain is broken, however, and the nation is redeemed and purified from the vile sin of slavery, and the dear old flag floats in the breeze from the granite hills of New England to the gold-veined mountains of California, and from the dark pine-woods of the icy North to the cypress swamps and cotton-fields of the sunny South, and the dark, thrice-accursed fiend of slavery is forever driven from the earth, the claims of this mammoth publishing enterprise, for occupying an advanced position on the great question of human rights, and as having given the Gospel-trumpet no uncertain sound in the darkest hour of great moral conflicts, will neither be great in themselves, nor reflect honor upon those who urge them.

It is not to be supposed, however, that there were

none in the army who could look beneath the surface of things and recognize, at once, the deeply-laid plans of wicked men and the rapidly-unfolding purposes of a righteous God. In the quarters of the men, at the picket-posts, in the hospital, on the march, anywhere and everywhere, the question of slavery, as affecting the interests of the country, and as having an important bearing upon the conduct and issues of the war, was freely and frequently discussed. One day, while visiting the hospital, one of the sick men called my attention to one of the tracts which I had distributed a few days before.

"Look here, chaplain," said he; "here 's a tract that's chuck-full of good common sense. Do n't pretend nohow to profess much religion, and do n't care much about dry, sermon-like tracts; but this one is none of your milk-and-water, tweedle-dee tweedle-dum affairs, that gives a poor sinner some scorching reproofs for taking a chew of tobacco, or shaking his foot in a ball-room, or ripping out some bad grammar—swear myself sometimes, chaplain—fact—bad habit though!—or finding fault with things that nearly every body condemns. There," said he, with emphasis, holding up the tract in question, which was: "What are we fighting for?" by Rev. J. A. Thome, of Cleveland—"that's the kind of reading the army needs. There 's truth in that, I tell you—and we have all got to come to it before the war is ended; and the sooner the better. No use dodging any longer. Better face the music at once. Just read that page there, chaplain—it 's true as preaching, an' a mighty sight truer than some preaching is, too."

The sentiments which were enunciated by the tract in question, and which elicited from the sick soldier such hearty commendation, were the following:

"Slavery curses the South, the North, the whole country. It has, at last, embroiled the nation in a destructive civil war. It has set brethren in deadly combat with brethren. Already fraternal blood has flowed, which never would have been shed but for slavery. Alas, more blood must be spilled, hundreds and thousands of victims must be sacrificed in this terrible fight between brothers! Slavery is responsible for this, and *the blood-stained monster must die.* It can not be suffered to live longer in this Republic, to foment another such war! We fight in vain, unless we aim at the extermination of slavery. . .

"We fight for the Flag as the symbol of Liberty and Union, and as the ægis of our citizenship throughout the Republic, whether in Boston or in Charleston, in Bangor or in Mobile. We remember that the flag was not for the first time struck down at Fort Sumter, was not for the first time outraged by the firing on the Star of the West, was not for the first time set at naught by the Ordinance of Secession passed by the Palmetto State. These were, by no means, the first acts of flagrant aggression upon our country's flag, and upon the sacred rights its folds shelter. For years it has afforded no protection to American citizens in one-half of the Republic. For years it has yielded no security to free speech, no guaranty to the rights of conscience, no safeguard to the irrepressible yearnings of humanity where these have been most called for. For years, beneath its witnessing stars, innocent beings have been chained, scourged, driven, sold, and worked like dumb cattle! For years, its stripes have blazed over slave marts, slave pens, and slave auctions, from Washington City to New Orleans. Since this flag has waved at all, it has waved

O'er the land of the free,
And the home—of the SLAVE!

"*These are the desecrations* that have covered our Star-spangled Banner with infamy in the sight of Christendom, before secession dared to insult it; and these are the grievances which ought to have aroused the fires of patriotism, and driven us to some form of united resistance long ago. These are the outrages which, so oft repeated and so tamely suffered, have left little for secession to do to our flag that has not already been done by slavery. To avenge *all these violations*, therefore, and to raise the flag of freedom to its rightful place of undisturbed supremacy, *is the aim of this war.* If the flag of freedom goes up, *that of slavery must come down.* We can no longer tolerate two flags in this Commonwealth. We can allow no further compromise between liberty and chattelism. We can no longer assent that a certain line of latitude shall divide this Republic into free and slave sections. No! No! The flag we fight for will frown upon the soldier who, under its folds, swears fealty to slavery."

As already remarked, the question of slavery, in connection with the rebellion, was now being freely discussed; and events, taking place almost every day, both in military and civil circles, were tending more and more to increase the interest and importance of the discussion. General Frémont's memorable order regarding the slaves of rebels in arms, declaring them free, had electrified the people at home, as well as the masses of the soldiers in the field. The President had thought proper to interfere with General Frémont in his somewhat radical, but really the only wise and practical method of dealing with slaveholding rebels, and so neutralized the celebrated general order as to render it practically null and void. This interference of the Executive, perhaps, more than any other circumstance, tended, at this time, to attract attention to the great question which, sooner or later, must be settled; namely, the policy to be pursued in dealing with the slaves of rebels in arms, and, indeed, with slavery itself, under any and all circumstances. Then Frémont's removal from the Department of the West, with all the accompanying circumstances, only tended to increase, both in political and military circles, the interest already felt in this subject. As if to show, however, that the entire question would, erelong, meet with a practical solution—that there was no design on the part of the Government to evade the responsibility of dealing with it in such a manner as to satisfy the more timid and conservative, if not the more courageous and radical—the President, on the 6th of March, sent the celebrated special message to both houses of Congress, recommending such legislative action as would secure compensation to those who should emancipate their slaves—a message which, to use a phrase which frequently occurs in it, might be well-named as the Initiatory Proclamation of Emancipation. This was soon followed by a general order, published throughout the entire army, as follows:

"All officers and persons in the military or naval service of the United States are prohibited from employing any of the forces under their respective commands, for the purpose of returning fugitives from service or labor who may have escaped from any persons to whom such service or labor is claimed to be due, and any officer who shall be found guilty, by a court-martial, of violating this article of war, shall be dismissed from the service."

Whether the men of the Eleventh were pleased with the President's message, and the general order referred to, may be inferred from the fact that a whipping-post which stood near the court-house, where Company B was quartered, was very speedily demolished; and on the question being asked of a group standing, one day, where the post once stood, what they would do were a slaveholder to tie up a slave in their presence, they promptly answered: "Do! Why we would give him such a dose of *blue pills* he would n't know what hurt him!" These matters are referred to, at this point, in order to show what were the feelings in the army upon the questions involved. Many a loyal heart beat joyfully on that day, when it was known that henceforth liberty, in the full and true sense of that blessed term, would no longer be ignored either in the cabinet or in the camp. It was seen that the issue was about to be met fairly and squarely, and every true patriot felt that God would bless the right.

ORGANIZATION OF A REGIMENTAL CHURCH.

Quite a number of those composing the Eleventh Regiment were professors of religion, and there were not a few who were anxious to keep up some visible bond of union, so that not only might there be mutual aid and encouragement in leading a religious life while in the army, but that direct efforts might be made to promote the interests of morality and religion in the regiment. In union there is strength. This is felt in religious as well as in other matters; hence the craving of the believing soul for Christian fellowship and communion. A few of the more spiritual and devoted of the men had arranged to hold two prayer-meetings during each week, and for this purpose had engaged a small room belonging to one of the citizens of the town. The first of these meetings I attended a day or two after joining the regiment; and such were the peculiarly interesting character of the services, together with all the accompanying circumstances, that it will never be forgotten. There was an entire absence of form or ceremony, and, seemingly, there was no room for any thing like the old stereotyped prayers or addresses which obtain so largely in more formal and, perhaps, more fashionable religious meetings. There were but few at that meeting—not more than a dozen, perhaps—but each countenance is as plain before me now while I write these lines as if the meeting had been but last night; and there were impressions made upon the minds of all present that will never be forgotten. It was nothing more than an humble prayer-meeting, held by Christian soldiers far from home, and deprived of the privileges of the sanctuary; but it was one of those precious seasons when the souls of believers rise superior to outward circumstances, and have fellowship with the unseen and eternal. One after another of those present engaged in supplicating the Throne of Grace, or spoke of the felt preciousness of the love of God in the soul; and so full of joy and comfort and gratitude seemed each one, that as soon as one stopped praying or speaking, another commenced! These were men who had endured incredible hardships during the previous summer and winter; had laid out in the open field or in the woods for sixty bleak, cold days and nights, without tents and with few blankets; had been fighting or marching, scouting or standing guard, day after day, and night after night, subsisting on a few hard crackers and a drink of muddy water! These were men around whose heads musket-balls had whistled like driving hail, and against whose bosoms had been pointed the glittering steel! The Lord had covered their heads in the day of battle, and His presence had cheered their hearts in the hour of suffering. For these they thanked Him as they knelt in prayer; and to the power of religion to comfort the heart they testified, as each arose to tell what the Lord had done for him. O, how true it is, that living, experimental religion—the love of God in the soul—is man's most precious treasure, at all times and under all circumstances! In the bright day of prosperity, when all is happy and cheerful, or in the dark day of adversity, when all is dreary and discouraging, religion is found to be the pearl of great price. In health or in sickness, among friends or enemies, at home or abroad, in life or in death, it is the same precious, priceless treasure of the soul. And amid all the changing scenes of life, the Christian can say, "I am persuaded that neither death, nor life, nor angels, nor principalities, nor powers, nor things present, nor things to come, nor hight, nor depth, nor any other creature, shall be able to separate us from the love of God which is in Christ Jesus our Lord." Blessed religion! Who would not gladly suffer all things, to realize the fullness of comfort, hope, and joy which these words of Christian triumph express!

At the close of the services, it was proposed to organize a regimental Church, and a committee was appointed to act with the chaplain in preparing some formal bond of union or Church covenant. This was on Thursday evening, the 27th of February, 1862.*

On the ensuing Monday evening, the 3d of March, a meeting was held in the Masonic Hall for the purpose of completing the Church organization. The record kept from that time till the regiment was mustered out, in 1864, contains the following minutes of that meeting:

"CAMP COX, POINT PLEASANT, VIRGINIA,
"*March* 3, 1862.

"Pursuant to notice, a meeting of the soldiers of the Eleventh Regiment Ohio Volunteer Infantry, U. S. A., was held in the Masonic Hall, Point Pleas-

---

* The general reader will, perhaps, excuse this apparent show of punctilious regard for dates. There are those into whose hands this unpretending volume may fall who will be glad to note these dates.

ant, for the purpose of organizing a Church in said regiment.

"The Chaplain, Rev. W. W. Lyle, was appointed Chairman, and M. L. Sheets Secretary.

"After devotional exercises, the business of the meeting was introduced, and the committee, appointed at a previous meeting, to prepare a constitution for the contemplated Church, presented their report, which was unanimously adopted, as follows:

"BOND OF UNION OF THE CHURCH OF THE ELEVENTH REGIMENT O. V. I., U. S. A.

"Believing it to be our duty, as the professed followers of the Lord Jesus Christ, to maintain a visible Church organization in our regiment, we, whose names are hereto appended, form ourselves into a Church, under the Designation, Articles of Faith, and General Rules, as follows:

"1. This organization shall be called THE UNION CHURCH OF THE ELEVENTH REGIMENT OHIO VOLUNTEER INFANTRY.

"2. The object of this Association is to bring into visible unity and organization the religious element in our regiment; to watch over, encourage, and comfort one another as brethren in the Lord, and, as much as in us lies, to promote good order, morality, and piety in our camp.

"3. Members of all Christian Churches shall be eligible for membership, and shall, in common with all applicants, be received on certificate or profession of faith.

"ARTICLES OF RELIGION.

"We believe in God the Father Almighty, Maker of heaven and earth, and in His Son, our Lord and Savior Jesus Christ, who came into the world to make an atonement for sin. We believe in the Holy Spirit, the Divine Comforter and Sanctifier; in the Scriptures of Divine truth, as the only sufficient rule of faith and practice, and in the necessity of repentance toward God, and faith in our Lord Jesus Christ, as conditions of salvation. We believe it to be the duty of every Christian to maintain a godly life, walk, and conversation at all times, and under all circumstances; and by gentleness, meekness, and fidelity, to commend the religion of Christ to the hearts and consciences of men.

"Candidates for admission will be addressed in the words of the following

"COVENANT.

"You do avouch the Lord Jehovah to be your God, the Savior Jesus Christ to be your Redeemer, and the Holy Spirit to be your Comforter and Sanctifier. You profess to have renounced the world, the flesh, and the devil, and are determined, through grace, to live soberly, righteously, and godly in this present world. In joining this Church, you promise to labor for the edification and welfare of your brethren; to attend as often as you possibly can the meetings for Divine worship; to labor for the conversion of your companions in arms, and to promote good order and morality in the regiment. [*Answer*—I do.]

"RESPONSE OF THE CHURCH—[*The Chaplain, in the name of the Church, will say*]—We receive you, dear brethren, into our fellowship and communion, and promise, through Divine Grace, to watch over you as beloved brethren in Christ; to sustain, comfort, and encourage you in the Christian warfare, and to discharge such duties as are incumbent upon us as fellow-believers in the Lord Jesus. And may the blessing of God our Father rest upon us all. Amen."

After the adoption of the foregoing, a committee, or Official Board—jocularly known ever after as "The Chaplain's Staff"—was appointed, as follows: A. Conklin, E. H. Eyer, C. J. McClure, M. L. Sheets, W. T. Burns, and J. B. Woolson.

An opportunity was then given for any who wished to join the new organization to do so, when some twenty-five immediately subscribed to the Bond of

Union. While the interesting services were being conducted, and one after another expressed a desire to be numbered with the little Christian band, an occurrence took place which was deeply affecting. A young man arose, and said: "I have known what it is to enjoy religion; I have known what it is to experience God's love; but since I came into the army I have backslidden from God. I have a praying father and mother, and when I left home my mother wept over me, and told me not to forget my God." While speaking, his voice faltered, and the tears trickled over his cheeks. "Yes," he continued, after a pause, "my mother is a praying woman—and, O, she is praying for me to-night! I know she is praying for me to-night; for when I said farewell to her, she said, 'I'll pray for you night and morning, my son, but, O, don't neglect to pray for yourself!'" These words, and the peculiarly tender tone in which they were spoken, had a thrilling effect upon every one present. After a moment's pause, he expressed an earnest wish to be prayed for; and we all knelt down to petition a Throne of Grace in his behalf. Another man arose, and said "he had long been a wanderer, but now he wished to be with the people of God—would we receive him?" "Yes, yes!" was the answer. "Come, and we will do thee good; for the Lord hath spoken good concerning Israel." Another season of prayer was held, after which a very sensible and spirit-stirring little address was made by the oldest soldier present—Mr. Nathan Whittaker, of Company E. How long that little, unpretending meeting might have been held, it would be difficult to say; but certain it is, the drummer's call for "tattoo" seemed to come too early that night. Services were again held the next evening. "The Savior's tender compassion for the penitent sinner" was the theme of discourse. At the close of the services, several were received into the Church, some on profession of faith, and others by certificate from their respective Churches at home. The meetings were continued every night during that week, and the interest manifested in religious matters generally was both hopeful and encouraging.

On the ensuing Sabbath, the ordinance of baptism was administered, when two young men, who had found peace in believing, publicly professed their faith in Christ. At the same services, six more joined the Regimental Church. Meetings were held each night during the succeeding week also; and such were the indications given of God's gracious presence, that it seemed as if the language of every attendant was, "It is good for us to be here." This state of things continued for several weeks, during which, services were held generally every night. The movement could not be dignified with the name of a revival, and yet not a few Christian soldiers were strengthened and encouraged, while several others, who left home thoughtless and godless, were constrained to give their hearts unto the Lord. There was an increased demand for Testaments, tracts, and religious reading generally, with which, thanks to Christian friends at home, we were abundantly supplied. On Sabbath, the 23d of March, the ordinance of the Lord's Supper was observed, for the first time, by our little Christian brotherhood, and, perhaps, for the first time within the lines of this portion of the army. It was truly a season of refreshing from the presence of the Lord—a time long to be remembered by those who participated in the solemn and interesting services. Perhaps the privilege of commemorating the sufferings and death of Christ, by those Christian soldiers, was all the more highly appreciated, because of the circumstances in which they were placed—away from the refining and elevating influences of home, and the sacred associations of home-Sabbaths and the home-sanctuary—together with the fact that such a privilege had not been enjoyed for a long time, while the expectation of an active campaign about to open gave no favorable promise of enjoying the same privilege very soon again. It was a time, too, of very solemn inquiry relative to the responsibility of professing Christians in the army, not only in regard to their own spiritual welfare, but also in regard to their influence upon their companions in arms.

CHAPTER III.

GAULEY BRIDGE—RALEIGH COURT-HOUSE—SUSPENSE—GENERAL COX AT FLAT-TOP—A POWERFUL BATTERY—HOSPITAL SCENES.

On the 16th of April, the regiment, with the exception of Company F, which was left to guard Government property, left Point Pleasant for Winfield, on the Kanawha River. We remained at Winfield till May 8, when orders were received to move to Gauley Bridge. At five P. M., six companies left, followed next day by the rest of the regiment. The transports could go up the river only as far as Cannelton, a landing near some coal-oil works, and about twelve miles from Gauley Bridge. At four o'clock next afternoon—Saturday, the 10th—the regiment encamped at Gauley Bridge, within a short distance of the camp ground occupied about five months before, and under the very shadow of Cotton Mountain, whose rugged summit the last lingering rays of the setting sun were illuminating with the soft, dreamy splendors of an early summer's eve, as we drove our tent-pins and stretched our cumbrous "Sibleys."

"In for another campaign, in this jumping-off place of creation," said one, as he dipped his tin-cup into the kettle of steaming coffee.

"Who wants to go on a scout to Sewell Mountain?" shouted another.

"Hold on, partner," said a third; "we are going to Richmond, by way of Greenbrier."

"What 'll ye bet," said another, "we do n't march straight for Newbern and cut the Conthieveracy in two, and distinguish ourselves generally?"

"Very likely," chimed in another, as he leisurely cut into a chunk of fat pork, using a piece of hard tack for a plate—"very likely, boys, we 'll distinguish ourselves generally, and some of us may get *ex*tinguished particularly."

"Did you hear the news, boys? The rebs are at Lewisburg and up New River," said another, who had just come from the camp of the Forty-fourth Ohio.

"Tell us something we do n't know," was the polite answer made in return for the information so freely volunteered. "Would n't be surprised if old Jenkins was n't considerably nearer than Lewisburg."

"Say, boys, do you remember when the rebs opened on us with that old smooth-bore from Cotton Hill, yonder?" said one.

"Guess we paid 'em back when we fired our ten-pounder ramrod at them. They did n't know what in thunder it was. Rather guess we knew, though. How they scampered off on the double-quick, seemingly scared to death at what they thought was a new gun, just got into position! Wonder if old Wise did n't think we were sending chain-shot after him, when our rammer went booming and splintering through the trees?"

And thus remarks, half in fun, half in earnest, referring to incidents and experiences of the preceding summer's campaign, were freely bandied about. But, with all the good-humored repartee and joke around the camp-fires that night, there was a very general disgust at the idea of another summer's scouting and bushwhacking in that bleak, dreary, forsaken region of Western Virginia.

Next day, Sabbath, May 11, the Forty-fourth Ohio moved up the east side of New River, toward Lewisburg, and on the following day, part of the Eleventh moved up the west side of the river by the Fayetteville road, toward Beckley or Raleigh Court-house. These movements fairly inaugurated the campaign of the Kanawha in 1862.

A few days after the movements above mentioned, Company E, Captain Douglass, and Company G, Captain Higgins, left Gauley Bridge also, and followed the regiment toward Raleigh. It was on Saturday, the 17th of May, that this detachment set out. It was a bright and beautiful morning, and but for the roll of the drum, which was answered by repeated echoes from the deep mountain gorges and frowning steeps of the New River and the Gauley, with an occasional bugle-blast, no one would have imagined that war's dread visage was darkening, even then, this wildly romantic but beautiful country. More stirring scenes have been enacted since that morning, and many a bloody battle has been witnessed by the writer of these lines, and by those who were his companions in arms, since then; but that morning's scene on the banks of the Gauley—the crossing of the river, the toilsome march up Cotton Hill, with all the attendant circumstances—will never be forgotten. Long before day the reveillé was beat, each note being taken up by the

> "Echoes wildly flying,"

and flung back again as if with tenfold power. In a short time the tents were struck, horses saddled, and baggage in the wagons, and we were on our way to the front. The "front," by the way, was, as usual, somewhat of a vague locality; for, as we afterward found, it was pretty near right and left, as well as before us. While the heavy supply-train was toiling wearily and slowly up the rough, rugged road that winds up and around Cotton Hill for some six or seven miles, I had ample time to survey the whole scene, and indulge in such reflections as it would naturally suggest. This is but a living picture of man's life upon earth, thought I, as the bustling, changing scenes of the past few days seemed to rise up before me. How true it is that life, at the best, is but a warfare; and he only is truly happy who hath taken to himself the whole armor of God, and in the strength which Christ imparts, struggles bravely on till the victory is obtained over the world, the flesh, and the devil. Glorious is the crown which the Captain of our salvation will give to those who conquer on the spiritual battle-field; and glorious even in this life are the rewards of him who daily says—

> "Fight on, my soul, till death
> Shall bring thee to thy God—
> He 'll take thee, at thy parting breath,
> Up to his blest abode.'

Toward evening, we reached the picket-posts of what I supposed was some regiment stationed at Fayetteville, and at first paid little attention to the matter; but on coming closer, I saw that something was in the wind. Here were some of our own men, who had preceded us some four or five days before, and whom I supposed were twenty miles further on. They had a keen, vigilant, wide-awake look about them, as much as to say, "Look out for bushwhackers, boys!"

"We have been expecting an attack all day," said the men at the picket-post, in reply to our questions—"Jenkins's cavalry have been scouting around, and fired on our pickets on the Raleigh road last night. And there was warm work up at Princeton, yesterday, too. General Cox had to fall back to Flat-Top, and the Thirty-fourth Regiment has been badly cut up."

Such were the reports given as we passed along. I could not help thinking to myself that "ignorance is bliss," sometimes—at least temporarily. I had been bringing up the rear—that is, half a mile behind—walking quite leisurely, in order to allow a wearied soldier to help himself along on my horse. On getting into the village, preparations were instantly made for both eating and skirmishing; which of the two duties would come first it was hard to tell.

The first stage of excitement was beginning to subside into coffee and crackers, when scouts came in, and reported a rebel force advancing toward Fayetteville in such a manner as to make a sudden attack during the night. The pickets were strengthened, additional rounds of ammunition distributed, and, having spread our blankets where we could, we went to sleep, and slept, if not comfortably, safely enough, for we were not disturbed. Early in the morning, orders were received from head-quarters to push forward with the utmost dispatch. This was a difficult matter, owing to the rough and hilly roads, and the heavily-loaded wagons; but, as there seemed to be trouble ahead, every thing was done to advance as rapidly as possible.

At night we encamped on what had been a farm-yard, and, after a late but delicious supper of crackers and coffee, threw ourselves down wherever there were the best indications of comfort. The greater number enjoyed the luxury of sleeping in the open air; a few, however, were fortunate enough to get into a dilapidated log-cabin. This cabin was the most thoroughly ventilated institution of the kind imaginable—fully equal to the demands of the most radical of hygienic reformers. The boys, had they not been accustomed to "roughing it in the bush," might, perhaps, have had some sympathy for the poor fellow, of whom we have all heard, who caught a severe cold by sleeping one night in the pasture-field with the gate open.

A thunder-storm came up during the night, and we had a plentiful supply of fresh water in addition to fresh air; but as it is not what a man has, but what he enjoys, that is really valuable to him, so, on the same principle, we valued very highly the opportunity of resting our aching limbs, even under such circumstances. It is not likely that any of us will make annual pilgrimages to that ancient log-cabin, as the followers of Mohammed do to Mecca; but I think, for one, that I will always look with considerable respect upon all log-cabins in general, and particularly upon those that are minus doors, windows, chimneys, clapboards, and chinking. We were just fully into the blessed enjoyment of sound sleep, when I was unceremoniously aroused with "Captain! Captain! here's a messenger from head-quarters." "That ain't the captain; that's the chaplain," said Henry Culbertson, who was occupying a neighboring board. "Where's the captain, then? Where's Captain Douglass?" By this time we were all at least half awake; and Captain Douglass, taking the dispatches from the orderly, read them hastily, and soon "Fall in! Fall in, boys!" awakened every sleeper, and made him start to his feet. In a short time the train was in motion, and away we went, over steep hills and through deep defiles, as rapidly as possible. In a few hours we reached Raleigh, and found every one busy at work preparing to receive, in a becoming manner, a rebel force expected every moment. General Cox had sent dispatches from Flat-Top to Colonel Coleman, informing him that a rebel force was reported moving around by way of Logan, with the evident intention of cutting our communications, and that it was probable an attack would be made on the garrison at Raleigh. Scouts were sent out in all directions, and every precaution was taken by the brave and ever-watchful Colonel Coleman to prevent a surprise. Log-houses were quickly transformed into tolerably good stockades; the court-house—a large brick building—was loopholed for sharp-shooters, and covered ways were made leading to the principal spring. It was, however, a time of no little anxiety; for, aside from our exposed position, there was but a handful of men to guard the post. Two companies, under command of Captain Lane, had been gone for three days on a scouting expedition, and had not been heard from. The expedition had started for a point somewhat east and south of where the battle of the Friday previous had been fought, and no little anxiety was felt for its safety. One company, as already stated, was at Fayetteville, while Company F was still on duty at Point Pleasant. There was quite a number of sick belonging to the Twelfth, Twenty-third, and Thirty-fourth Regiments in the hospital; and in case of any reverse, the facilities for their removal were very limited. Notwithstanding these somewhat perplexing circumstances, every one felt determined and hopeful. Not soon will I forget Colonel Coleman's reply to a remark I made to him, relative to the difficulty of falling back to any safer position, in the event of being attacked by a superior force. "The Eleventh do n't fall back from this point. We intend to stay here at all hazards, and advance rather than retreat!" Brave Coleman! He sleeps in the honored grave of a patriot soldier, but those words, spoken with such earnestness and decision, at a time when matters looked gloomy in the Kanawha Valley, will never be forgotten. The only expression indicative of anxiety which he uttered at this time was, "I only wish those two companies that are out with Captain Lane were back. They have gone too far. I am anxious about them."

Some of the more waggish of the boys had got a sheet-iron camp-stove—which bears no slight resemblance to a small mortar—and had placed it in such a position as to command one of the approaches! Others had mounted a joint of dangerous-looking stove-pipe on the fore-wheels of an old wagon; while in keeping with the brilliant military strategy displayed elsewhere, and which had such powerful influence on the ever-cautious McClellan in front of Manassas, some reckless wags in Company H had still another piece of stove-pipe duly mounted *en barbette*, on the top of their log-house lunette, on which they had painted, in staring capitals: THE LAST CHANCE!

As a tribute to a brave and worthy young man, now "sleeping his last sleep," it may be mentioned, in this connection, that Colonel Coleman had sent out Andrew Thompson, accompanied by a stalwart negro as guide, with dispatches for Captain Lane. Having each a rifle and a cartridge-box, and with three days' rations in their haversacks, they started out on their perilous mission. Over hills and through valleys, following bridle-paths and blind trails, they pressed on resolutely, and finally succeeded in finding the detachment. The confidence reposed in Andrew by Colonel Coleman, and the words of approbation with which he welcomed him, when he and the detachment came into camp, were alike honorable to both. How freely some of us breathed, and how comfortably brave and self-confident some of us felt, when the two companies defiled past, with their prisoners and genuine Union home-guards, and carrying any quantity of tobacco, I would not dare to say. Certain it is, however, that the thermometer of hope and confidence went up rapidly, and we all felt brave enough and strong enough to make Raleigh both the last chance and the last ditch. Whether the sentiment attributed to Napoleon—that "God is always on the side of the heaviest battalions"—be true or false, one thing is certain, people generally feel considerably more courageous and resolute when in a tight place, if they only know they have good backing.

Hospital Scenes and Incidents—"A Stranger Here."

While officers and men were attending to their appropriate duties, I commenced my work among the sick and wounded in the hospital, or rather hospitals, for there were two. In one of the wards I found a sufferer upon whose countenance Death had set his dark seal. I spoke to him, but he heard me not—he was too close upon the shores of eternity to hear words of earth. No one in the hospital knew him, or could tell where his home was, or whether any one called him son or brother. I knelt down at the side of his lowly bed, and commended him to the tender mercies of a gracious God. Was he prepared to die? Were the ministering angels hovering near to waft his spirit to the better land? Now, that no human language could reach his ear, was Jesus whispering peace and joy in his heart? and while his glassy eyes were closing upon earth, did he see the gates of glory opening to receive him? Or, was the harvest past and the summer ended—the Savior unsought and the soul unsaved? These were questions which it were vain to ask. O, DEATH! how solemn art thou! But much more solemn is LIFE; for it is the living that invests the dying either with the darkness of despair, or with the glorious sunshine of hope. If we live right, God will see to it that we die right, wherever we may be, and whatever may be our circumstances.

In a few minutes the poor sufferer breathed his last, and as we closed his eyes, I thought of some home-circle of loving hearts anxiously waiting for the return of the absent one, but whose face they would see no more. We got his knapsack, and searched it for any letters that might contain the address of relatives. One was found, written by a brother, to which a postscript was added by his father, as follows:

> . . . . "And now, my dear boy, do your duty to your country; and, above all things, remember your Creator in the days of your youth, that you may receive his blessing.
>
> "Your affectionate father,
>
> "J. FORSTER."

On the same evening—Monday, May 19—just as the sun was setting, we consigned to the earth the body of this young man; and, unless removed, there stands on his grave a board—placed there by our kind hospital steward, J. H. Harden—with the inscription:

"RICHARD FORSTER,
Company E,
Thirty-fourth Regiment,
Ohio Vol. Infantry."

"I WILL ARISE AND GO TO MY FATHER."

I was much interested in the case of a young man who was wounded in a skirmish with a guerrilla band, between Raleigh and Flat-Top. When I first saw him, which was about fifteen days after he was wounded, he was suffering very much. A large Belgian rifle-ball had passed through his lungs, and at every breath he took, the air and blood bubbled out through the wound. Our excellent surgeon, Dr. Gabriel, had pronounced his case hopeless, and did not expect him to live till the next day. I spoke to him of his condition, and found that he had a pious father and mother, and that he had been religiously trained. He was greatly discouraged, not so much on account of his bodily affliction as on account of his soul. I spoke to him of the love of God in Christ Jesus, of his tender mercy and long-suffering grace. The tears began to trickle over his cheek, and he whispered earnestly and sadly:

"O, chaplain, I wish it was with me as in months past, when the candle of the Lord shone upon my head. I was happy a year ago, but now"—

He could say no more. In a few minutes he recovered somewhat, and asked me to pray with him. I said to him that Jesus was able to save unto the uttermost all that came unto God through him, "seeing he ever liveth to make intercession for us."

"That 's very precious," was his reply.

"Well, here is another precious text for you: 'This is a faithful saying, and worthy of all acceptation, that Christ Jesus came into the world to save sinners.'" He was too feeble to reply audibly, and was in great physical distress; but he made signs, indicating how sweet and comforting were those words. Kneeling down by his side, I prayed for him, and for the wounded all around, that the joys of salvation might be vouchsafed unto them.

Toward midnight I visited the hospital again, and found that nearly all the sufferers were sleeping. I found my young friend, however, in great distress, and apparently sinking rapidly into the arms of death. Again I tried to soothe his troubled spirit by whispering in his ear the promises of a gracious God, and pointing him to the all-sufficient Savior. He expressed a hope that God would be merciful to him, and forgive his backslidings.

"I have been a professor of religion, a member of the Methodist Church," said he, in a whisper; "but, since coming into the army, I have neglected my duty. Darkness has come upon me; I am backslidden from God; but, O, I will arise and go to my Father, and I will say, "Father, I have sinned!'"

I pressed his hand, bade him good-night, and returned to my quarters, thanking God for the opportunity of speaking "a word in season to him that is weary."

The Wounded of the Princeton Fight.

The Post Hospital of the Kanawha District of the Mountain Department had been located at Raleigh, shortly after our arrival. Dr. Gabriel was in charge, assisted by Dr. Gill, and, for a short time, by Dr. Neal, of the Second Virginia Cavalry, and also by Dr. McNutt, the latter of whom was subsequently Second Assistant Surgeon to the Eleventh. On the 24th of May, Dr. Gabriel received orders from head-quarters at Flat-Top to make hospital arrangements for a number of the wounded of the Princeton fight. The court-house, which had been occupied as company quarters, was cleaned out most thoroughly. Bunks or cots were made of all the available lumber, which, at the best, was only the rough fencing-boards about the town; and as much straw as could be collected within several miles was used in making the rough bunks a little more comfortable.

The work was finished by Sabbath evening—next day—and on Monday the long train of ambulances with the wounded arrived, under charge of Dr. Gill. As quickly as possible the sufferers were laid on the cots provided for them, and every thing done to make them as comfortable as possible under the circumstances. But, alas! they were in a sad state. Many of them had been taken prisoners by the Confederates, and had had but little attention paid them. They had been brought forty miles after being exchanged, and for several days their wounds had not been dressed. When it is added that the weather was very warm and sultry, the reader will be able to form some idea of their terrible state. During that night and next morning the surgeons and nurses worked faithfully, and did every thing that skill and kindness could do to alleviate their sufferings.

Next day, their wounds having been dressed, and every thing done for their mangled bodies, I tried, through the help of God, to lead the wearied, exhausted sufferers to the healing streams of salvation, and to Jesus, the ever-living and ever-loving Physician of souls.

"I DON'T WANT TO THINK!"

An officer of the —— Regiment was among the first that attracted my attention. He had been wounded in the knee; mortification had taken place, and it was evident he had but a few hours to live. I spoke to him as kindly and soothingly as possible, and inquired how he felt.

"Very bad! very bad!" was his reply. He called incessantly for brandy; was restless, nervous, dying. I gave him some brandy and water, which the surgeon had ordered for him, and as I laid his head back on the pillow, and spoke to him of that loving Savior who died to redeem the world, I said: "Would you like me to read a little to you out of God's Word, and pray with you?"

"I'm too weak—I can't be troubled—some time again. Give me brandy! give me brandy!" was his reply.

"You are indeed weak, and seem to be dying, and that is the reason I asked whether you would not wish to be prayed for. Do you think you will get well?"

"I am afraid not," said he.

"I come to you," said I, "as a friend and brother, to speak to you in the name of Christ, who says to all sufferers, 'Come unto me, all ye that are weary and heavy laden, and I will give you rest.' It is a solemn thing to die. Do you think you are prepared to meet God?"

He seemed to quiver under the power of some untold agony, whether entirely physical, it were difficult to tell. He pressed his hands repeatedly on his forehead, as if trying to keep back unwelcome thoughts, and then exclaimed, through his clenched teeth, "*I don't want to think!*" There was a terrible energy in the manner he pronounced those sad words, and they conveyed a terrible meaning.

"God waits to be gracious; look to Him in this the hour of your suffering, and pray for pardon through the Savior's blood," said I, smoothing back the tangled locks from his clammy brow.

"I don't! I don't!" he exclaimed, in a loud whisper, at the same time grasping the blanket convulsively, and drawing it over his face. It seemed as if the poor dying man either did not wish me to speak about spiritual matters, or that the reference to them caused intense anguish. With a sad heart I turned away from this fearfully solemn and gloomy scene, with the intention of making yet another effort to point the dying one to Christ. But the second effort was, if possible, more hopeless than the first, and in an hour or two he had passed into the eternal world!

"He was an infidel," said one who knew him well, in answer to some inquiries I made concerning him.

And is this all the comfort that infidelity can give in the hour of suffering and death? Cold, cheerless, and dark as the grave is the skeptic's pathway! He begins by refusing to think of God and eternity. God is not in all his thoughts. He continues in the dark and cheerless pathway of unbelief, saying to the God of light and life, "Depart from me, O God, for I desire not the knowledge of thy ways!" And when he stands shivering on the brink of eternity, the poor, hopeless, homeless unbeliever exclaims, "I DON'T WANT TO THINK!" And does not this exclamation of this poor dying soldier contain the very essence, the very life, of all ungodliness? How many are there who every day and hour refuse to think on the everlastingly important and precious interests of their souls! They plunge madly into the rushing, deceitful current of worldly pleasure, alike forgetful of the claims of God and the interests of their immortal souls! We speak of their folly—their thoughtlessness. But why thoughtless? Simply because they *refuse to think* on the fearfully-important issues at stake. Practically, they say, "We don't want to think!" Were they to pause in their mad career, and think of their souls' eternal interests, they would be led to repentance. In fact, the enjoyment which any sinner derives from unhallowed pleasures depends upon the success with which he can keep himself from all serious thought. A godless life commences, and is continued in a refusal to think on those matters which affect the soul's happiness, and if persevered in till the light of eternity begins to flash upon the dying pillow, thought then becomes terrible. That dying scene will never be forgotten by those who beheld it. The terribly significant words will not soon be effaced from their memory!

A Brighter Scene—Christ Precious.

Turning away from the sad and gloomy scene just described, I went to a young man a few steps further on, who had been severely wounded in the foot. He had apparently been reading his Bible, for it lay near him, with several of the leaves turned down.

"I am glad to see you with your Bible," said I, as he welcomed me to his lowly cot, with a contented, cheerful smile. "You have been reading some of God's own words—I trust you feel them to be precious in the hour of affliction?"

"Yes," said he, "I feel that the Bible is indeed precious, when one is in suffering. I am not what I ought to be," he continued; "I have not lived as near to my Savior as I ought to have done; but I can say to-day, that what little religion I have in my soul I would not give for all the world!"

"I am glad to see you so happy and contented," I replied, "and trust that Jesus will be near you in all your sufferings. Don't forget this blessed text: 'I will not leave you comfortless; I will come to you.'"

"That is one of my favorite texts," said he, "and I know, from blessed experience, that it is true. Jesus never forsakes his people; He never leaves them comfortless. I have tried sometimes to preach a little, and if God restores me to health and strength, I intend to go on in my long-desired work of preaching the Gospel."

"What Church do you belong to?" I inquired.

"To the Methodist Church," he replied. "I was attending college, at Delaware, Ohio, when the war broke out, but I thought it my duty to shoulder a musket in defense of my country. I have done so, and feel I did right. If I die, all is well. I know that I love the Savior, and, blessed be God! I know he loves me, too." The tears rolled down his cheeks, while he added, "and I am certain, through grace, to have a blessed home in heaven."

Much more he said to the same import. He was truly happy, although suffering very much, and in expectation of undergoing a painful operation. Speaking a few more words of comfort to him, and laying my hand on his noble, broad forehead, I said:

"Now, Brother M——, don't get the least discouraged about your wound. Keep cheerful; be of good courage. God has work for you to do in the world yet, and, by and by, this head will be seen in a pulpit."

I turned away from this pious young soldier, thanking God for such testimonies to the living power of experimental religion, and feeling how closely connected are true piety and lofty patriotism.

"The only Son of his Mother, and She was a Widow."

There was one of the wounded men brought from Princeton who, by his uncomplaining, patient demeanor, notwithstanding his severe sufferings, attracted my attention from the moment he was removed from the ambulance and placed on the hard cot which had been prepared for him. The first words he uttered, except a suppressed cry of pain when laid down, were, "Thank God for this!"

On the following day, while visiting the lower wards of the hospital, where he was, and doing some little thing to make one of the patients comfortable, some one called, several times, "Steward, steward, come here!" Hearing the call frequently repeated, I looked up, and noticed that he was the person who was calling. Beckoning me to come to him, I did so, inquiring if he wished any thing.

"Yes," said he, "I do; are you one of the stewards?"

"No," I replied; "but that makes no difference, if I can help you. What can I do for you?"

"What are you, then?" he asked.

"The chaplain," I replied.

"Excuse me, excuse me," said he. "I didn't know; you don't dress like a chaplain."

"Nothing wrong at all," I replied. "You know a blouse is a fine thing to work in, and there is plenty to do here. What can I do for you?"

"I don't want any thing now. Please sit down; I want to talk with you. I'm glad you are a chaplain. I am much discouraged about myself. I don't think that I can get better."

Poor fellow! he was in a dreadful state. His leg had been mangled fearfully, and in addition to lying some forty-eight hours on the battlefield before his wounds were dressed, he had been neglected by the rebel surgeons to such an extent that they were rendered incurable.

"What are you discouraged about—your prospects of living, or is it about your soul?" I inquired.

"I think," said he, "that I can not get better; but

I am trying to put my trust in God. I am not so much troubled about myself; but, O, if I die, it will break my dear mother's heart!" And the noble, brave man turned away his head and burst into tears, while his whole frame shook with the violence of his emotions. "Poor mother! dear mother! her heart is bound up in me. I don't think of myself, I think of her; for I am her only son, and she is a widow. She has no one to depend on but me."

In a few moments he recovered himself somewhat, and requested me to pray with him. Kneeling beside his hard, lowly cot, I commended him to the tender mercy of that God who hath said, "Call upon me in the day of trouble; I will deliver thee, and thou shalt glorify me."

While talking with him, our excellent surgeon, Dr. Gabriel, came to him, and said that in a few minutes he would have to undergo amputation; that it was the last hope of saving his life; that although every thing would be done for him that was possible, yet he might not live half an hour after the operation, and that it would be well for him to consider all that might be necessary under such circumstances. Dr. Gabriel pressed his hand warmly, and spoke to him as tenderly as if he were his own brother. That little episode, at the side of that hard, rough cot, in the midst of all that was heart-rending of suffering and death, revealed to me the fact that, under all that was quiet, cool, and decided of medical skill, there could beat one of the warmest and tenderest of hearts. From that moment I felt attracted toward the doctor; and, singularly enough, from that very time till he left the army, we were hardly ever separated, either in the camp, on the march, or on the battle-field.

In about half an hour or so, the nurses came to take him into the operating-room. As he was carried out, he said: "Farewell, boys! farewell!" In two hours afterward he breathed his last! As I watched by him for a few minutes—a few minutes, reader, for I went from one dying man to another, and from the bedside of the dying to the grave, and from the grave to the bedside again—O God! this is war!—as I watched by him a few minutes, I thought of that brave, noble heart yearning for a mother's soothing voice, and the gentle pressure of a mother's soft hand, and whose last hours were troubled only by the thought of her loneliness and distress; and I wondered whether that mother, all unconscious, perhaps, of the condition of her dear boy, was, even then, praying *for* him as she used to pray *with* him, in other days, beside a little crib, while she taught him to lisp, "Now I lay me down to sleep."

As a fitting close to this hospital incident, I append the following extract from my note-book:

"*Wednesday*, May 28, 1862.—Corporal Thomas Johnson, Company D, Thirty-fourth Regiment Ohio Volunteer Infantry, died this evening, a few hours after having leg amputated. He was from Kenton, Ohio, and was wounded at the battle of Princeton."

CHAPTER IV

ANGELS IN THE HOSPITAL—WOMAN'S WORK—A REMARKABLE DEATH-BED—A MOTHER'S INFLUENCE.

THE wife who girds her husband's sword,
'Mid little ones who weep or wonder
And bravely speaks the cheering word,
What though her heart be rent asunder,
Doom'd nightly in her dreams to hear
The bolts of death around him rattle,
Hath shed as sacred blood as e'er
Was poured upon a field of battle!

The mother who conceals her grief,
While to her breast her son she presses,
Then breathes a few brave words and brief
Kissing the patriot brow she blesses;
With no one but her secret God
To know the pain that weighs upon her,
Sheds holy blood as e'er the sod
Received on Freedom's field of honor!

T. BUCHANAN READ.

MINISTERING ANGELS.

WE have had angel visits in the army. Angels have ministered to the suffering patriot soldier in many a camp and hospital, and on many a battle-field. Not angels direct from heaven, nor angels with white wings and golden crowns, as represented by poets and painters; not angels who are considered superior to some of the little frailties of humanity—no, nor angels whose visits are said to be few and far between—but angels of the earth who never were in heaven (unless Beecher's "Conflict of Ages" be true), but who, we earnestly pray, may yet be arrayed in white robes, be adorned with unfading crowns, and dwell forever in the city of God; angels in veritable human bodies, and—be it faintly whispered—not always superior to some of the frailties supposed to be incident to such habitations. Yes, to be plainer still, angels who have nimble fingers, and who rattle knitting-needles, and flourish scissors, and thrust with thimbles, in a way that looks as if they had a very close connection with something more practical than poetic. "Angels! Bah! You mean ladies!" sneers some cynical old bachelor, who never was pleased in his life, and never intends to be. "Angels! Pretty angels, forsooth!" exclaims some long-faced Pharisee, who thinks he is pious, when he is only bilious, and who considers it a special mark of virtue to make a sanctimonious outcry against the failings of men in general (except himself, good soul!) and of women in particular. Yes, angels! ye solitary croakers and ye canting Pharisees, who perform the double drama of saints at church and sinners at home! Yes, angels! all ye true, noble hearts who can understand the unspoken wants of the sad and suffering, and who can appreciate the noble efforts of mother and wife and sister to supply those wants. Yes, angels truly! all ye noble women of the loyal North, who have made sacrifices so heroically, and labored so faithfully and perseveringly in your Soldiers' Aid Societies, and done so much for God and humanity in the day of the nation's deepest distress.

But what has all this to do with the army, which, at the best, is not the most favorable place to meet with angels, either from heaven or earth? Very much, dear reader—very much indeed; and if you have never been in the army, perhaps you will understand my idea of the angelic in camp-life, if I paint you two living pictures as they might have been seen at the time referred to in the previous chapter.

First Picture.

It is a large room or hall, and running its entire length are six rows of rough cots or bunks. Come up stairs. Here is a room of similar dimensions, and containing the same number of cots. On each of these rough cots lies a wounded soldier. Here is one whose arm was amputated a day or two since. He is very weak and discouraged, for unfavorable symptoms have appeared. He has only a little loose straw laid on the boards for his bed, and his overcoat or knapsack is his only pillow. He is hungry, but can not eat the hard crackers and coffee, which is all he can get. Here is another, wounded in the breast, who, in his agony, rolls his head uneasily from side to side. He will die, likely, to-night. There is another near by. A ball went crashing through his leg, and you can see, from the appearance of the sufferer, that there is little hope of his recovery. Yonder is another, who has been gashed terribly. He is bleeding to death, and a few hours will close the scene. Close by you there is a mere youth, whose shoulder has been torn by a piece of shell. He looks deathly pale, and is wasted to a skeleton. He says if he had something nice, such as his mother would get up for him, he would get well right away. You see that poor fellow close by the window there, propped up by a couple of knapsacks? He may die any moment, for you could almost turn your hand in the gaping wound through his lungs. Go from cot to cot, and suffering is seen everywhere. Now, just look a little closer. Can you see a single pillow, or sheet, or bed-cover? Can you see a clean garment on those poor sufferers? No, not one! A coarse army blanket has been spread on the scanty allowance of straw; the wearied, wounded soldier has been laid down on it, and another coarse blanket has been thrown over him. Nobly the surgeons and nurses have been working to render the poor fellows as comfortable as possible, but the hospital stores are nearly exhausted. This large draft on our resources was totally unexpected, and we are forty-five miles from the nearest supplies. The men look haggard, dirty, and distressed. God pity them!

"Click! click! click!" goes the key of the telegraph instrument, and the electric messenger tells the tale of suffering and want and death to those who are in comfort and peace at home, hundreds of miles off.

Day succeeds day, and night, weary, dreary night, comes and goes. Cries of pain, moans of deep distress, labored breathings, murmured prayers for mercy, and long last sighs are heard every day and every night. The roll of the muffled drum, and the subdued, plaintive notes of Pleyel's Hymn, are heard frequently, as the soldier is carried to his long home. The large hospital is not so crowded now; but, see, yonder is a row of graves which tells a mournful tale!

Second Picture.

It is Sabbath afternoon—a bright, beautiful day, which reminds us of blessed meetings in the sanctuary, and dear friends at home in the enjoyment of many spiritual and temporal comforts. It reminds us, too, of the blessed, beautiful Sabbath of heaven—the fadeless splendors, the undying glory, and the unruffled calm of God's upper sanctuary. Let us visit the hospital again. Lo, what a change! Nice, soft pillows, white as snow, have taken the place of coats and knapsacks. Clean sheets and ample coverlets have been substituted for the coarse, dark army blankets, and the patients are all dressed in clean, white garments, which remind us of those robes in which John saw the saints arrayed as they stood before the great white throne. A subdued yet unmistakable cheerfulness is depicted on every countenance. The luxury of cleanliness has been enjoyed, and the patients feel not only more comfortable and cheerful, but absolutely better. The hospital, and all within it, has been entirely transformed, and you feel like asking whether the days of miracles are passed. By what means has this thrice-welcome change been accomplished?

There are marks on those snowy sheets and pillows

and soft quilts. Examine them, and see whether they will explain the mystery. Ah, yes, the mystery is solved! "Soldiers' Aid Society of Cleveland;" "Soldiers' Aid Society, Toledo;" "Sanitary Commission, Cincinnati," are the words marked on those pillows and sheets and other valuable articles; and they tell us at once who the good angels are who, unseen, performed this miracle. But this is not all. Fruits of different kinds, various cordials and delicacies, and many little tokens of sympathy are in abundance, and, for the past day or two, the sick have had something better than mere army rations. They now feel that they are not forgotten. Their hearts are cheered and encouraged. Beautiful visions of wives and mothers and sisters are brought vividly before them; a Sabbath calm pervades the whole scene, while we seem to hear, audibly, the words: "*Blessed are the merciful, for they shall obtain mercy.*" "*It is more blessed to give than to receive.*" Blessings, rich blessings—blessings in time and blessings in eternity—rest upon the noble women of the land, who remember the sick and wounded soldier, and who, for his comfort, ply the busy needle with such skill and industry! The blessings of him who was ready to perish shall come upon them, and their noble deeds will be had in everlasting remembrance! Never, till they stand before Jesus in glory, will they fully know the good they have accomplished, the hungry they have fed, the naked they have clothed, the sick they have visited, and the dying they have soothed.

Am I correct in saying that we had the ministrations of angels?

THE CHRISTIAN SOLDIER S LAST VICTORY—A THRILLING SCENE.

The circumstances under which any remark is made, or quotation repeated, often invest that remark or quotation with additional interest. This is specially true of some of the most beautiful and familiar of our sacred lyrics. How often does the reading or singing of some old familiar hymn awaken in one's bosom the tenderest memories of the past, or the sweetest remembrances of some dear friend, long since gone to rest! How often does some old, simple melody, which fashionable choirs, in the rage for operatic singing, have condemned as obsolete and in bad taste, carry us away back, by the mere force of association, to scenes of childhood, when we knelt beside a now sainted mother, and felt her hand laid affectionately upon our head, as we repeated the beautiful little prayer—

"Now I lay me down to sleep!"

We seem to see that dear mother again, and hear that loved voice that so often soothed our childhood's sorrows; and we again see that dear old home, and brothers and sisters, some in the grave, and others "scattered far and wide, by mountain, stream, and sea." We stand again in that peaceful old graveyard, where the grass is growing green on many a grave, and where, perhaps, we have shed many a bitter tear; or we are carried away by the force of association, to some little room, where a dear Christian friend calmly and peacefully entered the valley of the shadow of death, and we seem to hear again his shouts of triumph, as he neared the celestial city, "Thanks be to God, who giveth us the victory through our Lord Jesus Christ!"

There is one hymn which, perhaps, more than any other, awakens sweet and tender emotions in the truly Christian heart, because of its frequent association with all that is peaceful, hopeful, and glorious in death-bed experiences. The hymn referred to contains the following sweet and soul-thrilling lines:

"Jesus can make a dying bed
Feel soft as downy pillows are;
While on his breast I lean my head,
And sweetly breathe my life out there."

These lines have always been peculiarly interesting to me, as expressing the calm repose and childlike confidence which the believer enjoys while "waiting, only waiting, till the dawning of the day," when he shall be wafted to the realms of immortality. But to some whose duties called them to minister to the wants of the sick and wounded in the hospital at Raleigh, they are invested with more than common interest. Whenever I hear them read or sung, they bring before me one of the most thrillingly interesting and peaceful death-beds I have ever seen.

Among those brought from Princeton, spoken of in a preceding chapter, was a young man, very severely wounded. There was something about him which was very prepossessing. He had such an air of manly dignity, intelligence, and refinement, that no one could be long beside him without feeling a deep interest in him, and having the desire to render him as comfortable as possible. Shortly after he arrived, the surgeons decided that amputation of the leg was absolutely necessary. A few hours before the operation was performed, I had a long and interesting conversation with him. He said that he was blessed with kind, Christian parents, who had set before him a godly example. He made very special reference to his mother, speaking of her in the most respectful and affectionate language. With tenderest emotion, he spoke of his being a child of many prayers—the youngest of the family—and how peaceful and happy was home—dear, sweet home—sanctified by the daily offerings on the family altar! "And I may never see home again—I may die here, far from friends, and—and—O, if I could just get home!"

He spoke these words in a low, sad tone, while a tear glistened on his cheek and his whole body quivered in agony.

"And if you were to die here," I asked, "what do you think would be your prospects for eternity? Do you feel prepared to meet God?"

"No," said he, "I am afraid not. At least I don't feel happy in the thought of dying. I know that God is merciful, that the Savior died for me; and whether I live or die, I am determined, through grace, to put my trust in him, *yet I want something*."

"Have you ever been a professor of religion—are you a member of any Church?" I inquired.

"No, I am not," he answered, "and yet I think I have sometimes enjoyed religion. But I am not satisfied—*there is something wanting*."

"Are you trying to throw yourself, as a poor, lost sinner, on the mercy of God in Christ?"

"I am trying to do so," he answered; "for although I have not followed the example of wicked men in the army—such as swearing and drinking and gambling—yet I have not read my Bible, nor prayed as I should have done. I feel I am a poor, unworthy sinner, and I pray to God for mercy."

I tried to encourage him by repeating the blessed invitations of Christ himself, and urging upon his attention the glorious truth that "God is love." Poor boy! his sufferings were very great, but scarcely a murmur escaped his lips.

In the afternoon he was carried into the operating-room, and his leg amputated. While the wound was being dressed, he raised his hand, and laying it on my shoulder, as I moistened his lips with wine and water, he whispered to me:

"O, I have such a good mother! if she knew"—

A cry of pain, occasioned by the surgeon's needle, closed the sentence. I gathered from these words that, in the midst of terrible suffering, visions of home and of a dear, kind mother flitted before him, and, no doubt, he longed to lay his weary head once more on her bosom. O, the sweet, tender, holy power of a mother! How beautiful the web of love which she weaves and throws around her loved ones, so that, wherever they may wander, they feel as if mother is still near them! I have been among the sick, the wounded, and the dying, in the hospitals and on the field of battle, and have looked upon scenes of suffering which no pen can describe. I have gone from one dying soldier to another, hurried to the funeral of one and then of another, and back again to my post beside the hard, hard pillow on which others were struggling with the last enemy. I have knelt on the battlefield to pray with the dying soldier as his life-blood oozed away, and his eyes were growing dim in death. And I make this record for you, O mothers, that next only to the Savior—second only to the blessed name "JESUS"—the dying ones have murmured in their last moments, and breathed in their last prayers, the endearing words, "MOTHER! HOME!" Your son may be thoughtless and wayward, and it may seem as if your pious example and oft-repeated injunctions have been all in vain, and your prayers all unanswered; nevertheless, remember that you have not only the word of the Faithful Promiser to encourage you, but you have under your control the purest and most tender sympathies of the human heart, through which you may exert the most powerful influence for good, long after your son has left your roof, and even when the grass is growing green upon your grave.

Two days after the operation, it was my painful duty to inform my young friend that his days, yea, his hours, were numbered.

"Would you be disappointed," said I, "if you were told that you would not get better?"

"Well—yes, I would," was his answer. "Do you think I won't get better?"

Poor boy! even then Death's dark shadow was upon him. I answered, that it was not possible for him to live.

"If that is so," said he, with an anxious, disappointed look, "I hope God will have mercy upon me, and receive me unto himself. How long will I live, do you think—a few days?"

"No," I answered, "not many hours."

"I wanted to see father and mother—but—but—well, I'll try to be resigned. Pray with me, chaplain."

I knelt down beside him, and commended him to the tender mercy of that God who hath declared himself as the Lord God merciful and gracious, slow to anger, and plenteous in mercy. He followed the prayer audibly, and responded with fervor. I then repeated some of those texts of Scripture which seemed most appropriate to his condition, after which I inquired whether he could trust in Jesus as his all-sufficient Savior?"

"I don't want to deceive myself," said he, "but I think I can say I trust in Christ. I have nowhere else to go. I'm a poor sinner, but I think Jesus will not cast me off."

He then requested me to write, at his dictation, a letter to his father and mother. I did so; and from what he directed to be written, I was enabled to know more fully the state of his mind. Having finished his little worldly business, and requested his pillow to be adjusted, he said:

"Now I'm tired; I'll rest a little."

Others in the hospital required my attention, and I left him for an hour or so. On returning to him, I found that he was fast sinking—his sufferings were very great. As soon as he caught a glimpse of me, he gasped—

"You're the one I want. Come, stand by me, and

speak to me of Jesus. O, chaplain," said the dying boy, with thrilling earnestness, "you won't leave me, will you? O, don't leave me—wait with me till all is over, and speak to me! O, this pain! Jesus—Jesus, bless me—keep me!"

I repeated to him part of the fourteenth chapter of John's Gospel, and when I came to the words, "I WILL NOT LEAVE YOU COMFORTLESS; I WILL COME TO YOU"—a sweet but melancholy smile lit up his countenance. "Can you take these words and apply them to yourself?" I asked.

"Yes, yes, bless the Lord! I can—I can!" he answered, warmly.

"Do you remember any particular hymn your mother used to sing?" I inquired.

"Yes, a great many," he answered.

"Do you remember this—'Jesus can make a'"—

"I know it," said he—

"'Jesus can make a dying bed
Feel soft as downy pillows are;
While on his breast I lean my head
And sweetly breathe my life out there.'

"I'm trying to lean on Jesus. I think—yes, I know he won't cast me off."

"Do you think Jesus loves you?" I inquired.

"Yes, yes," he replied, with great earnestness, "Jesus loves me—I know Jesus loves me!"

"Here is a hymn I like," he continued, and immediately commenced singing—

"Say, comrades, will you meet me?
Say, comrades, will you meet me?

Say, comrades, will you meet me
On Canaan's happy shore?
Yes, by the grace of God, I'll meet you;
Yes, by—the—grace"—

He could sing no more!

"I'm too weak—I'm too weak to sing any more, chaplain—but I'll sing in heaven, won't I?"

The hospital was hushed, and the nurses, who had gathered round this wondrous scene, were in tears. Turning to the nurse who attended him—a member of his own regiment—he thanked him for his kindness, and, stretching out his hand to him, said, with deep pathos:

"Will you meet me in heaven?"

In a few minutes after this, Death's dark, mysterious shadow passed over him. I thought he was gone, but he rallied again for a short time. Suddenly looking up in my face, he said:

"What is your name?"

I told him.

"Well," said he, "I'm so glad you've been with me—we'll soon part—but, O! we'll meet—in—heaven—won't we?"

"Yes," I said, "by the grace of God, I'll meet you in heaven!"

"It's getting very dark, chaplain—I can't—see."

"It will soon be light," I replied, "for you will soon be where there is no night."

He asked for some water, and after he had taken a little, he stretched out both hands, and in a mournful, pathetic manner, cried out:

"Lord Jesus, come and take me! Blessed Savior,

take me in thy arms—I am so weary—I'm so weary! Come, dear Savior, come!"

"Is the Savior precious to you?" I inquired.

"Yes, he is precious," was the reply.

"Do you think he loves you?" I again inquired. With thrilling earnestness, though with feeble voice, he replied:

"I know he loves me—O! yes, I know he loves me. And now I'm going," he continued; "I'll soon be in heaven."

He fixed a long, wistful gaze upon me, and his countenance assumed once more the dark hue of death. Raising, with great effort, both hands, he clasped me round the neck as I stooped over him, and, drawing me down, kissed me affectionately, and whispered:

"When you see—my—mother, tell her—I—I—died a Christian and—and"—

The sentence was finished in heaven! Dear, patient boy! when torn, mangled, dying, thy brave heart yearned for home, and a mother's tender care and soothing words; but now thou art safely in the home of God. But if departed spirits ever look down upon this earth, perhaps thou art hovering near me, as I pen these lines to the praise of that Savior with whom thou art now dwelling! No wonder I contrasted the condition of this boy with the lines which he quoted:

> "Jesus can make a dying bed
> Feel soft as downy pillows are."

"Soft!"—a little straw laid on a few rough boards!

"Downy pillows!"—his weary head was laid on a hard knapsack! Yet Jesus made that hard pillow soft, and around that humble cot on which lay this suffering boy, angels from heaven were hovering, and, when his last battle was fought, they wafted him to the bosom of Jesus.

So died J. L. Ransom, of the Thirty-fourth Regiment Ohio Volunteers.

CHAPTER V.

"LISTEN! I hear the harmonies of heaven,
From sphere to sphere, and from the boundless round,
Reëchoing bliss to those serenest hights
Where angels sit and strike their emulous harps,
Wreathed round with flowers and diamonded with dew—
Such dew as gemm'd the ever-during blooms
Of Eden, winterless; or as all night
The Tree of Life wept from its every leaf
Unwithering."—FESTUS.

FLOWERS FOR THE SICK.

IF it could not be said of Raleigh and vicinity that it was a land flowing with milk and honey, it might, at least, be said to be a land abounding with flowers. Perhaps the veterans of some Ohio regiments who have often done picket duty on some of the bridle-paths leading to "everywhere and nowhere" in the woods, and whose eyes may glance over these pages, may say, "Yes, it was a land of snakes, too!" Well, it is conceded there were snakes in abundance. Ugh! the very thought of them makes one feel "shivery!" But, then, let us forget the snakes just now, and speak of the flowers.

If the writer were inclined to be a pantheist, his pantheism would be limited; that is, every thing would not be God, nor God every thing. He would make a selection from the elements of universal deity, and would be in danger of becoming an out-and-out heathen—even supposing pantheism to be only a more philosophical system of paganism. There would be but three elements—or, if it suit better, three idols—he would worship; namely, Children, Flowers, and Music. Or perhaps he might associate the three with the idea of unity, and thus have but one idol, a trinity; for children and flowers seem to be always associated together, and wherever there are children and flowers, there is music too. We might go further. Children, flowers, and music are associated with all our ideas of heaven, and there is not the least doubt that there are myriads of radiant, happy children in the better land, whose dwelling-places are amid scenery of exquisite beauty and fadeless splendor, and where there is breathed perpetually the sweetest music. Yea, may there not be infant choirs in heaven, whose melodies will forever be the glorious echo of the child-loving Redeemer's words—"For of such is the kingdom of heaven!" May there not be scenes of surpassing loveliness there?—and may not every hill and vale of that blessed land be beautified with the richest treasures of the floral creation? And what of heaven's music? What shall be said of those grand oratorios performed by the innumerable hosts of angels and redeemed saints before the great white throne, when the grand choral symphonies will be as the voice of many waters?

Speaking of flowers has led my erratic pen from the line of narrative. This is somewhat natural, although it is generally admitted that there is not much of poetic sentiment, except the epic, perhaps, about camp life. What I intended to say was, that one of the most pleasant employments I had while at Raleigh was to go out to the woods every morning and gather as many flowers as I could carry, and make bouquets for the sick and wounded in the hospital. The bouquets were given in the name of mother or sister, or *somebody else's sister*, whose likeness they had laid away snugly in their knapsack, or placed securely in their bosom. A glad smile and warm pressure of the hand often told, more eloquently than words, how acceptable the little gifts were. Some of the most pleasing remembrances of hospital duties and experiences while at Raleigh are connected with the distribution of those flowers among the sick and wounded, and not a few truly pathetic scenes rise up before me as I pen these lines. Too hallowed, however, by the sweeter and more tender and sacred of human sensibilities, to be revealed to every eye, they are vailed and laid away in the sanctuary of the heart, with other sacred memories of the past.

Gathering Flowers under Difficulties—A Pleasant Position.

On a beautiful morning in July, in search of flowers, as usual, for the sick and wounded, I got my friend Byron to accompany me to the woods, a little north of the camp.

While we were busy at our pleasant task, we were startled by the report of a musket and the whiz of a ball in too close proximity for our comfort. Bang!

whiz! hum! whir-r! There goes another right over our heads. Instinctively we make for the nearest trees, and get as close to mother Earth as possible. While talking, whiz goes a ball between Byron and myself. We crawl closer to the tree. Bang! bang! whir-r! shug! The ball struck the tree I was leaning against, and I felt the jar very perceptibly! What in the world does all this mean? Bang! bang! whiz! hum! whir-r! again, and the balls come thicker and faster. There was, after a few minutes—it seemed hours—a lull; and, deeming discretion the greater part of valor, we threw a hill between us and the place whence we thought the firing proceeded—at least, we put ourselves behind the hill, which amounts to the same thing. I never let go my flowers; but, somehow or other, whether they had wilted by being kept in the sun, or whether they had been too roughly treated for their delicate organizations, or whether my sense of beauty had been disturbed somewhat by being under fire, or whether the ideal had given way to the intensely actual, I will not undertake to determine. Certain it is, however, my flowers were not so beautiful as usual that morning; and hereafter wild honeysuckles, forget-me-nots, blue-bells, and fox-gloves will forcibly remind me of Minié balls. The whole was caused by a mistake of Captain T——, who had just come into camp with his company. They were firing off their pieces, and only mistook the target—that was all! I have a quarrel with the captain yet for that, and I here revenge myself by putting his initials—S. T.—in good type, and wishing him swung off into—matrimony! Hope I'll be there to perform the execution. Rather guess the knot won't slip.

Apropos to the foregoing, I may give the following as

A Solemn Joke at the Chaplain's Expense.

One morning, when visiting the hospital, and speaking an encouraging word to each patient individually, I came to one who had been severely wounded, and whose sufferings the day before, while having his wounds dressed, were very severe. He was deathly pale, and had a very sad, desponding expression of countenance. Believing more in a good-humored smile and a genial, encouraging word, as being better, both for moral and physical health, than demure looks and sanctimonious sighs, I did the best I could to comfort and encourage him. In doing so, both religion and patriotism were spoken of. Among other encouraging things, I told him—"That very likely he would go home a cripple; that he would have but one leg on which to journey along through life; that he might, perhaps, have some serious difficulties to contend with, but it would always be a great comfort for him to reflect that he had suffered in a good cause; that he had shouldered his musket in defense of his country; that his wounds were honorable to him, and that God would bless him"—and so on.

"He's a secesh, chaplain—he's a secesh!" said a wounded boy, occupying the next bunk. "He was wounded when bushwhacking us on the Flat-Top road. I got shot by some of the cusses myself. Yes, chaplain, he's a secesh!"

"Ah! hem! well! yes—hem!" stammered I, feeling somewhat up a stump. "Secesh! ah—considerable of a mistake," I continued, trying to recover my equilibrium, and as gracefully as possible remove the underpinning of the consolatory edifice I had been so industriously and hopefully building.

"But he is sorry for what he has done, and says he did wrong in joining the rebs," said the boy, apologizing as much as possible for the wrong-doer, and magnanimously trying to take the edge off his keen accusation.

Knowing that this little incident would likely get thoroughly ventilated, and be a standing joke, the chaplain was very careful to tell it to two of the most remorseless jokers of the regiment—Colonel Coleman and Captain Duncan. As it was, however, the chaplain was bored slightly, now and again, by a good-humored reference to the circumstance.

CHAPTER VI.

A WOMAN'S ESTIMATE OF A WOMAN'S VALUE—PRACTICAL MECHANICS AND ENGINEERS—OFFICIAL THEORIES AND UNOFFICIAL REALITIES—BRIDGE AND FERRY ENGINEERING—A SOUTHERN BAPTIST BROTHER'S PITY FOR UNCLE SAM'S SOLDIER-MECHANICS.

WHAT IS A WOMAN WORTH?

DON'T screw your mouth into a contemptuous sneer, nor draw down your eyebrows into a disdainful smile, my bachelor friend, at what, perhaps, you think the ominous title of this paragraph. It is not intended to give a homily on woman's rights nor woman's sphere. By no means. Such work would be superfluous now. If woman has not asserted both her rights and her sphere, since this war commenced, then it will likely never be done. The author would state, however, with becoming modesty, that he considers himself quite orthodox on the "Woman's Rights" question, and that he is a firm believer in the doctrine first proclaimed in Eden, that woman is man's ministering angel, and that hers is a ministry of love and joy.

True, woman sometimes falls from the high and holy position in which God himself placed her; and when she does fall, she falls as an angel of light—her descent is terrific! When fulfilling her blessed mission of love and gentleness, she diffuses a heavenly calm and peace all around, and makes the scene of her special ministry—home, sweet home—

"The dearest spot on earth."

But when her fine feelings are blunted, her sympathies chilled, her gentleness destroyed, her generous, unselfish spirit quenched, then is she seen, not as an angel of light, but as a fallen spirit, scattering firebrands, arrows, and death. The histories of our Marthas and Marys are beautiful pictures of love and gentleness—the most beautiful seen outside of heaven. The histories of Herodias and Cleopatra are dark pictures of malignity and pride—the darkest outside of hell. A wicked man is barely endurable; a wicked woman is shocking. Low brutality in man excites your indignation and scorn; in woman it fills you with feelings of unutterable shame. A swearing, blustering man, who deals in human souls and bodies, is simply a loathsome brute, whose very existence you feel to be a huge excrescence on the body politic, and a ghastly mockery of modern civilization. A vulgar, boastful, cruel slave-mistress is a fiend incarnate, whose very delicacy of organization and acute sensibilities enable her, not to bruise with a club the human body, but to sting with the keenest anguish the human heart. The sight of a drunken man wallowing in the mire causes a feeling of pity, or, at most, of disgust; the sight of an intoxicated woman causes your cheek to mantle with shame; and, for the sake of woman's honor and holy position, you have an instinctive dread of others seeing the abhorrent sight or hearing the dread tale. When men conceal themselves behind trees, logs, or fences, and murder unsuspecting Union men—as has been done every day in rebeldom—the most intense indignation is aroused in every noble heart, and swift punishment is demanded for every such murderer; but when women perform the same dastardly deeds, we stand aghast at the fearful revelation of female cruelty and degradation.

At one time, two men were discovered by our "boys" putting poison in the springs near one of the camps in the valley—they were caught in the very act. In twenty minutes these same would-be assassins were hanging on the nearest tree. A few days afterward, a woman sold poisoned cakes to some in our regiment, and two purchasers were brought to death's door by them—and what was done? Nothing. Why? I don't know, unless it was on the principle that the woman who could fall so low as to become an assassin, was certainly in that state spoken of by the poet—

"Where'er I am, 't is hell! myself am hell!"

These remarks are induced by the remembrance of an incident which took place during our campaign in the Kanawha Valley. Once, when traveling between Gauley Bridge and Charleston, on special regimental business, I applied at what was styled a first-class Virginia mansion for supplies for the inner man. The cavalry escort with which I had been favored from Raleigh had turned back, and as they had led me on the gallop for thirty miles, I felt disposed to rest as well as eat. The information had been volunteered to me by a half-secesh trader from the North—who hadn't soul enough to see his country's interests except as they were connected with his two hundred per cent. profit—that the mansion in question was inhabited by the genuine Virginia chivalry from the eastern part of the State; that the old gentleman was an aristocrat of the "first families," and the daughters were no disgrace to the old "Norman blood"—and much more to the same sort.

Dinner being over, I entered the parlor, and, taking up a richly-gilded book from the center-table, I proceeded to make myself comfortable for an hour or two. A dreamy, pleasant calm soon began to settle down upon me, the words were oddly running together, and "Nature's sweet restorer, balmy sleep," was gently wooing me, when I was startled by a shrill voice, speaking so harshly and abruptly that I concluded some sweet domestic misunderstanding had taken place among the fair representatives of the chivalry. Bang! went one door, and slam! went another, and, in a twinkling, a fair young lady of some five-and-thirty summers—or winters, if you like—was standing, or rather *stamping*, before me, in the most approved style of feminine scolding.

"Dog-on them niggers! Thar again—I'll be dog-on'd if they hain't torn my collar, and spoil't my handkerchief—and—and—blast 'em all, they ain't worth their necks! O, if I had the training of 'em, I'll be bound I'd make 'em mind! You Sal, thar! tote them 'ar things this way, or"—

What the terrible "or" was designed to convey to Sal I don't know; but the fair beauty's foot went down on the floor with such an emphasis, that it seemed to say, "You'll catch it, by thunder!"

Thinking this exhibition of ruffled temper was not designed for strangers' eyes or ears, I made a slight movement by way of announcing my presence. But this was entirely unnecessary, and I might have saved myself some little sympathy I felt for the lady caught in the undignified position of a termagant, for she was aware of my presence, and turned toward me with flushed face—not of shame, but of passion—and apostrophized me thus:

"What a plague them niggers are! Talk about 'em taking care of 'emselves, and all that 'ar! Dog-on't, they don't know nothin'. I've got to follow 'em up, and follow 'em up everywhar, and show 'em how to do this and how to do that, and ef I don't watch 'em, and see that every thing is done as I want it, why it ain't done at all. They are a lazy, good-for-nothin' set—now that's p'intedly so. An' the more you do for 'em, the worse they get. They have no gratitude—not they."

Much in the same polite and lady-like style she rattled off her eminently gracious remarks, and thus gave free vent to her overtaxed and amiable temper—as much, perhaps, for her own comfort as my edification—and she finally subsided into a calmer mood and into the sofa at the same time. I frankly acknowledge that I felt first amused, and then mischievous. Keeping my face as grave as any New England deacon's, I blandly questioned her regarding slaveholding kindness, the strong bond of affection between master and slave, so pathetically dwelt upon by novelists and ministers of the South-side school, and finally wound up by inquiring into the market value of human property in the Kanawha Valley. All of this seemed to have a very soothing effect on her irritated nervous system, and she spoke and acted very much as a high-toned, noble Virginia lady might be expected to do. In fact, she became quite communicative, and chatted away as if nothing had transpired to ruffle her amiable temper. In answer to a question relative to the value of slave property, she said:

"Women don't bring as good a price as men. You can't buy a man for much less than fifteen hundred. But, law me! men ain't worth that no-how. Women ain't worth near as much."

"What is a woman worth?" I politely inquired.

"Well, that woman thar"—pointing outside to a colored woman busy with laundry work—"cost pretty high. You can't buy much of a woman for less than eight or nine hundred—no, sir, a woman that is any thing of a woman can't be got for much less."

This last was too much for me. It seemed as if some horrid monster, half brute, half devil, had hissed in my ears, "*You can't buy much of a woman for less than eight or nine hundred dollars!*" And this was spoken of woman by a woman! I had read and heard much of the horrid character of the God-accursed institution of slavery, but I never felt such a thrill of horror, such a painful sensation of outraged womanly dignity and honor, as I then experienced. "MUCH OF A WOMAN!" Woman, her personal appearance, her age, her abilities as cook or laundress, her affections as daughter or wife or mother, her keen sensibilities, her womanly delicacy—herself, soul and body, put in the balance, and her price estimated by woman at so many hundred dollars, more or less! If a low, coarse, blear-eyed villain of a slave-trader had uttered these words, perhaps the revulsion of feeling would not have been so great; but that a lady should utter such sentiments, in a cool, deliberate manner, was absolutely horrid. I had a decided impression that I was rapidly falling from grace—that is, the grace of believing every lady an angel—and, lest such a calamity might befall me, I rose and proceeded on my journey. For days the words seemed to hiss in my ears, and I felt that this apparently trivial incident was additional proof that slavery pollutes whatever it touches.

Rough and Ready Engineers—Axes and Rifles.

In April, 1861, when the Massachusetts troops, under command of glorious old Butler, marched through Annapolis, on their way to Washington City, determined to gain the Capital either *through* or *over* traitor mobs—it made little difference which—they found the only locomotive in the dépôt disabled, the railroad track torn up, and the bridges burned. It was the work of a few moments to find men in the regiments who could both build, repair, and run a locomotive. Others could be found who had experience in laying railroad track, while any number of practical mechanics and engineers stepped out of the ranks, and volunteered to rebuild the bridges. What occurred then with the brave Massachusetts soldiers, has occurred a thousand times since, in all portions of the army. Unlike the armies of the older and more warlike nations of Europe, which are composed mostly of professional soldiers, who practically know but little more than the duties which pertain to a military life, our armies have been made up of practical and experienced mechanics from our machine-shops—carpenters from our factories and boat-yards—molders and workers in iron from our foundries—practical engineers, conductors, and brakesmen from our railroads—steamboatmen and sailors from our rivers, lakes, and sea-coasts—lumbermen from our pine forests, as familiar with the ax, the drag, and the saw-mill as a lady is with her thimble and scissors—editors, printers, dentists, doctors, and dancing-masters—shoemakers, tailors, and bakers—not forgetting even preachers, with all their reported leanings in the *chicken* direction. The Eleventh Ohio was a fair representative of the army in general for mechanical, scientific, and literary resources. Bridges could be built, locomotives repaired, railroad track laid, ferry-boats built and navigated, saw-mills erected and kept running, roads surveyed and made; ovens built, and bread, that would have driven a Frenchman mad with envy, baked in them; watches repaired, *but not* accurately timed; teeth extracted, and dental work performed generally; type set up and newspapers printed—*vide* the *Weekly Invincible* or *Semi-Weekly Eleventh*—could all be accomplished within the limits of the regiment.

There were two occasions when the more practical of mechanical and engineering skill was brought into more than usual prominence. One was when the

Army of the Kanawha, under command of General J. D. Cox, moved for the first time up the valley. The first obstacle that required the special attention of the engineers was the Poco, or Pocotaligo River. The rebel General Wise had burned the bridge on his retreat up the valley, so as to retard the progress of the Union troops. When Cox's division arrived at the river, it could be easily forded at several places, but, as it was necessary to concentrate the troops and receive supplies at that point before advancing further, several days elapsed before it was deemed proper to cross. In the mean time, the river had been swollen by heavy rains, and was running bank-full. It was necessary, therefore, to adopt some means to effect a crossing, as orders had been given for an immediate advance. The professional engineer, upon whom the duty of bridging the stream devolved, received orders to construct a bridge immediately—in obedience to which he proceeded to select a site, and ordered a detail of men to commence the work. The discovery was made, however, that while there were workmen in abundance, there were no tools with which to do the work. An order was immediately dispatched to Ohio for the necessary tools, and the prospect was that the army would be detained for at least a week or ten days.

It was suggested to General Cox that Captain Lane, who was a practical mechanic himself, and in command of a company mostly made up of experienced workmen, might be of considerable service in erecting the bridge. The captain was ordered to report immediately at head-quarters. The General stated the necessity of moving forward without delay, and expressed his regret that the bridge could not be completed for several days after the tools did arrive, and thus the movements of the army be very seriously retarded. Captain Lane had already surveyed the ground, and formed his own opinion as to the best plan of bridging the stream, and consequently was prepared to give any suggestions that might be necessary. He, however, only asked the privilege of controlling the work of building a bridge, promising, at the same time, to have it completed next day. The proposition seemed so absurd, both to the General and his professional engineer, that they could not refrain from expressing their incredulity. No time would be lost, however, even should Captain Lane fail to accomplish the undertaking, as either success or failure would be demonstrated before the tools which had been ordered could possibly arrive. He was ordered, therefore, to proceed at once with the work, and the Assistant Adjutant-General was directed to furnish him with a detail of men. At Captain Lane's request, his own company was detailed.

Near the site of the contemplated bridge a raft of logs was found in the stream, fastened together in the usual manner. There were also two or three good dwelling-houses near, which had been deserted by the occupants on the approach of the Federal troops. On examination into the mechanical resources of the company, several axes and two or three augers were found. These were all the available materials and tools that could be relied on for the construction of the bridge. But, if it be true that a Yankee adrift on a log is sure to succeed in making port, and even in successful "diskiveries," if he have just his jack knife in his pocket, there was no reason to doubt that the Poco would be bridged by the extemporized engineers.

The logs were floated to the proposed site, and placed side by side; poles were securely fastened on the ends of the logs, so as to keep them in place; all the log-chains that could be found in the neighborhood were used as anchors, and, when the supply of chains failed, strong poles were spliced together, and so arranged as to reach from different points of the bridge to the shore, so as to keep the structure from being floated off by the strong current. The deserted houses were then torn down, the hewed frame timbers were fastened on the logs for string-pieces, and boards were laid on these again to form the floor or covering, green withes being used to bind them together. The work was commenced at nine o'clock A. M., and at two o'clock next morning Captain Lane reported to General Cox that the bridge was completed. By daylight the army was in motion. The troops, with the artillery and supply-trains, passed over without delay and without any accident, so that before the tools ordered from Ohio could have been much more than packed, the army was safely across the river and thundering on the heels of Wise. The bridge was used during all that summer, without any special attention being paid to it to keep it in repair, and the supply-trains continued to cross on it till the heavy rains and high waters of the ensuing fall rendered it unsafe.

In keeping with the foregoing, was the work at

PACK'S FERRY.

As stated in a previous chapter, the Kanawha campaign of 1862 was opened in April, by the forces under General Cox moving from Gauley Bridge and vicinity nearly due south, with the intention of cutting the Virginia and Tennessee Railroad, at or near Wytheville or Newbern, and destroying the bridge across New River, so as to sever that important line of communication. The rebels had been able, by means of this great central road, to concentrate their troops at almost any point with so much secrecy and celerity as to strike heavy blows on different points of the Federal line, and by hurling superior numbers against some given point, not unfrequently causing serious disaster to our forces before reinforcements could be brought up. Having the interior line, they could, with one army, fight on the Potomac to-day, and, before a week or ten days elapsed, fight again with the same army on the Mississippi. The necessity of severing this important line of communication was, therefore, obvious. As already stated, the Kanawha army moved forward in two columns—one, under command of Colonel (now General) Crook, passing up on the east of New River, toward Lewisburg, and the other, under command of General Cox, in person, passing up on the west by way of Raleigh and Princeton. The head of the column, under General Cox, reached a point within a few miles of the railroad, had a severe fight with a greatly superior force, but, being unable to maintain its position, fell back to Flat-Top Mountain. As a tribute to a noble regiment, it is worthy of note, in passing, that the Thirty-fourth Ohio fought desperately on this occasion, and so resolutely did they guard the trains, that, at one time, they had to cut their way through the rebel lines at the point of the bayonet. The hospital at Raleigh told the tale of their bravery and endurance. The other column, under General Crook, met the rebels near Lewisburg, and achieved a brilliant victory—the Forty-fourth Ohio, under Colonel Gilbert, covering itself with glory. This affair took place on the 23d of May. General Cox proceeded to maintain his positions on both sides of the river, his left resting on Lewisburg, and his right on Flat-Top Mountain. To secure this, however, it was necessary to open direct communication between the two wings of the army, and a point on New River, known as Pack's Ferry, was the only available crossing-place. Floyd, in his retreat from Cotton Mountain, in the fall of 1861, had destroyed all the boats that could be found on New River, and had obstructed the roads by burning bridges, felling timber, and by rolling huge rocks down from overhanging cliffs in narrow gorges, thus rendering them impassable. The roads were obstructed, more or less, in this way, from Shady Springs to Pack's Ferry, a distance of some eighteen or twenty miles.

On the 25th of May, orders were issued to Captain Lane to take Companies G and K, and proceed immediately to clear the roads, put in repair the ferry, and build a boat capable of carrying five hundred men. In making preparations for the expedition, it was found that the tools necessary for the work contemplated had been left at Gauley Bridge, and no implements could be had but spades and axes. The orders, however, were imperative—it was an absolute necessity that communication be opened without delay. The two companies, numbering one hundred and thirty-seven men, immediately left Raleigh for the scene of operation. Company G, composed of as brave and efficient men as ever shouldered musket or swung an ax, was under command of Captain Higgins—an old Californian of enlarged experience, true as steel in the hour of danger, always cool, calm, and collected, and, be it whispered, a dry old wag, whose jokes were as spicy as pepper-sauce. Company K was in no wise inferior to their comrades, but, composed of intelligent mechanics and practical engineers from Cincinnati, their intelligence and experience were only equal to their pure patriotism and unflinching bravery. Perhaps no officers were ever prouder of their companies than Captain Lane was of Company K, and Captain Higgins was of Company G.

On the first day the expedition advanced twelve miles, halting for the night at Shady Springs. Next morning the work of clearing the road commenced in earnest. One-half of the men were kept under arms, with rifles loaded and capped, ready for any emergency, while the remainder were busy at work removing the obstructions. These were of no ordinary character. The road wound round precipices, ran zigzag with a rocky mountain stream, and, in its general outline, resembled an immense "W"—the apex, or apices, striking through some deep, precipit-

9

ous gorges in the mountains. Floyd's rear-guards deserved the credit of being skilled in the art of obstruction, if nothing more. Trees were cut on the sides of the mountain and thrown across the road in such numbers and in such a manner as to form an immense network of logs and branches. Added to this, huge rocks had been rolled from the overhanging cliffs and rugged precipices, making the entanglement so perfect that the natives declared it could never be removed. Even the commanding officer of a reconnoitering party sent out from Flat-Top to examine the condition of the road, and the possibility of building a ferry, had reported that less labor would be required to open a new road than to remove the obstructions from the old one; and, moreover, that there were no materials in the vicinity for building a ferry. On the evening of the fifth day, however, the expedition of unprofessional, but eminently practical, sappers and miners, formed their line on the bank of New River, at Pack's Ferry, having cleared the road and made it available for artillery and supply-trains. The greatest caution and vigilance were necessary, however, for the expedition was now in front of the enemy, and it was not less than twenty-four miles to the nearest support. The very first work, on reaching New River, was to have the position thoroughly reconnoitered. In doing so, it was found that at a point called Blue-Stone Creek, about four miles above, there was a tolerably good ford, and also a road leading to the rear of the detachment. Another road and ford were also discovered at the mouth of the Greenbrier, about five miles below. Both points were picketed as strongly as the force would permit, and the men so disposed and such general precautions adopted, that whatever disasters or misfortunes might happen the expedition, a surprise would not be one of them. These matters having been disposed of, the work of building the ferry-boat was at once commenced.

New River, for nearly its entire length, is a rapid, rocky, mountain stream. At the point where the crossing was to be effected it is about two hundred yards wide, and the current runs at about ten miles an hour—a slow pace for New River. About two hundred yards above the ferry, and as many below, the river rushes roaring and foaming over and between immense ledges of rocks, and even at a low stage is an angry mountain torrent, rushing along with irresistible power. The difficulties of the undertaking will at once be apparent. One of the scouts, having received information that two gunwales for a boat were concealed in a creek about ten miles up Greenbriar River, a small party was instantly dispatched to bring them in. This important work was accomplished in about twenty-four hours, and was the result of hard and incessant labor. An old "dug-out," or canoe, was also found, which answered the purpose of crossing the river, and was perfectly safe for three or four men—provided they were all experienced swimmers.

In the vicinity lived a local preacher of the Hard-Shell persuasion, who was possessed of the happy faculty of always occupying the right side of the fence, no matter what troops occupied the country.

Captain Lane took a squad of men and made the clerical diplomat a visit—not, we opine, either for a "sarmint" or prayer-meeting. There was something else in the wind than either of these—something considerably more tangible and carnal, but, very possibly, considerably more useful and available just at that time. The preacher received Captain Lane with all the politeness and sanctimonious unction imaginable, and seemed anxious to show his visitors that he was too good for any thing merely sublunary. He was asked whether he knew of any lumber in the neighborhood. He replied, innocently, that he knew of no lumber nearer than a certain point some forty miles up the river. That point being within the enemy's lines, the information vouchsafed was not of the most valuable character, seeing the lumber referred to could not be made available for present necessities. But something else was needed as well as lumber. Captain Lane having noticed a quantity of flax in the barn, he informed the preacher that he would be under the necessity of having some of it, for the purpose of calking the boat he was now building. The preacher expressed great surprise at this request, stating, at the same time, that, there being no materials with which to build a boat, of course there could be no necessity for having flax to calk it with. When he found, however, that he was dealing with one who was thoroughly in earnest, and that the flax would have to be forthcoming, he blandly promised to send some to camp next day. Captain Lane informed him that he would save him so much trouble as that, and would only take his (the preacher's) team, then at the door, and, with the aid of Uncle Sam's boys, he could easily manage the flax. "In the mean time," said the captain, "I will look around the premises, and see whether I can find any lumber suitable for our purpose."

The party accordingly proceeded to the barn, and, on turning over the flax, lo and behold! a large quantity of fine planking was discovered, of the very quality and dimensions suitable for boat-building. It had been very carefully hidden away, and, of course, the loyal preacher did n't know any thing about it! By this happy discovery sufficient material to finish the first boat was very soon secured, as well as other articles, such as tools, which materially aided in the general work. On the evening of the fourth day after the arrival of the detachment, a boat sixty feet long was successfully launched, amid the shouts and cheers of the one hundred and thirty-seven men, which made the woods and rocky sides of New River reëcho again and again. Two days had been spent in getting the gunwales out from their place of concealment on Greenbrier, and in collecting lumber, etc., so that only two days were occupied in building the first boat.

Preparations were immediately made for building another boat eighty feet long, which, in due time, was accomplished; the two were joined together, thus making a ferry-boat one hundred and forty feet long. By the time this was accomplished, a rope had arrived from Gauley Bridge to work the ferry-boat, as it could not be managed with oars in such a strong current, and in such a stage of water. The design was to make what is known as a "flying bridge," or ferry, propelled by the current, having the boat fastened by means of a long cable to an anchor placed in a proper position up stream. The working of such a ferry will be familiar to most of our readers, but to the natives on New River, it was one of the wonders of the world. Some of them shrugged their shoulders and knit their brows dubiously, and even hinted that the devil, or some of his special friends, must be in the Yankee camp. The Hard-Shell brother had owned both the ferry and the old negro who worked it for a number of years; but such a profound mystery as an immense ferry-boat, moving from bank to bank so rapidly and regularly without oars or other visible means of propulsion, was something beyond either of their wise heads. The old slave frequently sat on the bank watching with intense interest the movements of the Yankee ferrymen, but he would never consent to take a trip in the new boat, although frequently invited to do so. He would shake his gray head, and mutter something about "De old Debil pushin' dat 'ar boat," and that he "wasn't gwine ober dar, lest old Split-foot should cotch him." The preacher crossed several times, and finally took such an interest in the spiritual welfare of the boys, that he kindly offered to preach to them on Sundays. The boys, however, were not hungering after such righteousness as they thought he possessed, and preferred literal *immersion* to preaching on Sundays, believing that cleanliness of body was closely connected with purity of mind.

Thus ended one of the half-civil, half-military accomplishments pertaining to the Eleventh while lying at Raleigh, in the summer of 1862.

CHAPTER VII.

CHANGE OF LOCATION—BATTLE OF BULL RUN—THE TWELFTH OHIO—FREDERICK CITY, ETC.

Change of Location.

On Friday, the 25th of July, six companies of the Eleventh Regiment left Raleigh for Gauley Bridge—two companies, under command of Major Jackson, being left to guard stores till relieved by the Thirty-seventh Ohio. They left at seven o'clock P. M., and marched all night. Demonstrations had been made by the rebels during the previous few days, indicating a movement on our base of supplies. Heath's rebel cavalry had made a dash on Summerville, capturing quite a number of the Ninth Virginia, and rumors were afloat of a rebel column moving into the valley by way of Logan. But other and ulterior objects were in view; for a detachment had gone to Pack's Ferry, on New River, to destroy the ferry-boat which had been constructed by Companies G and K a month or two previously, while all means of water transportation, such as skiffs and canoes, all along the river, were also destroyed. On the following Sabbath orders were received for the remaining companies, A and E, to start for Gauley at three A. M. on Monday. In the mean time, the Thirty-seventh Ohio had arrived from Flat-Top. All these movements indicated a change of programme.

FAREWELL SERVICES IN THE HOSPITAL.

In the evening religious services were held in the different wards of the hospital for the last time at Raleigh. Strange as it may seem to those unacquainted with army life, I felt loth to leave the poor fellows; and when the "farewell" and "God bless you" were repeated by many a wan, wounded soldier, whom I never expect to see again till the Judgment of the Great Day, my feelings nearly overcame me. The inmates of that hospital had suffered in behalf of home and country; but many of them, thank God! had chosen the Savior as the Captain of their salvation, and had been enabled to rejoice in the hope of heaven. The prayer of penitent souls had been heard calling upon God for mercy; the joyful shout of victory over sin and death had been frequently heard amid the suppressed groans of mortal agony; and, while to the physical senses the whole scene was indescribably sad, melancholy, terrible, the inner eye—the eye of faith—beheld the angels of God hovering over this dread scene of suffering and death, ministering to the dying Christian soldier, and ready to waft his wearied spirit to the bosom of the Redeemer. And O! was it not so? During many a long, weary night, when every sound was a groan, and every look was agony—when the brave heart yearned for one last look of wife or sister, or father or mother, and thought so fondly and lovingly of the dearest spot on earth—HOME—and wished but for one earthly boon—that of dying there—O! was there not ONE standing beside each sufferer, and, pointing to his own wounds received on Calvary, saying, "I am the resurrection and the life: he that believeth in me, though he were dead, yet shall he live: and whosoever liveth and believeth in me, shall never die?" Who that has ever experienced the love of God can doubt it? Who that understands the deep sympathy and tender mercy and loving-kindness which form the essential elements of God's character, can, for a moment, doubt that the dark, dreadful scenes of agony and death were illuminated by his gracious presence?

The sacrament of the Lord's Supper was also observed on this our last evening in Raleigh. We had secured a vacant room in a dilapidated house, and there we made preparations, few and simple, to observe the Christian Passover. A rough table was procured, and for a table-cloth we used a copy of *The American Wesleyan*. We had no Christian sisters to prepare the communion bread, and see that every thing was neat and orderly as becometh every thing pertaining to this holy ordinance; nevertheless, matters were so managed that the communion-table, and all that appertained to it, was as becoming as the exhibitions of Christian taste and attention I have seen in some churches. True, the table-cloth was only a newspaper, but then it was *clean;* the decanter was only a glass wine-bottle, but it looked at least a little better than a whisky-flask, which I had seen more than once on the communion-table of churches, any one of the members of which could have purchased a silver-plated tankard or crystal decanter with what he spent in six months for tobacco.

At the appointed hour for the services to commence, a goodly number of Christian soldiers assembled to enjoy the wished-for meeting. After the communion services were finished, a short time was spent in singing and prayer, and in speaking of religious experience. One little incident connected with these exercises will not soon be forgotten by those who were present. A young soldier, who had been severely wounded in the chest, and who, seemingly, had hovered between life and death for several weeks, and whose heart the Lord had opened to receive the truth as it is in Christ, was supported to the meeting, and there, with tearful eyes and a countenance indicative of spiritual joy, he testified his faith in a sin-forgiving Savior, and publicly acknowledged his discipleship by fulfilling the Savior's command, "This do in remembrance of me." Weeks before, he had said, "I will arise and go to my Father, and will say, Father, I have sinned against heaven and in thy sight, and am no more worthy to be called thy son." He had put his resolution into practice; he had sought reconciliation with God through the finished work of Christ, and now he could testify that "He is able also to save them to the uttermost that come unto God by him, seeing he ever liveth to make intercession for them."

The regiment remained at Gauley Bridge from the 26th July till the 17th August, when nearly the whole of the Kanawha division was withdrawn from the valley. The Eleventh, Twelfth, Twenty-third, Twenty-eighth, Thirtieth, and Thirty-sixth Ohio Regiments, under General Cox, reached Washington City on Sunday, the 24th—and the Thirtieth and Thirty-sixth Regiments having passed through to Warrenton, the remainder of the division encamped in the vicinity of Alexandria. We were now, for the first time, numbered with the grand Army of the Potomac, and great were the expectations of seeing military life in its most finished and scientific forms. Newspapers, east and west, had been filled with glowing accounts of the perfect organization of that army—of its efficiency in all military duties, its perfect discipline, and its unbounded confidence in its leaders. But circumstances were such that, however efficient and highly disciplined that army might have been, an unfavorable impression was almost certain to be made. Just at that time every thing seemed to be in confusion. With regimental guards in the camps, provost-guards on every street-corner, guards patrolling the city from one end to the other, and with apparently the strictest discipline everywhere, it seemed as if order and discipline existed nowhere. Without any reflection whatever upon the well-known and well-established bravery and devotion of that army, it seemed as if the causes for such a lack of discipline and general good order were not hard to discover. It was at the time General McClellan's troops were returning from the Peninsula, and when army movements generally seemed to be involved in inextricable confusion. The general appearance of the men indicated the exposure, fatigue, and privations they had endured, while their battle-rent flags told the tale of that heroic bravery they had so often manifested in the face of danger and death. But, whether by mere accident, or on account of the incompetency or neglect of general officers, there seemed to be a lack of every thing the men required to make them feel as if they were treated with that honor and sympathy which they had a right to expect as men and as soldiers. Many of them, utterly reckless, gave way to their passions—mean, money-making sutlers, traders, and adventurers supplied them with liquor, which only added to the general confusion and disorder, while the utter absence of any real effective check, even on many of the officers, showed that something more serious existed than a mere momentary disregard of good order and discipline. The truth was, that the movements on the Peninsula, spoken of as being "profoundly strategic," "brilliant," "well-timed," "inimitably grand," "successful," and even "unheard of prior to the existence of the genius of Napoleon," were but a series of huge blunders, and, but for the heroic endurance and unflinching devotion of the rank and file, together with the pure, unselfish patriotism and military skill, as well as bravery, of such men as Sumner and Hooker and others, would have resulted in disaster and ruin. That men, under such circumstances, should give way, if even for a brief period, to discouragement and recklessness, is not a matter of surprise.

As one instance among many that might be cited, indicating the want of thorough intelligent order and discipline, it may just be stated that while the largest liberty was taken by the more reckless of officers and men, a general officer, who was in command of an army corps, ere one week had elapsed, was arrested on the streets of Washington, and lodged in the guard-house! One of the most exemplary of men, as diffident as he was brave, a total abstainer, recognized by all in his command as a good, religious man, as well as an efficient officer, it is not difficult to tell either his own or his friends' feelings when he was thus welcomed to the hospitalities of Washington!

Our camp equipage had scarcely arrived, when two regiments of the Kanawha division were ordered to move to the front. Who gave the orders it was rather difficult to tell. It has not yet been very clearly ascertained, owing, perhaps, to the fact that there were many aspirants for command, and that there existed many and bitter jealousies consequent on McClellan being superseded by Pope. Be this as it may, however, the matter has not been very satisfactorily explained, although official reports recognized the orders and movements referred to.

On Wednesday, 27th of August, at dawn of day, the Eleventh and Twelfth Ohio Regiments, according to orders received an hour or two previous to starting, moved out by the Orange and Alexandria Railroad toward Manassas, as it was reported a rebel force was making demonstrations in that vicinity. Colonel Coleman had been summoned to Washington on official business, and, of course, knew nothing of the movement. The expedition was under the command of Colonel (now General) Scammon, of the Twenty-third Ohio. Before reaching Bull Run Bridge and water-station, the rattle of musketry and boom of cannon told us that fighting had begun. In a few minutes, we moved forward, crossed Bull Run, and took position on the railroad and in the woods above the water-station. A New Jersey brigade, under command of General Taylor, had been engaging the enemy for about an hour, and by this time were falling back in large numbers—doggedly refusing to rally to the support of the Ohio troops. It was hardly any wonder. They had been recklessly pushed forward, without even the precaution of having skirmishers thrown out in front, and when exposed to a raking fire from batteries on both flanks, were so poorly handled by their general, that they lost all confidence in him. Some of the officers, it is said, begged him to order a charge, but he refused, asserting his belief that the batteries were not rebel, but Union, and that their mistake would soon be corrected. To stand almost in solid column, and be plowed by grape and canister, is more than men can endure, especially if refused permission to return the fire or take the batteries by storm. General Taylor himself fell mortally wounded, and the ranking colonel immediately ordered the command to fall back. It was just at this juncture that the Ohio regiments reached the scene of action.

Major Jackson had command of the Eleventh until Colonel Coleman arrived on the field, which he did about an hour after the regiment went into action. Not soon will I forget his appearance, nor the words he spoke when he came to where I was dressing some of the wounded. The day was very hot and sultry,

He had walked some five or six miles, and, as he paused a moment beside me, the perspiration rolled in great drops from his face.

"Where's the Eleventh, chaplain?" said he.

"Round that curve of the railroad, and just across the creek. You'll find Company E in the ravine down there."

"Have they been engaged long?"

"About an hour and a half. That's our regiment that has fired that volley."

"I could have cried," said he, earnestly and bitterly, "when I came to camp and found the regiment gone. No one knew any thing about it at Cox's head-quarters."

Away he went, with redoubled speed, and, in a few minutes, a hearty cheer, that made the welkin ring, told of his arrival and warm-hearted reception.

But the contest was unequal. The little band of scarcely three thousand, all told, were contending with an army of not less than thirty thousand, under Jackson and Fitzhugh Lee—in fact, a powerful column, moving up by way of Fairfax, with the intention of cutting Pope's communications and threatening Washington City.

The heroic stand maintained by the little Union force, and the peculiar nature of the ground, which favored bold movements without exposing our weakness, induced the rebels to believe that we were but the advance-guard of McClellan's army, swinging round to the support of Pope. At about two o'clock we had to commence falling back toward Fairfax Station, taking the most of our wounded with us.

Adjutant Alexander, who was wounded severely, had to be left, as was supposed, in a dying state—two men having volunteered to remain with him. In a day or two these, with others, were released on parole, and returned within our lines. Before falling back, an incident occurred which raised the two Ohio regiments very much in each other's estimation. The Twelfth had made a charge on a portion of the enemy's lines, and, while doing so, were taken in flank and rear by a regiment sent out to cut them off. The Eleventh, seeing this, instantly rushed to the assistance of their comrades, charged bayonet on the exultant rebels, and thus enabled the Twelfth to cut their way out, which they did in splendid style. A few minutes after this, the Eleventh was in nearly the same predicament, and required similar assistance, which was as promptly and as gallantly rendered. In several severe battles after this, the Eleventh and Twelfth fought side by side, and they vied with each other only in bravery and in mutual good-will.

Having reached Fairfax Station, the troops were formed into a large hollow square, the railroad station being near the center, filled with the wounded. The word was passed around that no speaking louder than a whisper would be permitted during the night, and that the utmost vigilance would have to be observed. In the mean time, the surgeons were busy attending to the necessities of our wounded, the greater part of whom had been brought off the field. By ten o'clock every thing was quiet, save the low moan of some sufferer, or the suppressed whisper of some hospital attendant. There were no camp-fires kindled—not even a candle glimmered in the profound darkness that enveloped the little band—and each one, anxious, gloomy, yet hoping for the best, threw himself down, if not to sleep, at least to rest. Following the example of others, I lay down in a vacant corner, expecting to rest with tolerable comfort. Very soon I was passing dreamily and sweetly into a delicious state of oblivion, when I was suddenly aroused by Dr. Gabriel, who informed me, in a low whisper, that we would leave in about twenty minutes. It was now about half-past ten. On looking around, I found the column already formed; but, with the exception of the long dusky outline against the darker shadows of the woods, there was nothing to indicate that two brigades were formed in line, ready to march. Moving down the railroad toward Alexandria, in the most secret and cautious manner, we had not gone far till our advance-guard was halted by the rebel pickets. So they had us surrounded, without doubt! "About—face!" was given in whispers, and our steps were speedily retraced. Halting for fifteen minutes near the place where the column had been formed, we struck to the right, by an unfrequented road, through a strip of woods, and toward daylight reached the main turnpike, within two or three miles of our fortifications. It was afterward discovered that the rebels did have us completely hemmed in—their ignorance of this by-road alone securing our retreat.

It was a matter of deep and lasting regret to all in the regiment that our brave and gentlemanly adjutant had been mortally wounded. He had endeared himself to every one in the regiment by a uniform kindliness of manner, and by a general deportment which showed him at once the brave soldier and the generous, upright gentleman. The sorrow of the whole regiment—especially of Company B, of which he had been lieutenant—was as honorable to them, showing, as it did, their appreciation of a good man, as it was to him whose early death they mourned. He was brought within our lines in the course of a day or two, taken to one of the hospitals in Alexandria, where he died on the 25th of September. Peace be to his memory! A martyred patriot, he fills an honored grave!

A Cup of Cold Water.

One little incident I feel inclined to narrate here—one simple enough in itself, perhaps, but not without some little interest. If circumstances often invest words and deeds with an importance and interest they otherwise would never possess, then the circumstances under which the following incident occurred will, perhaps, be a sufficient plea for its being recorded here.

Dr. Gabriel and Dr. McNutt were dressing the wounded, at or near a little house to the right of the railroad, and, seeing me engaged on the left of the road, Dr. Gabriel had sent me a hospital knapsack, with what bandages he could spare. During the stampede which followed an attempt on the part of the rebels to flank us, a man who had assisted in the arduous work of bringing off another, rather severely scratched in one finger, and who had gladly volunteered to hold my horse, had rather suddenly disappeared. A little colored boy had taken his place, and, while holding my horse, was observing, with great apparent interest, the work of dressing the wounded. At this juncture, orders were given to have all the wounded sent to the rear without delay; and, as if to give emphasis to the hint, a volley was suddenly poured in on our left, which sent Minié balls whirring and humming around us. Not having any particular desire, just then, to see Richmond, and noting the rapid changes going on in all directions, I prepared to "change the base of operations" also. The wounded were speedily removed to a place of security, and I was making preparations to follow, when, feeling somewhat exhausted from the intense heat as well as labor, I had recourse to my canteen for a draught of water. Finding it empty, I gave it to the little colored boy who had been so bravely and patiently holding my horse for nearly two hours, requesting him to have it filled. With evident pleasure, he started in quest of water, but soon returned, saying that none could be found, manifesting, at the same time, serious disappointment at his want of success.

At this juncture, Dr. Gabriel sent me word that a number of wounded had been removed to a certain point, but that there was no one to attend to them. He also suggested the propriety of having them removed still further to the rear, apprehending a flank movement, of which there was every indication. In accordance with such suggestions, I started for the place indicated, and got the wounded there sent further down the railroad. An hour, perhaps, had elapsed—nearly the entire force had fallen back to Fairfax—

when this boy came up to me, with a canteen in his hand, and, looking up wistfully in my face, said, "Will you have a drink now, sir?" Poor child! he had followed me at least two miles to give me a cup of cold water! Perhaps some will say this is a very trifling matter to write about, but to me it was inexpressibly affecting. I felt as if the Lord had sent this little one to give me a cup of cold water, when faint both with hunger and fatigue, on the battlefield of Manassas! May that Savior who promised a rich reward to those who would give a cup of cold water in his name, have this unknown little one in his holy keeping, and give him to drink of that "Living water, of the which, if a man drink, he will never thirst."

Next day–Thursday, the 28th–late in the afternoon, the great and disastrous conflict known as the second Bull Run battle may be said to have fairly commenced. Our regiment rested on that day; but on Friday the entire division again moved to the front, and took position near Falls Church. Although comparatively quiet along our lines, a terrific battle was raging elsewhere, and Pope was fighting against fearful odds. On Saturday, the battle was renewed at ten o'clock A. M., and from that hour till nearly six in the evening the roar of that terrible conflict continued. Nearer and nearer came the fearful sounds of that bloody field, showing that our forces were being pressed back. That Saturday was, indeed, a gloomy day. The roads leading from Washington to Centerville were thronged with supply-trains going out, and with ambulance trains, loaded with wounded, coming in. And not only was Government transportation crowded to the utmost, but all the livery stables in the city were pressed into service, and every carriage sent out to the field for the wounded. It was, indeed, a mournful sight—those seemingly endless trains of crushed, mangled humanity—all the more mournful when the fact was learned that a contemptible jealousy, if not absolute treachery, had prevented re-inforcements reaching that struggling army when pressed back by superior numbers.

On the 4th of September, demonstrations were made by the enemy in our immediate front. Our pickets were driven in, and considerable artillery firing was kept up for a short time. The troops were under arms all night, artillery in position, and every thing in readiness for battle. But those demonstrations were only a feint to draw attention from other movements the rebels were making on the Upper Potomac. Next day passed quietly, with the occasional exception of picket-firing.

A Short Sermon—Preparations to Move.

As the army was now in the midst of an active campaign, and opportunities to hold religious meetings were but few, it was very desirable to improve the few hours of quietude that were given us on the evening of this day. Accordingly, the bugler sounded the "church-call," and very soon a large congregation had assembled within the fort, and we had the prospect of an interesting meeting. Preliminary services had just been finished, however, and the text fairly announced, when Colonel Coleman sent me word that marching orders had just been received. This, of course, had the effect of bringing our services to a sudden close, and the brief sermon was, "Now, comrades, we have got orders to march, and I must stop. God bless you, and make you faithful soldiers for God and your country!"

Soon the camp-fires were replenished, and every man was busy in preparing rations for three days. At the appointed hour, next morning, the various columns were put in motion, and our faces were turned toward Washington City. This confirmed our suspicions that the reported crossing of a rebel force into Maryland was true, and that the National Capital was seriously threatened. It had also been reported that the rebels were in possession of Frederick City and Hagerstown, and that they were holding high carnival in the beautiful and fruitful valleys between the latter city and the Potomac.

The authorities being anxious seemingly to secure the safety of the Capital, the various columns were moved out toward Maryland, very slowly. Indeed, for two or three days, it seemed a matter of doubt whether the enemy was within five or ten miles of the city, so slowly did the army move. A day's march was usually from five to eight or ten miles, and it seemed as if there were a constant "feeling the way" through from one point to another. Marching at this rate, the column under command of General Cox passed through Ridgeville, on Thursday, the 11th of September—the rebel pickets retreating from the vicinity of the town as we approached. We halted till next morning, and, at an early hour, were again pushing forward on the Frederick road.

About one o'clock the rebel pickets in the neighborhood of Frederick City were driven in, and the artillery opened on both sides. Simmons's and McMullen's Ohio batteries were both brought into position, and opened on the rebels posted at and near the stone bridge which crosses the Monocacy on the east of the city. The column was formed in three divisions. One division moved across the fields on the south, another formed in the woods to the east and north, and advanced on the city from that direction, while the center column moved on the turnpike and across the stone bridge. Our artillery and musketry being mainly directed to clearing the bridge, the rebels were soon compelled to retreat in no little confusion. They re-formed again still nearer the city, and in such a position as to command the bridge and approaches. But the three columns pushed on steadily, nevertheless. The center, with the Eleventh in advance, took possession of the bridge, and drove all before them. At this juncture Colonel Moore, of the Twenty-eighth Ohio, who was commanding the center, ordered a charge, himself bravely leading. Two pieces of artillery were at the same moment wheeled into position, in such a manner as to sweep the road—the intention being that the party charging should open right and left, so as to allow the gunners to plow the ranks of the rebels on the road. The order seemed to be misunderstood—a momentary confusion ensued, and some of our cavalry (among them Colonel Moore and his aids) were driven back. The artillerists, with guns loaded and lanyard in hand, were waiting orders to fire. In the rush, some one drove against one of the gunners, jerking the lanyard in his hand and discharging the gun. By this accident several of our own men were severely wounded, and a momentary confusion ensued. The rebels, seeing their advantage, made a charge, and captured both pieces, and, with them, Colonel Moore. General Cox's voice was heard shouting to Colonel Coleman, "Will the Eleventh recover those guns?"

"We will!" was the instantaneous reply of Coleman. "Now," said he, addressing his men, at the same time waving his sword over his head, "now, Eleventh! we must take those guns! When I say 'Charge!' I want you to charge with a rush, and drive those devils from our guns. Forward!—double-quick—charge bayonet—march!"

With a deafening cheer, they rushed on the rebels like an angry wave of gleaming steel, drove them precipitately from the guns, and, the columns right and left moving simultaneously, kept charging on the double-quick, cheering as they rushed on and on, up the road, through the main street of the city, and halted not till the enemy, routed and scattered, were fleeing in all directions! As the rebels rushed through the main street, with the Eleventh thundering at their heels, and the noble Twelfth, Twenty-eighth, and Thirty-sixth coming down like tornadoes on their flanks, it seemed as if the pent-up loyalty of the citizens burst out everywhere, and in every form of demonstration. As the head of the column advanced, doors were flung open, windows were raised, and flags unfurled by the score, while handkerchiefs, in the hands of hundreds of the citizens, were waved continuously. Young and old—boys that could just toot "Yankee-doodle," and gray-haired patriarchs, on the verge of the grave—fresh, rosy-cheeked maidens, all the more beautiful from the blush of joyful excitement that suffused their cheeks and added luster to their eyes, as well as more matronly ladies, rushed out impulsively, heedless of gleaming bayonets and prancing steeds, and warmly welcomed their deliverers! Men and women, more thoughtful of the physical wants of the Union soldier, came running out of the stores and dwellings with water and other refreshments; and so overjoyed and grateful were they, that many of them rushed into the advancing column, and thrust their gifts into the hands of the soldiers! As if by magic, the whole city was arrayed in holiday attire. Flags were waving from every house, and hats and handkerchiefs from every balcony and window, while cheer upon cheer went up with such hearty good will, and with such a genuine "ring," that no one could doubt either the loyalty or lung-power of Frederick's sons and daughters. I noticed some elderly ladies wringing their hands in ecstasy, while the tears that trickled over their furrowed cheeks told how deep and fervent were their emotions. One, still more demonstrative than the others, pressed her hands together, and exclaimed, in true Methodist style, "Bless the Lord! O! bless the Lord!"

It was one of those eras that come but seldom in a man's lifetime—one of those strangely grand, sublime hours, or moments, rather, so full of all that is touching and pathetic, yet noble and elevating, when a man who has any manhood, any soul in him, springs to the higher and purer atmosphere of the heroic in thought and action! The thrill of gladness, the inexpressibly *delicious*—that's the word—delicious feeling of satisfaction which fills the heart under such circumstances, is second only to that which the truly good and great experience when victories are achieved on the great moral battlefield, and when the Christian warrior comes off "more than conqueror through Him that loved us." The thrill of deep and intense joy may be but momentary, but it awakens in the heart new emotions, opens up new well-springs of thought, and brings into play dormant energies. Any one who could not feel deeply and nobly under such circumstances, and aspire to fuller and clearer views of duty in regard to daring and doing in every true and righteous cause, would be unworthy the name of man. Unlike the emotions of the merely professional warrior who exults over a blood-tarnished victory, simply because it is a victory and no more, the feelings of the Union soldiers at Frederick were those of men who peril their own lives to save others, and who strike for victory because victory brings life and liberty.

There are times when men live a lifetime in a few moments. Life is not so much days and years as it is thought and action.

"Life's more than breath and the quick round of blood—
It is a great spirit and a busy heart.
The coward and the small in soul scarce do live.
One generous feeling—one great thought—one deed
Of good, ere night would make life longer seem,
Than if each year might number a thousand days—
Spent as is this by nations of mankind.
We live in deeds, not years; in thoughts, not breaths;
In feelings, not in figures on a dial.
We should count time by heart-throbs. He most lives
Who thinks most—feels the noblest—acts the best."

CHAPTER VIII.

THE night after the rebel forces were driven out of Frederick, our army bivouacked in the rich valleys which stretch away in such beauty and magnificence, till they are hedged in by the blue, hazy mountains, or lost in the dim, dreamy outlines of far-distant cloud and sky. No movements took place, save by the cavalry, till late in the forenoon of the following day, when again the various columns were in motion toward Middletown. By six o'clock that evening the advance reached Catoctin Creek, about two miles beyond Middletown. Cox's division lay in line of battle close by the creek, and commanding the main road leading from Middletown to Hagerstown.

Cannonading had been heard nearly all day in the direction of Harper's Ferry, intimating that some demonstrations were being made against that stronghold. Little did we think that, through the treachery or cowardice of Colonel Miles, in command there, the post, with the valuable stores collected there, would pass into rebel hands, and that the arms and ammunition would be employed on the following day against Union forces. As if to mark, however, the fact that he who basely seeks his own personal safety at the expense of honor and truth, often lose both life and honor by such conduct, Colonel Miles fell, mortally wounded, while waving, it is said, with his own hands, the white flag of an ignominious surrender.

On Sabbath morning—14th September—at an early hour, the forward movement commenced. It was known that the rebels had taken a strong position on the hights commanding the Hagerstown road, a part of the Blue Ridge known as South Mountain. At seven o'clock the first gun was fired, shelling the woods on the right and left of the road, so as to find out the position of the enemy. And thus was ushered in the day of sacred rest—the weekly memorial of that day when Jesus Christ, the Prince of Peace, rose from the grave, the conqueror of death and hell! It was a lovely morning. However much the passions of men might be raging, and however fearful might be the shock of war that would yet make the very earth tremble ere the shadows of evening would descend, nature, at least, was calm, peaceful, and joyous. The dreamy blue haze that covered, as with a gauzy vail, the mountain ranges; the deeper and brighter vapory covering that hung like a glory over the far-stretching valleys; the grass and the flowers, yet dripping and sparkling with nature's dewy baptism; the glad songs of the birds, not yet driven from their woodland homes by War's fierce visage, which filled the woods with gushing, glorious melody—all told of Sabbath—sweet, sacred Sabbath—the day of rest and peace! And we thought of *home-Sabbaths*, too, and the sanctuary of God, and the voice of prayer and the songs of praise. Amid the roar of the opening battle, we thought of brethren dearly beloved and longed for, perhaps praying at that very moment for those about to enter the very jaws of death; and one great comfort in that dread hour was the thought that, in answer to such prayers, coming generations would reap the fruits of the day's unwonted and unwelcome work in a fuller and holier and more permanent heritage of civil and religious liberty. Many a prayer went up that morning from the embattled hosts of freedom for loved ones at home! Many a brave, good heart breathed the wish into God's own ear, that if no more earthly Sabbaths should see them and dear ones nestling once more at home, sweet home, they might at last all meet in the home of God, where war's fierce tumults shall never be heard, and where the calm of an eternal Sabbath shall never be disturbed.

Before forming in line of battle, there was sufficient time for a few who loved prayer to engage in devotional exercises. The 86th Psalm was read—the following verses being both appropriate and comforting: "Bow down thine ear, O Lord, hear me: for I am poor and needy. Be merciful unto me, O Lord: for I cry unto thee daily. Rejoice the soul of thy servant: for unto thee, O Lord, do I lift up my soul. For thou, Lord, art good, and ready to forgive; and plenteous in mercy unto all them that call upon thee. Give ear, O Lord, unto my prayer; and attend to the voice of my supplications. In the day of my trouble I will call upon thee: for thou wilt answer me."

At about eight o'clock the bugle sounded the advance, and, after crossing the Catoctin Creek, and moving a short distance up the turnpike, our division filed off to the left through some fields and an orchard, where the artillery was already in position. Here we formed in line of battle, partly concealed by a strip of woods at the foot of the hill, on which the enemy had taken position behind a series of stone walls. By this movement our division was thrown to the left of the gorge known as Turner's Gap. The forces of Generals Wilcox, Rodman, and Sturgis followed close up in our support, while the cavalry connected our left with General Franklin's right—he being engaged with the enemy at a mountain pass a few miles further down.

It was while we were lying in this position, expecting to engage the enemy every moment—the shot and shell from our own and the rebel batteries passing over us in all directions—that a little circumstance occurred that has often been spoken of by all in the regiment. Sergeant Wilson, of the Quartermaster's Department, arrived on the field with the mail, and, permission having been granted by Colonel Coleman, it was distributed—the men, however, keeping in ranks. What hasty tearing open of envelopes! What a fluttering of letters all along the line! Then what absorbed attention! Little did the writers of those "love-notes" think, when writing them, that they would be opened and read amid the booming of artillery, and the explosions of shell that made the very earth tremble! Little did they think how opportunely they would reach some anxious ones, who, perhaps, would never see home nor friends again. Perhaps as little did they understand how much true comfort those letters would give in the hour of peril, nor how much they would strengthen both the heart and hand of the patriot soldier on the field.

Perhaps I ought to apologize for obtruding any thing of a merely personal character into these Lights and Shadows, when reference is made to personal experience, under such circumstances. A sufficient apology will, it is hoped, be found in the fact that acknowledgments of benefits received, both from the Infinite Father and from our brother man, are eminently proper, and have a salutary influence both upon ourselves and others. Among other letters received that morning, was one from Professor James McEldowney, of Adrian College. I read it while the shot and shell were screaming and bursting in all directions, and while the earth was trembling under the fearful roar of musketry and artillery. Nothing could have been more in keeping with my circumstances than the tone and spirit of that letter, and I felt a new impulse of humble faith in God's protecting care when I read the following lines: "We continue to pray and hope for your preservation. Under the protection of Heaven we know you are safe, as even the hairs of your head are numbered." It was as if an angel had spoken, or as if the Savior himself had come near to cheer and strengthen in anticipation of the trials and dangers of that fearful day! I felt greatly refreshed in spirit; and in the two or three minutes of communion with God, during which I tried to rise to the full appreciation of those precious words, I felt as much, if not more, of heaven and of heaven's peace, than I remember ever to have enjoyed even when blessed with the hallowed privileges of the sanctuary. But the tide of battle rolled toward us, and in a few minutes the regiment was facing the enemy.

Dr. Holmes, brigade surgeon on General Cox's staff, having selected a suitable place—not very suitable, as was soon discovered—for a temporary field hospital, at the request of Dr. Gabriel I went down through a ravine to our regiment, to give directions to the hospital corps for bringing off the wounded. The Eleventh and Twenty-third Regiments having made a movement threatening some South Carolina troops, in position behind the stone fences on the ridge, drew the enemy's fire, which sent the musket-balls hissing and whizzing all around, and which cut the twigs and leaves like a storm of hail. I had just called the attention of the hospital assistants to the directions indicated, and was turning to leave them, when this unpleasant salute came in our faces. For a short time it was exceedingly doubtful whether some of us would not require assistance before getting out of that place. As it was, there were very sudden exhibitions of profound humility on the part of all; for we crouched very closely and lovingly beside some low friendly rocks. We could hear the spent musket-balls pattering, like rain-drops, on the huge bowlders for several minutes, while others hissed and hummed in most uncomfortable proximity to our ears. Another tremendous volley was fired, followed by the cheers of the Twenty-third Ohio, as it dashed on the Twenty-third South Carolina, which was holding a strong position behind a stone wall. Another cheer, and no more South Carolina bullets hissed among those boulders and trees for that day! "The psalm-singers of the Western Reserve"—as the Twenty-third Ohio was nicknamed—from the hotbed of Abolitionism in the North, had met the boastful champions of wrong and robbery, from the hotbed of oppression and treason in the South; but Freedom's steel, stronger than Slavery's bullets, had signally triumphed! Meantime, George—do n't know his surname, if he had one; very likely he had, but surnames in the South are not always very honorable to those from whom they are derived—George, our bright, sharp-eyed contraband, came staggering along, with a wounded artillerist on his back. It was Corporal James, of McMullen's Battery, a young friend of mine from Troy, Ohio. He was very pale, but cheerful and bright as ever. His replies to my inquiries were characteristic.

"Why! is that you, Charley? Where are you wounded?"

"O, it's only a flesh-wound. Would n't have left, only could n't stand. The lieutenant was wounded too. We peppered them, though!"

With all his cheerfulness, however, he was quite severely wounded, a musket-ball having passed through his leg. I learned afterward, from those who noticed the splendid workings of McMullen's Battery, that Corporal James had distinguished himself by his coolness and bravery. He had stood by his gun till the last, and when he was shot down, there was not another left to reload the piece. The two batteries—Simmons's and McMullen's—were, perhaps, the most exposed of any of our batteries on that part of the field, and they suffered accordingly.

A short time elapsed, and I returned to the ambulances, to assist the surgeons in caring for the wounded. Dr. Gabriel was engaged near a little house on the left of the road, and Dr. McNutt and myself took charge of those brought to the place first indicated, a few hundred yards further to the left. I had just finished dressing Charley's wound, and commenced attending to the wants of another, when Andrew Thompson, of Company H, was brought off, severely wounded. By this time, the battle was raging fearfully. The indescribable noise of the contending hosts, as they swayed to and fro, like the surging billows of the ocean; the sharp, continuous roll and rattle of musketry; the deep, deafening boom of the artillery, and the crashing, shrieking shell, together with the short, sharp hiss of grape and canister, told a fearful and bloody tale. The wounded were being brought off in large numbers, and every available help was required. It was then that Andrew was carried to us. We had just put our fingers on the spot where the musket-ball—having pierced his lungs—was lodged in the muscles of the shoulder, and were about to extract it, when a shell hissed close by us, exploding in an instant. Another and another succeeded, in quick succession, until it seemed as if the rebels had taken our ambulances as their target. In the trees, over our heads, on our right and left, shot and shell, and finally grape, raged and roared around and above us like some fearful, driving storm. During a momentary lull we tried to get the ambulances moved to a point which seemed to promise greater security, but the drivers either got confused or frightened, and a few minutes—which seemed hours—elapsed before we got them to understand what was wanted. We had just got the ambulances fairly in motion, when again the artillery opened, and the iron hail was plunging and shrieking once more among us. Some of the wounded were brought to within a few yards of where surgeons were at work, only to be torn in pieces by grape-shot or fragments of shell. One poor fellow, perfectly helpless, was laid down, as was supposed, in the safest place, and scarcely had the assistants turned from him, when a shell cut him nearly in two! For a few minutes, it seemed as if the very gates of perdition itself were opened, and as if the unquenchable fires were hissing and roaring around and above us. There seemed to be no avenue of escape—no shelter from the incessant, pitiless, fiery storm. We were literally surrounded with fire. There was scarcely any hope that either ambulances or wounded, or, indeed, any one, would ever get out! George was holding my horse, under shelter of a rock; but he could stand it no longer, and he bolted as speedily, if not as gracefully, as possible. At the same instant, almost, some grape went plowing under my horse, throwing dust and gravel all about him, and away he went, snorting and scampering over the field. Dr. Gabriel was faring no better. A fragment of shell had come close enough to tear his coat; another piece struck him lightly on the leg, while another passed harmlessly under his horse. At last, the ambulances, with the wounded, were got into the road by which we had entered the field, and a new and safer place was sought for a field-hospital. While descending the hill, on the left of which was a strip of heavy timber, the rebels began shelling the woods with the evident intention of clearing them of troops getting into position, and it was not till one of our batteries—McMullen's it was afterward discovered—seeing the danger, opened a concentrated and continuous fire on the rebel battery, and finally silenced it, that troops could be moved up. A large stone house at the foot of the hill, belonging to a Mr. Vincent Sanner, was selected for a temporary hospital, and thither the wounded were carried. It proved to be a most admirable location, for it was near enough the scene of action to secure attention to the suffering; yet not so near as to unnecessarily expose either the wounded or those attending to them.

Single-handed, yet Brave.

While the incidents just narrated were taking place, a circumstance occurred which the boys delighted to tell. During one of the movements made by the Eleventh, to drive the rebels from their position, Colonel Coleman, unfortunately, was cut off from the regiment, and, on emerging from a dense thicket of pine and laurel bushes, found himself confronting some ten or a dozen rebels, having in charge several Union soldiers as prisoners. In an instant, he flourished his sword over his head, dashed right at them, and in a stern, commanding voice, ordered them, in no very complimentary terms, to surrender. Down went every gun, and up went every hand, and, ordering them to fall in, he marched them within the lines—the Union boys and the rebels, meanwhile, having changed positions considerably.

The Eleventh Hour.

"Can't you do something for me? O, this is awful!" said a young man, suffering greatly from a wound in the breast. I tore open the blood-soaked blouse and examined his wound. It was truly a fearful gash, and reluctantly I had to tell him it was likely he would die. Poor fellow! he looked up so piteously in my face, and said, very sadly, "Then I am lost—I must go to hell!"

"Why are you lost?" I said to him.

"O!" said he, in answer, "I have sinned against God—I have resisted the spirit—I have been a very wicked boy—I am lost! I am lost!"

"God so loved the world," said I, repeating one of the most precious texts of Scriptures, "that he gave his only begotten Son, that whosoever believeth on him might not perish, but have everlasting life. God is gracious. Look to him for mercy; he will in no wise cast you out."

"What is the use of trying now, after sinning as I have done? God won't accept of such a miserable sinner's prayer as mine is for mercy, now, at this late hour. O God! what shall I do? What shall I do?"

"Believe on the Lord Jesus Christ, and thou shalt be saved."

"Are you a chaplain?"

"Yes."

"Then, will you pray for me?"

"Yes, I will, comrade. Let me put this wet cloth on your wound first. There, you'll feel easier now. And take a little of this wine, too—it will do you good."

Kneeling beside him, for a few moments, I tried to preach to him Jesus and the resurrection. I told him that, sinful and unworthy as he might be, he was precious in the sight of God; that the Savior had suffered and died for him, and that salvation was freely offered, on condition of trusting in Christ as his all-sufficient Savior.

Others requiring attention, I left him for a short time. In the mean time, he was placed in a more comfortable position. Returning in the course of perhaps half an hour, I asked him if he had ever prayed, and whether he could not pray now.

"Yes," said he, "I have tried to pray many times, when I was a better boy than I am now; and I have been trying to pray since I have been wounded. O, Lord Jesus, have mercy upon me! Here, Lord, I give myself away; 'tis all that I can do."

As his eyes grew dim, and death's dark shadows were passing over his countenance, it was evident that this dying soldier craved but one earthly boon—that of being at home in this his young life's last hour! He whispered something about his far-off Michigan home, and sighed sadly as he expressed the wish to see home and friends before he died. But already the wheels of life's fountain were moving slowly—were about to stand still, and the silver cord was just being loosed! Death's mysteries were being solved no less solemnly, on this fearful field of carnage and death, than in the peaceful chamber, where the dying are soothed with love's ministry!

"Won't you stay beside me till the last—won't you, chaplain?"

"Yes, certainly I will."

"Pray for me, then—pray that God may have mercy on me."

I engaged in prayer with him. Soon all was hushed and quiet around us, save the stifled groans of the sufferers and the roar of battle. Surgeons and assistants paused, for a moment, and a little sanctuary was found in that place of indescribable horrors.

"Did you hear the prayer?" I asked.

"Yes," said he, "I did—and I have thrown myself as a sinner into the arms of Jesus, and he will save me. Lord, I believe, I believe! Bless, bless the Lord!"

In a few minutes the suffering soldier ceased to breathe. He rested from all earth's battles—he slept his last sleep!

Patriotic till the Last.

While the battle was raging fiercely, among the many wounded which were brought off, was a man who had received a mortal wound, and was evidently in a dying condition. As soon as he was laid down on the grass, I went to him to see what could be done for him. Life's crimson current was ebbing fast away; his face was ghastly pale, and his eyes were already dim.

"Raise me up—raise me up once more!" said the dying man, earnestly, but feebly. "Now—there—that will do. Give me water—water—water!"

Water was put to his lips, but he would not drink. "Stop!" said he, seizing the tin-cup with great eagerness. "Here's to my country! Here's to the glorious Stars and Stripes! I die for my country! Boys, never give up!"

His lips quivered, and he fell back exhausted. My attention was called away by Dr. Gabriel, who wished me to assist him, and, as I left this noble, dying soldier, I felt to say, "This is a scene of patriotism indeed! One thing more would make it complete, and shed upon it unfading luster—and that one thing is, the dying patriot-soldier looking to the crucified Savior as the Captain of his salvation." Perhaps, poor, suffering, noble man, thy brave heart was resting on Christ, and thou couldst be all the braver in the hour of battle and in the agony of death because thou didst trust in him!

That scene will never be forgotten by those who beheld it. There was something about it so thrillingly pathetic, so truly noble and grand, and yet so natural, earnest, and honest, that it seemed more a scene of martyrdom than an event on the battlefield.

He was buried, along with others, in the orchard near which he fell. Over his honored grave will the apple-blooms fall in fragrant showers of beauty, and the summer birds will warble the notes of a holy requiem.

"Hushed be the song and the love-notes of gladness
That broke with the morn from the cottager's door—
Muffle the tread in the soft stealth of sadness
For one who returneth—whose chamber lamp burneth—
No more.

"Silent he lies on the broad path of glory
Where withers, ungarnered, the red crop of war;
Grand is his couch, tho' the pillows are gory,
'Mid forms that shall battle, 'mid guns that shall rattle
No more.

"Soldier of Freedom! thy marches are ended—
The dreams that were prophets of triumph are o'er;
Death, with the night of thy manhood is blended;
The bugle shall call thee—the fight shall enthrall thee
No more."

Many a time I have felt to contrast the hearty zeal and devotion of that soldier who had laid his all, even life itself, upon the altar of his country, with the craven, cowardly croakers who, safely at home, and protected by the patriot braves on the field, were, nevertheless, sympathizing with traitor hordes—not, perhaps, because they really desired the ruin of the country, but because they placed their own personal selfish interests above country and liberty and humanity. If posterity will ever do justice to the memories of the Union soldiers who bared their bosoms to the battle-storms of an accursed slaveholders' rebellion, and placed themselves as a living, breathing wall around freedom's sanctuary, and faltered not when the day was darkest and the storm of treason howled loudest, then posterity will also do justice to the memories of those who, through a wicked pro-slavery spirit, sought, with remorseless hate and blind prejudice, to overturn the holy places of Liberty and Truth, and rear upon their ruins the polluted altars of Wrong and Outrage! The former, crowned with undying laurels, will go down to posterity as the cherished of every noble heart; the latter, covered with eternal shame and held in deepest abhorrence by all the good and great of all ages, will be numbered with the Judases and the Arnolds of the world.

On Monday morning, at an early hour, the work of removing the wounded was resumed. Going over the field, it was easy to see the sanguinary character of the struggle of the previous day. In many places the dead lay in great windrows, which seemed as if some remorseless reaper from Death's dark domain had come, and, with unerring aim,

"Wielding a sickle keen"—

cut down, with one fell sweep, the ranks of living, breathing humanity, and left them ready to be garnered into the silent, rueful shades of the grave! In one place—a long, narrow lane, protected by a low stone wall, from behind which the rebels fought stubbornly, and where the Eleventh and Twenty-third Ohio Regiments made some of their most desperate assaults, and finally drove the enemy at the point of the bayonet—the rebel dead lay two and three deep, just as they fell! In another place—nearer the corner of the open field, and close by a small log-house, where the most desperate fighting, perhaps, ever known, took place between Ohio and South Carolina troops, already referred to on a previous page—fifteen rebel dead lay within a space of three steps! Some were lying with their hands stretched toward heaven, as if imploring mercy, or calling down vengeance upon the heads of those who had led them into rebellion, and brought them to a traitor's fate. Others were in the act of firing, having been shot dead while pointing their guns at the bosoms of those who were defending righteous government. Others—friends and foes—had rolled over and over, as if trying to escape from the fiery blast, and in their untold agony had gnashed their teeth and bitten the dust reddened with their own blood! Others had crawled away into the shelter of some pine and laurel bushes, and, unseen by mortal eye, unsoothed by words of comrade or friend, had breathed their last! O! it was a terrible sight! Not in poetry or painting, or mere description of the historian, who deals only in "brilliant charges," "glorious victories," "serried hosts rushing to victory," and "gleaming sabers and nodding plumes," but, O! in stern reality was this a battlefield! The horse and his rider, "in one red burial blent," were here! and "garments rolled in blood," and corpses, stark and stiff, heaps upon heaps, were all here! And as I looked over this bloody field, and gazed upon the lifeless forms of friend and foe—those who had fallen under the glorious Stars and Stripes, and those who had met a traitor's death beneath a traitor's flag—I asked, "O God! who slew all these?" and the answer came back to me, as if in the low wail of a funeral dirge, "THESE WERE ALL SLAIN BY THE INFERNAL SPIRIT OF SLAVERY! AND THERE SHALL BE NO PEACE TILL OPPRESSION IS DESTROYED. THE SWORD SHALL DEVOUR TILL SLAVERY IS NO MORE!"

CHAPTER IX.

THE IDEAL AND THE ACTUAL—A THRILLING SCENE—MY BROTHER! O, MY BROTHER!—ANGELIC WORK.

Mind must love mind: the great and good are friends;
And he is but half great who is not good.
And O! humanity is the fairest flower
Blooming in earthly breasts; so sweet and pure
That it might freshen even the fadeless wreaths
Twined round the golden harps of those in heaven.

FESTUS.

THE POETRY AND REALITY OF WAR.

THE poetry of war! exclaims some one, in surprise. Has war any thing poetic about it? Yes, it has; but, as poetry is essentially ideal, not actual, so the poetry of war is war only in idea. There is a great difference between the ideal and the actual in every thing; and that which is simply ideal is one thing, and that which is actual is entirely another. Ideal war, as presented to us on the pages of the historian, the canvas of the painter, or the dashing, brilliant, spirited letters of "special correspondents," is vastly different from actual war, as exhibited on the battlefield and in the hospital. Ideal war has tinsel and plumes, waving banners and flashing swords, wreaths of flowers and silver medals, the plaudits of brave men and the smiles of beautiful women. Actual war has hunger and thirst, cold and weariness. It has the saber-stroke deep in the quivering flesh, and the bayonet-thrust in the beating heart. It has the bursting shell and the hissing shot, crashing and tearing through solid ranks of living men like the furious storm-blast in the forest. It has ghastly wounds and "garments rolled in blood," the agonizing cry of the wounded, and the stifled moan of the dying. It has the crowded hospital, with wearisome days and still more wearisome nights for the sick and wounded, and where oftentimes—as after a battle—every look seems to be agony, and every word a suppressed groan, a petition for help, or a cry for mercy. It has the tearful eyes of those who look wistfully for absent ones who will return no more, and it has the sad, sad sigh of burdened, broken hearts. It has Rachels weeping for their children, and refusing to be comforted because they are not. It has lonely widows and desolate orphans. And whosoever may causelessly and wickedly initiate war, has the execration of all the truly good, and the curse of a righteous God.

Even when waged for a good cause—when it is for the defense of truth and righteousness, and is absolutely necessary to roll back the dark tide-wave of human oppression, and to destroy the foulest treason—war is still a terrible reality, as the bloody field of South Mountain showed on this eventful day.

Glad though I was that our arms had been successful—that the wily, unscrupulous foe had been driven back—it was, nevertheless, with saddened heart that I gazed upon the fearful scene. Time and again I felt to say, "O! Prince of Peace, come once more to our bleeding country, and say to the waves of strife, 'Be still!'"

"My Brother! My Dear Brother!"

Would that my pen could paint a picture seen on the field where our regiment had been engaged. While passing through a clump of laurel bushes, through which the skirmishers had been pushed forward on the afternoon of the previous day, I found a member of our regiment leaning over the dead body of a brother soldier, while the tears were trickling over his cheeks. The countenance of the dead was calm and placid, as if stilled in sweet repose, or as if lighted up with the sunshine of happy dreams. At first sight I could hardly believe that from that body, apparently just composed to sleep, the spark of life had fled forever. But so it was. A fragment of shell or a grapeshot had crashed through the side and back of his head, tearing away a large portion of the brain, but leaving the face untouched. And there leaned, or rather knelt, the brother of the fallen soldier, his hands pressed upon his face, and the hot tears trickling between his fingers—weeping as only brave men weep—and exclaiming, "My brother! O, my dear brother!"

That scene was too sacred for intrusion. Words of common condolence would have jarred like a discord amid the subdued tones of anguish that burst from the lips of the living over the placid face of the dead. In its sublime pathos—its mingled bravery and affection, manly courage and womanly tenderness—it was one of those scenes that can not be described, and which the beholder feels to be so sacred he must needs draw a vail over it, lest it be profaned by the gaze of some thoughtless intruder. It reminded me of that scene once beheld on the gloomy mountains of Gilboa, the very thought of which wrung from the heart of the poet warrior and king a requiem for the fallen brave, so inimitably touching and tender that it will find an echo in every generous, manly bosom till the end of time.

During this day our division lay partly on the crest and partly on the slope of the hill, from which, after desperate fighting, the rebels had been driven on the previous day. The Eleventh was posted in the woods, on the summit close by a somewhat level plateau, where Simmons's Battery had been driven, with consummate strategy, to within fifty yards of the rebel artillery, and, being well supported and well manned, did much toward driving the enemy from that formidable position.

It was while the regiment lay here for a few hours that Colonel Coleman wrote his last letter to loved ones at home. I can see him yet, sitting under a small oak tree, with pen in hand, a book on his knee for a desk, improving the few minutes' repose in recording for the comfort of others his hopes and desires. With that frank, decided manner for which he was distinguished, he told me, in glowing terms, of the brave conduct of the regiment on the previous day. He had been somewhat chafed and chagrined at some disparaging remarks concerning the Ohio troops, reported to him as made by some thoughtless officer, with more brass than either brains or bravery. After he had ventilated his opinion about comparative merit, he exclaimed, with great earnestness, "I guess the old Kanawha division showed some of them how to fight within the last week, and we will show them again. The boys are eager for an assault—a regular storming of some battery—and they'll have the chance, too, before long. There's a big fight or a big run before us yet. I am just as much afraid of death as any one, but I'll lead the old Eleventh as far as any one dare go, and I'll do it, too, before long!"

The Wounded cared for at Middletown.

As soon as the more severely wounded were attended to on the field, they were sent back to Middletown, to general hospitals established there. It was about two and a half miles from the battlefield. All the churches—Methodist Protestant, Lutheran, and Presbyterian—and also the Academy building and some private houses, were occupied as hospitals. And not only were those buildings crowded to their fullest extent, but many of the poor fellows had to be laid on the grass outside. The Methodist Church, in which Dr. Gabriel and I worked for several days and nights, was not only crowded, but on Monday night—the night after the battle—the audience-room, and lecture-room below, were filled from end to end, and even the aisles and pulpit and platform were crowded with the wounded and the dying, so that it was with the utmost caution and care that the attendants could move among them. What a sad and terrible scene! And yet, like the silver-lined storm-clouds of the early spring, this fearfully dark and dreadful scene of suffering and death had its bright gleams of sunshine also—the sunshine of Christian hope and joy. Yes, and Christian effort, too—genuine, practical, large-hearted sympathy! While great numbers of men were busy collecting bandages, preparing mattresses, bringing hot tea and coffee, assisting to unload the ambulances as they drove up in quick succession with their loads of torn, bleeding humanity, the ladies were also at work amid those terrible scenes of suffering and death, ministering to all with that tact and delicacy of sympathy of which woman alone is susceptible. Like pitying angels from the better world, intent only on fulfilling some mission of love and gentleness, they moved amid those dread scenes of mortal anguish, literally dealing bread to the hungry, giving drink to the thirsty, soothing the suffering, and speaking peace to the dying. The objects of their pity and kind ministrations lay there, in all the stern realities of fiery battle, helpless and bleeding, their faces begrimed with powder and their garments rolled in dust and blood—sometimes giving vent to their anguish in low, suppressed groans, or in sharp, short, piercing shrieks, all of which seemed to render the place and the circumstances unfit for woman's keenly sensitive and sympathetic nature. But, although some of them had blanched cheeks and quivering lips, they resolutely went forward in their blessed work. There was one whose great personal beauty and lady-like deportment, as well as her kind attentions and winning, soothing language, seemed to invest with more of heaven than earth. Dressed in a robe of pure white, her only jewelry the ring on her finger and a small brilliant with which her collar was fastened, she moved now here, now there, as an angel of light. Her husband, the Rev. ——, was there also, aiding in the good work. Several times I noticed that her lips quivered and tears dimmed her bright eye, but she strove heroically for the mastery, and only once did she give way to her feelings—when she knelt beside a dying youth, whose last words were of mother and Jesus and heaven. Seemingly, by tacit consent, she superintended the whole work of that ministry of love and sympathy. Her clear, mellow voice, soft and musical as a lute, could be heard now here, now there, during that day and the greater part of the night, condoling with one, encouraging another, and even breaking out into a low, musical laugh as some rough, rollicking fellow, with a ball through his arm or leg, told her how he "Had put a spider in the dough of some of the graybacks before he came so near having his own chunk knocked out!"

If even a cup of cold water given in the name of Christ shall in no wise lose its reward, then those noble women, who ministered to our brave soldiers on that trying and terrible occasion, will not be forgotten by the ever-living and ever-loving Redeemer.

CHAPTER X.

ANTIETAM—ASSAULT ON THE STONE BRIDGE—DEATH OF COLONEL COLEMAN—VICTORY AND RESULTS—DISSATISFACTION WITH GENERAL M'CLELLAN.

BATTLE OF ANTIETAM.

ON Wednesday, the 17th of September, the great battle of Antietam was fought. It is not the design of this unpretending volume to give minute or even general details of engagements to which reference may be made. As the title indicates, it is but Lights and Shadows of army experiences. Little glimpses of sunshine here, and little darkening clouds yonder—little incidents now and then—are all the author aspires to give. Hence, general details will not be given, being entirely outside the scope of this little work.

But a word or two relative to the share taken in it by the Eleventh and other regiments.

On Monday, after the battle of South Mountain, the army moved forward toward Sharpsburg. General Richardson's division of Sumner's corps was in the advance, and moved through Boonesboro' to Keedysville. The splendid Eighth Illinois Cavalry, under Farnsworth, was attached to Sumner's corps, and, as usual, pushed on in the advance. During that day little more was done than to reconnoiter the position which Lee held, and post the troops as they came up. The forenoon of Tuesday passed without any general movement, but, between two and three o'clock in the afternoon, Hooker, who was in command of the right wing, crossed the Antietam by the upper bridge and by a ford near Pray's Mill. Extensive cornfields, in the fullness and freshness of the early autumn, stretched away to the north and west. In these, concealed by the tall, tasseled corn, were the rebel pickets and sharp-shooters. Hooker drove in the enemy's pickets, opened briskly with artillery and musketry, keeping up the skirmishing till dark, and that night his advance lines occupied a portion of the cornfields and woods in which the enemy had taken position on the morning. Meanwhile, Burnside, who was in command of one of the grand divisions of the army, had his troops posted on the left, the most difficult position in the whole field, the greater part of it being rough and broken, and shaded here and there by dense oak woods. During the night the Kanawha division, under General Crook, was brought into position near the lower bridge—Simmons's and McMullen's batteries being so placed as to command the bridge and bluffs beyond. That night the troops lay on their arms, prepared to move at a moment's notice.

On Wednesday, the 17th, scarcely had the gray dawn of the early morn revealed the dim outline of the Sharpsburg hills, when the loud, roaring echoes, rolling along the mountains and through the valleys, announced that the dread work of death had begun. Hooker opened on the right, replying to the rebel batteries with tremendous and almost uninterrupted explosions. The green cornfields in his front were soon ablaze with musketry, while dusky forms were seen to move hither and thither, or spring into the air with a deathly shriek, spin round, and fall to rise no more. For nearly four hours Hooker alone engaged the enemy. For some reason or other, the left and center did little more than maintain their skirmish-line, although the rebel artillery sent the missiles of death thundering and crashing over and among them continually as they lay in line of battle. Finally, at about ten o'clock, Burnside received orders from McClellan to advance. The order was:

"You are to carry the bridge, gain the hights beyond, and advance along their crest to Sharpsburg, and gain the rear of the enemy."

The command was instantly given, and the extreme left was soon in motion. McMullen's and Simmons's batteries opened with grape and canister, varied now and then with solid shot and shell. Rodman's division was ordered to cross by a ford about a quarter of a mile below the bridge, and the Kanawha division, under Crook, supported by Connecticut and Pennsylvania troops, were ordered to storm the bridge. The Eleventh Ohio, which had been deployed as skirmishers, was withdrawn from the skirmish-line preparatory to the desperate work, and the entire brigade formed in line under cover of the woods.

The position held by the rebels at this point was the strongest on the whole field. It was a steep bluff, part of it a limestone ledge, along which the rebels had made extensive rifle-pits, and thrown up fortifications of logs and stones. The bluffs and the ridge beyond were bristling with cannon, which commanded all the approaches, while along the stone walls and in the cornfields the rebel infantry lay massed in thousands. The bridge was a massive stone structure of three arches, and about twelve or fourteen feet wide. A short distance from the bridge, and half-way up the bluff, was a limestone quarry, in which were sheltered sharp-shooters. The work to be done, therefore, on the part of the Union forces at this formidable point, was of no ordinary character.

The fearful moment arrived. Skirmishers were advanced to clear the bridge and ledges of rebel sharpshooters. "Forward!" rang out along the lines, and the assaulting column charged on the bridge. The opposite bluffs and ledges and ridge were instantly lighted up with one long sheet of flame. Volley after volley of musketry was driven into the faces of the advancing columns, while the artillery swept the bridge with one incessant, pitiless storm of grape and canister. The head of the column pushed on bravely, but was seen to waver and literally melt away before such a murderous blast. In vain the heroic champions of freedom struggled against the driving storm of iron and lead that tore remorselessly through their ranks! In vain they attempted to gain the bluffs which, from end to end, were enveloped in one long line of flame and smoke! In vain they threw themselves forward with desperate energy to seize the guns from whose brazen throats were belching forth destruction and death! After a heroic struggle, they had to withdraw from the unequal contest, and fall back to the shelter of a wooded ridge.

At this juncture, an aid from General McClellan rode up to General Burnside, with the short, decisive order:

"Assault the bridge, and carry it at all hazards!"

To accomplish this was an absolute necessity. Hooker, who had now been fighting seven or eight hours on the right, was being pressed by the massed forces on Lee's left, and the bridge must be stormed and the hights carried, at whatever cost, in order to turn Lee's right, and relieve Hooker. Burnside had but twelve or fourteen thousand men covering his entire line. The bridge and the bluffs alone were held by six thousand rebel troops, even before being reinforced by Hill's command, which, ere this, had come up to their support. Burnside sent for reinforcements. McClellan replied he could send none. Burnside, whose eagle eye took in the whole position at a glance, saw that on that bridge hinged the fortunes of the day, and that the position must be gained at all hazards.

"That bridge must be taken," said he to Cox; "but you have n't force enough to do it."

"I can take it, General, if you order it," said Cox, in his quiet, unassuming manner.

Burnside was cautious—he was dubious.

"If you order me to take that bridge," said Cox, "I 'll do it! I know my men—I know what they can do!"

The order is given, and again preparations are

made to storm the bridge. In the grand assault the Eleventh Ohio, supported by a Pennsylvania regiment, is to advance so as to form a strong skirmish line, or storming party, as circumstances may dictate, while Connecticut and Maryland troops are also formed for the same purpose. Colonel Coleman has formed his lines; the regiment is moving forward—steady, determined, and hopeful—toward the bridge, from behind the massive stone parapets of which, as well as from the rocky ledges beyond, the rebel skirmishers and sharp-shooters are again keeping up a continuous volley of musketry. Just at this juncture Colonel Coleman falls mortally wounded, while leading and cheering on to victory those whose steady tread he knows so well, and whose tried bravery he can ever trust. Almost at the same instant Captain Weller, of Company H, is wounded, and both officers are removed to the rear. The regiment is, for a moment, paralyzed; for they have learned to trust the skill and bravery of their fallen chief, and this is a trying hour. But there is no time to pause on this dread field of death, even although the good and brave may fall; and, vowing to avenge the death of their officers, the troops rush forward, a noble band of brave men. Onward, still onward, sweeps the roaring tide-wave of battle. The bridge is gained, and the rebel skirmishers are driven back. Simmons and McMullen now rain a perfect storm of grape and canister on the massed forces, who, with desperate energy, are striving to hold the position. The rebels, on the other hand, are playing on the bridge, and the stones fly from the parapets and arches. Splinters of wood and stone are flying in all directions, while the shell and grape-shot scream and hiss over and through the ranks of the advancing columns. But at last the center of the bridge is gained; then the western extremity. Cheers go up from the struggling heroes, which are answered by others further down the creek. Simmons wheels two guns so as to sweep the ridge. "Hurrah! forward! forward!" is the cry. The bluff is gained. Up, up the struggling heroes climb, or crawl, digging their hands or bayonets into the steep sides in their efforts to reach the top. They are successful! The bridge is secured, after a desperate struggle. The rebels are driven from their rifle-pits and batteries on the ridge, and the glorious Stars and Stripes now gleam in the slanting rays of the afternoon sun! Lee's right is turned by this costly but brilliant movement, and the issues of the day are decided.

The boastful slaveholding rebel — the notorious Toombs, who proudly prophesied he would see the day when he would call the roll of his slaves at the foot of Bunker Hill Monument—was in command of the rebel forces at this point. But the "Sword of Bunker Hill" gleamed that day in his traitor face, and he shrunk from its keen, conquering edge. So let it gleam, and never let that sword be sheathed till the last traitor foe is subdued, and the last slave is free!

That night, after one of the most sanguinary battles of the war, the Union forces rested upon the field, from every point of which the enemy had been driven, scattered, and confused. It was truly a great victory, but, alas! at what a cost of precious lives!

DEATH OF COLONEL COLEMAN.

Colonel Coleman was wounded in the arm and side, the ball lodging against the spine. At first, neither he nor his attendants apprehended that his wounds were of a serious nature; but, two hours after his removal from the front, his brave spirit passed away. He was sensible till the last, and, although suffering acutely, he uttered no complaint. His death cast a gloom over the entire regiment, every man of whom had learned to respect him for his manly, open frankness, and for his well-known military skill and bravery. Had he lived, no doubt he would have risen to distinction in the service of his country; for, to natural talents of a high order, he added those derived from a West Point education.

> "He sleeps his last sleep, he has fought his last battle;
> He ne'er shall awaken to glory again."

Peace be to his memory! He fills the honored grave of a patriot soldier, and his noblest monument is the affectionate remembrances of brave men.

THE FIELD AFTER THE BATTLE.

There was something inexpressibly saddening in the appearance of the Antietam battlefield. This was especially true of the right and center. On the right of the Sharpsburg road, where the gallant Hooker was engaged, the carnage was fearful, and the sight that met the eye everywhere was of the most ghastly and terrible character. Among solid shot—fragments of shell, broken caissons, splintered artillery wheels, overturned gun-carriages, empty ammunition-boxes, cartridge-cases, and the mangled carcasses of artillery horses—lay hundreds upon hundreds of the wounded, the dying, and the dead. On the night after the battle, and during the succeeding day, twelve hundred wounded soldiers were brought to one barn and barn-yard. In another barn, not far from this, were six hundred, and in another, seven hundred. It is no exaggeration to say that, on that day of dreadful conflict, the dead lay in heaps, and the wounded in thousands. While the battle was raging most fiercely, the rebel artillery could be seen mowing down Hooker's veteran troops, leaving great gaps, which were instantly filled up, only to be opened again as the murderous shell or grape was hurled against them. And even on the various roads leading from the field, the sad tale of suffering and death was told; for the ambulances were constantly engaged in carrying off their loads of bleeding, dying men, whose life-blood was trickling down through the ambulance floors and mingling with the dust of the hoof-trodden field, or staining the hard granite bowlders and broken stones of the turnpike! No one, with common feelings of humanity, could look upon such terrible scenes unmoved, nor forget that around each one of the thousands of killed and wounded clustered many warm affections, and that there was no one on this bloody field so lonely, wretched, or forsaken as that for him throbbed no loving heart, and for him no tears would be shed. As I looked upon the hundreds on hundreds of killed and wounded, I thought of the distant homes of these men, and how the sunlight of hope and joy would be quenched in grief, and how mother and wife and sister would clasp their hands in speechless agony, and fathers would bow their heads and weep, as only strong men weep, when the names of loved ones were announced as among the killed or wounded or missing. Not alone on the battlefield was there agony that day! Ah! no. There was untold agony in thousands of hearts, and deepest gloom in thousands of homes far from that field of blood. Who could refrain from breathing a prayer that the Angel of the Covenant might visit every weeping household, and comfort every stricken heart? and that soon, O soon! the olive-branch of peace might wave over our bleeding, distracted country, truth and righteousness flourish in our midst, and the people,

> "Walking in the light of God,
> In holy beauty shine."

A Glorious Victory—What were the Results?

"But, then, 'twas a glorious victory!"

So said a certain moralist, when debating with himself between the feelings of national pride and exultation over a great victory and the instincts of humanity, which revolt at the dreadful carnage of the battlefield. The Army of the Potomac achieved a glorious victory over the legions of traitors and defenders of human oppression during that memorable week in September, when, it might be said, in literal truth, that the very earth drank blood. The glowing accounts of the valor and unflinching devotion of the patriot soldiers, which appeared in the papers and magazines, were, by no means, exaggerated. Emotions of sadness, however, were mingled with the transports of joy; for, "glorious" though the victory was, there were several things connected with it that subdued the otherwise joyful feelings. First of all, the victory was purchased at a fearful sacrifice of human life. When the last gun was fired, on the evening of that bloody day, there could not have been less than twenty-five or thirty thousand torn, bleeding men lying on that battlefield! General McClellan reported, officially, a loss of seventeen hundred and forty-two killed, and eight thousand and sixty-six wounded. The rebels acknowledged a loss of fourteen thousand killed and wounded. What a fearful record of suffering and death!

Another thing that tended rather to depress than elevate the hearts of both officers and men, was the inexplicable conduct of military officials in holding back the victorious Union army, when it was known to every man, and published to the world, that the rebels were routed and demoralized. General McClellan telegraphed to the War Department to the effect that the Union troops had been everywhere victorious, and that the enemy, routed and demoralized, was retreating in great confusion. To all of which it was added, that he—McClellan—would push forward vigorously, and follow up his advantages. But, notwithstanding such official announcements of a complete victory, and the promise made to follow it up, the fruits of that victory were never reaped. It was the general expectation that the army would have moved forward on

Thursday morning—next day. Thursday passed; still no movement took place. Then there *must* be an advance on Friday morning—perhaps some grand strategic combination was being perfected, and a movement would inevitably take place. There was a moral certainty of that, of course. But Friday came, and no advance. Saturday also passed—and then intelligent men in the army, from corps commanders down, who saw and felt that then and there were both the time and place to strike one last tremendous blow on the routed, demoralized rebel army of the East—freely yet bitterly denounced the as yet unknown authors of that unnecessary delay.

"There is something rotten in Denmark," was the significant remark made by some of the bravest and most accomplished officers in the Potomac army.

"Why do we not move forward?" said I to a certain staff officer at corps head-quarters, on the afternoon of Saturday.

"Move forward!" he exclaimed, bitterly. "Cowardice or treachery would, perhaps, be the answer. We have been asking that question for the last two days. Lee has been retreating since Thursday, and this is known, or ought to be, at head-quarters."

This was a fact. Major Jackson, in command of the Eleventh, had made the report, through the proper channels, that his pickets reported the enemy crossing the river, evidently on the retreat. At the mess-tables of officers, and around the camp-fires, the question was repeated, time and again, "Why don't we move, and destroy the rebel army?" But day succeeded day, and week succeeded week, and still the army lay inactive. What the design was in thus holding in check as brave an army as ever fought, and that, too, while there was an enthusiastic eagerness to follow up the advantages gained, and thus end the rebellion, is already patent to all who have studied the political events of 1864. The Chicago Platform, with its supporters under it, and its candidate once *on* it, but now under it, too, throw considerable light on many things hitherto shrouded in mystery. Never, since the Pilgrim Fathers landed on Plymouth Rock, has any one had such a clear, open, easy path to honor and usefulness as General McClellan. Never has any one man had such influence and power as he. Petted, praised, courted—his very foibles were imitated, and he could hardly sneeze, certainly he could n't wash "his fevered brow at a roadside spring," to use the words of a correspondent—without its being duly reported all over the land. But he is politically as well as militarily dead—dead by his own acts. Traitor hands buried him, and over his grave they placed the wreck of his and their platform of principles—a platform so weighty with treason and oppression, that it will lie heavy on his grave till both he and it are forgotten in the lapse of years.

Unnecessary Sufferings of the Wounded—Inefficiency Somewhere.

Another thing that tended to modify exuberant emotions was the lack of prompt and efficient attention to the wants of the wounded, thus greatly increasing their suffering.

No army in the world has been so well cared for

in every respect as the Union army. No nation has ever so freely and bountifully supplied its defenders with the necessaries and comforts of military life. No nation has done so much for its soldiers when in health, or taken such tender care of them when sick or wounded. The Army of the Potomac, however, in 1862, was not, in any respect—except its heroic bravery—what it is in 1865. There was not a little of the elements of flippancy, arrogance, and official *hauteur* in the various departments of the army. The medical staff was by no means free from such unfavorable influences. Young, soulless, incompetent medical tyros had wormed themselves into the army, and thus occupied positions in which they might, with comparative impunity, play the petty tyrant, and, under the specious plea of military or medical rule, oppress those committed to their care. Not soon will some of those flippant gentry be forgotten by the soldiers who came in contact with them during the campaign of 1862. Incompetent, careless, and haughty, they were more intent on showing off their brass buttons and shoulder-straps, and maintaining professional dignity, than in attending to the wants of the suffering soldier. There were then, as there are now, many true, noble, skillful men in the army, who toiled day and night for the benefit of the sick and wounded, and who, uniting a pure patriotism, profound medical skill, and a tender sympathy, labored industriously for the good of others, and thus made their presence, on field or in hospital, fall like sunbeams around the sad and suffering. But these could not do their own work and that of others also; there must, therefore, be some who would be necessarily neglected and uncared for.

One or two incidents by way of illustration.

Captain Duncan and myself went to a large log house in search of some of the wounded of our regiment. We found it filled with the wounded of different regiments, but principally of those belonging to the regular army. Quite a number were also in a barn adjoining. Two days had elapsed since the battle, and yet their wounds had never been dressed, no surgeon had been to see them, and there was no one to give them a drink of cold water! I will never, to my dying day, forget the piteous words which one poor fellow spoke to us as we turned away:

"Are you going away to leave us here?" said he, in tones that told of his anguish and hopelessness. "For God's sake, don't leave us here alone, to die like dogs!"

"No," I replied, "I will not leave you; but I have no bandages with me, nor any thing else to afford relief. I'll go and get assistance and supplies, and do what I can."

I went to our brigade surgeon and reported the case, and asked for some bandages. Alas! all our hospital supplies were exhausted; our own surgeons had been working night and day; and what, therefore, could be done? Dr. Holmes looked distressed.

"It's too bad—it's too bad! but what can I do?" said he. "We are entirely out of bandages, and supplies in general, and it is the same in other divisions, for they have sent to me for supplies till I have none left. The surgeons of our own division are worked down; but I'll see after those wounded; I'll report the case, at least, to head-quarters."

Not knowing any more necessary or important work to be done than to take care of the suffering, I started to Middletown immediately—nearly ten miles off—applied to the Sanitary Commission for supplies, and returned to the field with what my servant and self could carry on our horses.

Next day, and in another part of the field, I found a dozen or more of our wounded in a barn, if possible in a more hopeless and deplorable condition. Their wounds were in a horrible state. As I washed and dressed the worst of the cases, it required the calling forth of all my powers of endurance. The stench from the foul, festering wounds was sickening to a degree that is indescribable, and the whole scene was as disgusting to the beholder as it was terrible to the sufferer. I rushed out to breathe a purer atmosphere, only to meet with festering limbs and blackened corpses, from which emanated a deadly exhalation.

To show that there was no lack on the part of the Government or of the Sanitary Commission in caring for the wounded, it may just be stated that on a box or bench were packages of farina, essence of beef, different kinds of cordials, crackers, etc., and yet those noble sufferers had had no breakfast, and it was now between two and three o'clock in the afternoon! There was no nurse, no attendant, and it was a matter of doubt whether any thing was being prepared for them. This case was reported to the proper authorities, and the barn was speedily inquired into, and it is said that language, more emphatic, perhaps, than polite, was used by the powers that be.

In making these statements, I do not wish to be understood as making even a general complaint against our army surgeons as a whole. By no means. I think, from what I have seen, that these were exceptional cases. A very large majority of those surgeons with whom I was acquainted, and with some of whom I was in close and constant association, were men of principle, honor, and humanity. Nobly did they work to relieve the suffering soldiers, and I heartily make this record to their honor.

It may be added, just here, that, on the battlefield of Antietam—as on all battlefields—there was much suffering and privation, aside from sickness and wounds, that was unavoidable. And it may also be added that every one who enters the army, intelligently and thoughtfully, makes calculations to meet with just such privations as are inseparable from military life, and he goes forth bravely to endure them, if needs be. But it must be conceded that at Antietam, through the blunders of some, the carelessness of others, and the incompetency of many who were invested with the sacred responsibility of seeing that our brave men were cared for when sick or wounded, the sufferings of our soldiers were greatly increased. The great want was a *corps* of strong, humane nurses for field and hospital—especially for the field—to attend to the wounded and dying. Another want was a greater number of skillful surgeons; both of which necessities have been measurably removed.

CHAPTER XI.

A GLEAM OF SUNSHINE ON A DARK SCENE—THE ELEVENTH HOUR—THE LOVED ONE REMEMBERED IN DEATH.

In one of the art galleries of Europe there is a most remarkable picture. It speaks less to the eye than to the heart. It seems to express much, but it suggests more, and is one of those rare works of a refined and elevated genius that seldom dazzle the eye, but leave such impressions upon the heart as render them ever after not so much tangible realities to be seen by the eye, as living ideas to be recognized by the mind. They are, so to speak, painted thoughts. They are abstract truths in outline—ideas on canvas.

The picture referred to is nothing more than a landscape—earth and sky. The background is a dark, pine forest, with a dense undergrowth of briers and alders. In the foreground are moss-covered rocks, with here and there tufts of fern and wild flowers. In the center, and nearly hidden by the interlacings of the wild rose and common bramble, are two solitary graves, marked by broken, crumbling tombstones. The scenery all around is gloomy, weird, and wild. Dense, black clouds float in a dark and troubled sky, while away in the far distance the tall pines are seen bending before the gathering storm. But, out from a rifted storm-cloud there streams down one broad, bright beam of sunshine, which, falling upon the lonely graves in the dark wildwood, lights them up with rays of glory. The dim outlines of a rainbow are seen fitfully glimmering against the dark shadows beyond. The lesson of the picture is, that there is some sunshine on the darkest pathway, and rays of glory on the most lonely graves.

This picture was realized in the barn already spoken of, where Hooker's gallant corps fought so desperately on the right wing. As already stated, a number of wounded soldiers had been brought to the barn in question, and left there without having the attendance either of surgeon or nurse. Whether through gross neglect or necessity this occurred, it is not necessary to hazard any opinion. But there they were, a helpless, sad, suffering company of noble men. Being supplied with every thing necessary, I went to work to relieve them as much as possible; and if ever there are times in men's history when the reflexive influence of making effort to help the needy is most salutary in all respects, then that effort was not in vain. One poor fellow, whose sufferings were very great, was the first who attracted my attention. As I washed off the clotted blood, and cleansed his wounds, and arranged his lowly pallet so as to render him a little more comfortable, his eyes filled with tears, and, with thanks which were totally unmerited, he said it was the first thing that had been done for him since the surgeon of his own regiment had hastily dressed his wounds during the heat of battle, and that he had felt as if forsaken both by God and man.

"Thank you! O, thank you for this!" he continued to say. "I feel so much easier already."

When I had finished, he asked me earnestly what I thought of his wounds, and whether they were dangerous. When I told him he might possibly live a day or two, but that, humanly speaking, his recovery was impossible, he looked disappointed. From a few remarks he made, I perceived that his thoughts were away far off to his New England home, and that he was yearning once more to see loved ones, and "that dearest spot on earth—home, sweet home!" Any one could see that a struggle was going on in that brave heart. The great spiritual victory was, at length, attained, and the language of resignation burst from his lips. I conversed with him on the fatherly character of God, and of His deep and abiding sympathy for man. I spoke of the peace which believers enjoy through faith in Christ Jesus, and encouraged him to place himself fully and freely in the hands of a gracious God. As I turned to leave him, he asked for a drink of water, and as I raised his head, and placed the cup to his pale lips, mortality! O, mortality! revealed itself more painfully and sadly than I care to tell. Perhaps, as I write these lines, the redeemed spirit, freed from that torn and broken tabernacle, is drinking of the fountain of living water in the City of God, and the battlefield and the bloody barn floor have been exchanged for the everlasting rest and joy and glory of that heavenly home.

"Will you please attend to me?" said a young man lying in another part of the barn, and who was, if possible, in a worse condition than the one previously mentioned. I spare my own feelings, and those of my readers, by refraining to give a minute description of the sad state in which I found this suffering soldier. Suffice to say, that he was lying—just as he had hastily been laid down—on a pile of wheat and straw. A piece of shell had torn a fearful gash in his side, and driven a part of his clothing into the wound, which, not being removed, occasioned him great pain. His blouse was hard and stiff with the dry, clotted blood, while his face was besmeared with dust and powder. Like the others around him, he had received no attention since being brought there, and had neither supper the night before, nor breakfast that day. And yet there was an air of peace and happiness around him, that measurably relieved the sad picture from its otherwise truly dark and hopeless appearance. By his side lay an open pocket Bible, which, to all appearance, he had been recently reading.

"Is this your Bible?" I asked, while removing the hardened bandages from his wounds.

"Yes, it is my Bible," he replied. "I 've managed to carry it with me ever since I left home."

"Have you found its promises to be precious to you in this your time of suffering?"

"O, yes! very precious—very comforting to me."

"Have n't you been in great pain? I would think you could n't read much while here in this sad state."

"The worst was at night," said he, "especially last night—it seemed so long and so dark; but I tried to think over all the comforting texts I had ever read, for I could n't sleep. O, it has been terrible here!"

I spoke a few encouraging words to him, and repeated some of the Savior's own blessed promises, while bathing and bandaging the deep and, apparently, mortal wounds, and then passed to others needing attention. During that day, and for several days afterward, fearful scenes of human suffering—glorious scenes of heroic devotion—peaceful scenes of Christian triumph, hope, and joy, were brought before me; but that one glorious picture—would that I could paint it!—of the young patriot soldier, wounded and dying, far from home, and suffering from hunger and thirst, turning his dim eye to the sacred page of the Divine Word—the gift of a pious mother—and drawing therefrom consolation and hope—O! it was the most vivid and glorious of all! and it will ever be to me as a sunny memory of the battlefield. Think of it! That poor, torn, dying soldier—no one to give him a drink of cold water in the hour of his deep distress, or wipe the dew-drops of agony from his dust-begrimed brow—no one to soothe his hard pillow, or speak a word of cheer to him in the lone midnight hour!—and yet, in his deepest anguish and loneliness, he turns to the Fountain of Life, and drinks of the precious, priceless waters of salvation! And, through the long, weary night, surrounded with fellow-sufferers, in pain like himself, he whiles away the dark and weary hours in thinking over the precious promises of the loving Savior! And O, what a testimony was this to the priceless value of God's Word! O, it is not the dry, severe, didactic book that many suppose it to be; but it is a book full of warm, generous sympathies, and cheering promises, and is the unchanging friend of man in every condition of life! It comes to us as the guide of our youth, our support and counselor amid the busy scenes and engrossing cares of maturer years, and our comforter and most welcome companion when, with wearied steps and dim eyes, we near that land "where the wicked cease from troubling, and the weary are at rest." And what a comfort, too, is such an incident to praying parents! O, ye Christian mothers, who have given your sons to the country, and sent them forth baptized with your tears and consecrated by your prayers, cease not your supplications in their behalf, and part not with your hopes concerning them! The Angel of the Covenant will have them in his holy keeping; and, although your loving hands may not lave their burning brow, nor moisten their parched lips in the dark hour of their anguish, Jesus will give them to drink of that living water of which, if a man drink, he will never thirst. When they have fought their last battle, they may also sleep their last sleep, far from the other graves of your household, and you may not have the melancholy satisfaction of visiting the spot where the beloved dust reposes; but remember that the pure in heart will meet again, and the shining shores of the better land will reëcho with the shouts of joy as redeemed friends meet each other there.

A Few Minutes' Warning—Was it Heeded?

While dressing the wounds of Captain Weller—a brave and efficient officer, mentioned in a previous chapter as being wounded at the stone bridge—an incident occurred, which, although by no means uncommon, will help to give an idea of the circumstances in which a minister in the army has often to try and preach Christ. Two men staggered into the crowded house with a stretcher, on which was a wounded man. Laying him on the floor gently, and adjusting a handful of straw under his head, one of them turned to me, and asked if I would attend to his wounded comrade as quickly as possible. I immediately went to him, and found that a musket-ball had penetrated his stomach and bowels. Indeed, he was in a dying condition. He told me that he had been lying two days and two nights in a cornfield before he was found; that he had suffered greatly from hunger and thirst; that his wound did not pain him, and if it was dressed, and he had something to eat, he would be better. Taking his hand in mine, and speaking to him as soothingly as possible, I told him he was very near eternity, and that he had but a short time to prepare to meet his God. He would not believe it—insisted that he felt better, and was sure he would not die. I plead with him to think of his position as a dying man, and press upon his attention the solemnity of death and judgment. But it seems unavailing. In twenty minutes he breathes his last! As I look upon his lifeless body, I think of the long, lonely hours of suffering he has passed in the cornfield, and whether he tried to lift up his heart to God, and whether he had found pardon. And the answer is only a doubt. Ah! how many souls, unwashed in the fountain of redeeming mercy—unprepared to meet God—are being ushered into eternity! And I turn away with saddened feelings.

Going Home.

In one of the temporary hospitals there was a wounded man, with whose last hours were connected many circumstances of a peculiarly interesting and pathetic character. My attention was first directed to him by one of the attendants, who informed me that he seemed to be dying. Approaching where he lay, I asked whether he wished any thing done for him. At first he could not answer me. It was evident he was near his last. The perspiration stood in large drops on his pale, massive forehead, his breathing was short and difficult, and his sufferings were very great. At last he was able to speak, although but in whispers, and at intervals.

"Chaplain, I'm in great pain—O, I'm in great pain!"

"I see you are in great pain," I replied, "and wish it were in my power to help you. There is One, however, who can always help in the hour of trouble, and who is ready now to help you. How do you feel? Do you think you will get well?"

"Yes, I think I will."

"Would you be displeased if I should tell you that you can live but a short time?"

"No," said he, "I would not; for if I die, I feel that I am ready. Jesus is my Savior. I would rather have been at home, however," he added; "for I want to see mother before I die."

In further conversation with him, I learned that he had, while a youth, sought an interest in the Savior, was a member of the Methodist Episcopal Church, and that he was blessed with godly parents. Toward midnight, his sufferings increased, and he sent for me, as he said, to speak to him again of Christ.

"I want you," said he, "just to tell me of Jesus. I can't speak much—I'm so weak. I can hear—tell me, tell me of Jesus!"

In the midst of low moanings, and sharp, short screams, I bent over him, and repeated parts of the fourteenth chapter of John's Gospel, and the Twenty-third Psalm. Beside that lowly pallet, in the midst of suffering and death, the Lord was found to be "as a little sanctuary." The gloomy scene was irradiated with the sunlight of Christian hope and joy, and, for the time being, the horrid scenes of war and tumult were forgotten amid the peaceful triumphs of Christian faith. It was noticed that he had a hair bracelet on his left wrist, and that he was holding something in his hand, attached to which was a small cord, which passed around his neck. As he seemed to be anxious about this, whatever it might be, I asked him what it was. With great effort, he raised his hand to his face, and looked at something, with a long, yearning look; it was a small gold locket. Closing it tightly in his hand, he whispered:

"This bracelet is a lock of my lady-love's hair."

"Would you want it and the locket taken off and sent home?"

"No, I want to be buried with them."

The last request he made was, "I wish you to see that this bracelet is not taken off my arm."

I watched by him as he neared the shores of eternity, and it seemed as if his joys were momentarily increased. "I'm going home to heaven—yes, to heaven!" were the last words I could hear distinctly. In a few minutes, he peacefully fell asleep in Jesus.

O, blessed religion! precious in youth and old age; precious in health and in sickness; precious amid the endearments of "home, sweet home," and precious when neither wife nor mother is near to assist or comfort the lone sufferer! Precious in the "house of the Lord," among "brethren dearly beloved and longed for," and precious on the battlefield, amid bloodshed and death! O, Savior! bless the reader of this, whoever he may be, and grant that he may enjoy thy blessed presence here, and enter into thy glory hereafter.

CHAPTER XII.

DIVINE SERVICES ON THE FIELD—WHAT DOES RELIGION DO FOR THE SOLDIER IN BATTLE?

Where shall we Worship?

"Our fathers worshiped in this mountain, and ye say that in Jerusalem is the place where men ought to worship," were the words which the woman of Samaria addressed to the blessed Savior, as, wearied with his journey northward to Galilee, he sat resting at the well of Jacob. Defective religion has always more to do with the outward form than the inner feeling, and the place and surroundings of religious service are more anxiously attended to than the worship itself. Such was the case with the Samaritan woman. Perceiving, from the Stranger's heart-searching questions, that he was a divine teacher, she was more anxious to be assured that Mount Gerizim was as good a place as Mount Zion in which to worship God, than to have her own heart searched, or her sins reproved by Divine Truth. Genuine religion is more intent on having the heart right, than in having the body in any prescribed devotional position. And it can find an altar or a temple in every valley and on every hill-side. "The hour cometh, and now is, when the true worshipers shall worship the Father in spirit and in truth; for the Father seeketh such to worship him."

Such was the answer which Christ gave to the woman of Samaria; and it not only sets forth the spirit and object of Divine worship, but it also teaches the truly spiritual and simple character of our holy religion. No magnificent cathedral, with groined arches and stained windows, is necessary to constitute a place of worship; neither are sacerdotal vestments and floating incense and responsive choirs indispensable aids or accompaniments to the sublimely simple and spiritual services which the infinite Father requires of his children. Jacob found a Bethel, the house of God, in the lonely wilderness, as he journeyed toward Padan Aram, and he found it again as he wrestled all night with the Angel of the Covenant at the fords of Jabbok. Elijah, the heroic reformer of Israel in troublous times, found a house of prayer on the top of Carmel, and a peculiarly glorious sanctuary on the wild and rocky sides of Horeb, while "the still small voice" soothed his chafed and wearied spirit, and revived his failing courage. And on the Christian Sabbath, in later times, "that disciple whom Jesus loved" worshiped with angels and the spirits of just men made perfect, even though banished from "brethren dearly beloved and longed for;" and, while the waves of old ocean were dashing around his rocky prison, he was permitted to look down the long vista of futurity and see the consummation of all things. Paul and Silas had a more glorious meeting in the dark Ephesian dungeon, than was ever held amid the gaudy tinselry and pretentious devotions of the grandest cathedral ever built; and in the gloomy days of persecution, many of those who

> "Lived unknown
> 'Till persecution dragged them into fame,
> And chased them up to Heaven—"

found a sanctuary in many a lonely glen and gloomy cave, while their hearts were filled with rejoicing and praise because of the presence of the Lord.

And so has it been in the army. The question has been oftentimes, not Where shall we worship, but When shall we worship? It is one great blessing connected with our army, that, during the war, wherever there has been a genuine desire to engage in religious services, the opportunity to do so has usually been afforded; and not only so, but services in camp are often of a peculiarly impressive and interesting character—not only from the fact that they are associated with many things of an exciting and novel nature, but, divested of all stiff, starched formality, they are frequently seasons of spontaneous outbursts of genuine religious emotions. The Sabbath after the battle of Antietam was a day of rest for both the body and the soul. The circumstances in which the army had been placed during the past week, as well as the events which had transpired, were all conducive to make this day sacred and impressive. The troops had been in several heavy skirmishes, and in at least two, if not three, pitched battles during the previous week or ten days. Many a soldier had been called to his final account during that time, and very hard must that heart have been that felt no emotion of gratitude for deliverance in the hour of peril.

Early in the day, Colonel Andrews, of the Thirty-sixth Ohio, came to the camp of the Eleventh, and suggested that the two regiments unite in religious services, seeing there was but one chaplain in the entire brigade. His proposition was gladly accepted, so that the two regiments, and, indeed, portions of the whole brigade, united in the sacred services. The "Church-call" was made at ten o'clock, repeated again in fifteen minutes, and we met on the two slopes overlooking a small ravine close by the Antietam Creek. But four days ago the fierce storm of battle had raged furiously on this very portion of the field, and death and destruction had held high carnival here; but now the song of praise was heard instead of the rush and roar of battle, and a Sabbath's calm and peace followed the fierce tempest of war. And, judging from the interest manifested, and the order and decorum everywhere visible, the services were appreciated by all. Indeed, throughout the entire camp the quietude and good order were very marked. It might be added here, that, while encamped on the Antietam, and latterly on the Potomac, there seemed to be a very general religious interest in the army. On every Sabbath, and two or three times during the week, there were religious services held in the Kanawha division, and the attendance at every meeting was quite large.

THE PHILOSOPHY OF CALMNESS IN THE HOUR OF BATTLE.

One evening, shortly after the Antietam battle, a little informal meeting was held in the chaplain's tent, when the question of calmness and presence of mind during battle was incidentally introduced. Nearly all present made reference to their experiences during the battles of the previous week. One spoke as follows: "Immediately before going into action, I felt excited and fearful. I could not get away to any secret place to pray or meditate, but, as I stood in ranks, I lifted up my heart in prayer to God, and it seemed as if I never enjoyed such a clear and refreshing sense of my Savior's presence. I committed my all to him, and asked that, whether I lived or died, I might be his true follower. I felt to consecrate myself again to his service, and, in so doing, I felt an indescribable peace and satisfaction fill my heart. During the few minutes thus engaged," he continued, "I enjoyed more happiness, and a clearer conviction of my acceptance with God, than I ever did before. My fear and trembling disappeared, and I felt calm throughout the entire day."

It might just be added here, that this Christian brother was not only calm and peaceful, but was truly brave in the hour of peril. At one time, when there was not a commissioned officer to take command of the company, and that, too, at a time when the battle was hottest and the carnage most fearful, he took command of his comrades, rallied them for another charge, and led them onward, till relieved by a superior officer.

It is said—with how much truth there is not the means of knowing—that, during the Crimean war, strong suggestions, amounting almost to positive orders, were made by general officers in the English army, that the chaplains, when conducting religious services, should, as much as possible, refrain from introducing the subject of Death, as such a subject might have the tendency to induce a fearful, despondent, and even cowardly spirit! Blind leaders! Their suggestions were as irreligious as they were unphilosophical. No man can be as brave without the consciousness of God's favor as he would be with it. Who can afford to be so brave as he who hath placed his all in the hands of God, and feels prepared either to live or die? He who has made his peace with God can afford to dare and do noble deeds of heroism, for "he endures as seeing Him who is invisible." And the bravest unconverted man that ever lived could have been braver still if he had possessed the blessed consciousness that, "whether he lived or died, he was the Lord's." Nothing strengthens a man in the hour of deadly peril, and nerves both heart and hand, like a firm faith in God. In every walk of life is this true. The wife and mother, in the privacy of the domestic circle, engaged in her holy ministry of love, is all the more happy in her own soul, and all the more successful in her blessed work, if she have the consciousness of the favor and presence of her God. The man of business, who, necessarily, has to come in contact with the sharp angles and the unpleasant phases of human nature, can have a clearer intellect and a stronger heart, if he has consecrated himself and his business to the glory of God. The general who commands the armies of a nation, and the private in the ranks, can be all the braver in the hour of peril if they have experienced the love of God shed abroad in their hearts by the Holy Ghost. The most cowardly man I ever saw, while connected with the army, was a great, robust, two-fisted fellow, who, from his physical proportions, ought to have been a Hercules for strength and a Hannibal for bravery. On a certain battlefield, where his pluck was tested, I had serious doubts whether he had nerve enough to pull trigger even once. He certainly had not enough life left in his one hundred and eighty pounds of physical substance to gasp out an incoherent assertion that he was too sick to stop and help me lift a comrade whose leg had been shattered by a cannon-ball! If he did n't go at a two-forty pace to the rear, it was n't because he did n't try! He neither feared God nor regarded man—except just at that time, perhaps!

CHAPTER XIII.

MOVING WEST—A TERRIBLE MARCH—SUFFERING OF THE TROOPS—USE OF ARDENT SPIRITS IN THE ARMY.

AFTER the withdrawal of the larger portion of the troops from the Kanawha Valley to reinforce McClellan's army, the rebels sent large forces into the valley, which drove the small body of Union troops there to near the Ohio River, and destroyed large quantities of Government property at Gauley Bridge. They had, also, been running the salt-works, near Charleston, for some time, and otherwise securing needed supplies for their larger armies, which they transported by way of Fayetteville to the Virginia and Tennessee Railroad. General Cox had been ordered back to the Kanawha, or rather to the Ohio, to take command of a new department, which embraced Western Virginia. At his own urgent request, he was to have his old and well-tried Ohio veterans with him.

The division under command of General Crook broke camp, on the Potomac, near Sharpsburg, about nine o'clock, and, passing through Sharpsburg, took up the line of march toward Hagerstown. The day was excessively hot—unusually so, considering the lateness of the season. The little air that stirred seemed to come from the mouth of a furnace, while the hard limestone turnpike was covered with hot dust, which, being kept in constant motion by thousands of feet, and by the artillery and wagon-trains, induced a burning thirst, which water, seemingly, could not quench. There had been considerable sickness in the army while camped on the Antietam and Potomac, consequently the men were not in the best condition for a fatiguing march. They were all suffering, more or less, from the noxious exhalations of the contiguous battlefield, not to speak of scarcely less deleterious agencies caused by insufficiently policed camps. Taking the whole circumstances into consideration, it was the most fearful march that any of the regiments composing the division ever made—and they all knew, from experience, what forced marches were. The burning sun, the hot, stifling dust, the scarcity of water, the defective arrangements for the relief of the sick, the wretched order of march for the ambulances, the debilitated condition of many of the men, to all of which was added an unnecessarily rapid rate of march, with only brief halts, and those at long intervals, made this march from the mouth of the Antietam to Hagerstown one of intense suffering.

If it had been the design to save Hagerstown from imminent peril at the hands of rebels, it would have been scarcely possible to have made much more of a forced march. By noon, there were hundreds out of ranks. In fence-corners, under trees, on logs or stones, all along the roadside, soldiers were lying utterly exhausted, and so completely broken down that many of them seemed careless either about life or death! And these were no stragglers or shirks—as almost every regiment has, more or less—but they were men who would scorn to fall out of ranks—men who never before sank down on the march, and never asked to be excused from duty or to be assisted in any way. Company officers, who had neither gun, cartridge-box, nor knapsack to carry, only as they might manfully help some exhausted private, even they, many of them, had to succumb to the terrible ordeal, and sink down, weak and fainting, by the wayside. Scarcely one-half of the distance had been traversed, when two men fell down, never to rise again. One died instantly; the other in a few hours. Yet, on and on pressed the dispirited, exhausted column, through the blinding, stifling dust, that burned and blistered the feet and filled the eyes and throat, producing a painful, burning thirst.

It has been said that, on entering the army, chaplains have generally lost what little religion they ever had. The author frankly acknowledges that if all anger is sin, then he sinned woefully that day, for he was both sorrowful and angry—yes, may as well confess it—right down angry! Good, efficient, energetic Dr. Gabriel had gone home, on account of his own failing health. Dr. Gill—a soldier, every inch of him, and good as he was brave—had been transferred to another regiment, and their places had been supplied with—with—the boys said, "Checking Powders"—which means, being interpreted, inefficiency and heartless indifference! Noble men, who, in all that pertains to true manhood, as well as in talents and accomplishments, were infinitely superior to some of those who were paid to care for them, were rudely and shamelessly insulted and neglected on that terrible day, because they sank down utterly exhausted. They asked for help, and received, instead, a bitter taunt, that burned into their very soul. There are times when a man may have patience under wrong and insult; but, assuredly, it is not always when his back is to the wall, and when his very helplessness should secure to him better treatment at the hands of his fellows. It is not, therefore, a very marked indication of exalted piety to stand quietly by and see the good and brave wronged because they are incapable of helping themselves. The man would not only be less a man, but less a Christian, could he have seen some of the scenes of that march, and had no throbbing heart and no flashing eye.

There was one genuine outburst of good, healthy indignation. With the exception of some decidedly bad grammar, it was both refreshing and edifying. A soldier was lying in a fence-corner exhausted—thought to be dying.

"Shorty"—beg pardon, Mr. Shaw—"Shorty," a bristling, bustling, humane-hearted but rough old sea-dog, was there, too, blazing with wrath, and he was putting in all the exclamation points and all the three-cornered adjectives he could think of, in spite of staff-buttons and shoulder-straps, that speedily knocked an M. D. beside him into a cocked hat!

But, finally, that march came to an end. About five o'clock in the afternoon the column filed off to the right into some gently-sloping fields, near Hagerstown, where arms were stacked and camp-fires were soon blazing. It is said—whether as a veritable fact, or as a bit of biting sarcasm, can not now be decided—that, on reaching camp, General Scammon, who had been in the advance, inquired of the cavalry, with evident solicitude, *how their horses had stood the march!*

The General had better make special arrangements, in his last will and testament, for masses to be said for his soul perpetually, for assuredly he will never get out of purgatory, if soldiers' prayers avail any thing.

Next morning reveillé beat at an early hour, and, shortly after dawn, the column was again on the march. Lessons had been gained by the experience of the previous day. General Crook was in the advance, and the march was conducted with great care and regularity. Early in the evening, the division encamped in or near a strip of woods on the National Road, and about three miles west of Clear Springs. The sick—and there were many of them—were well cared for by the loyal citizens of that town and vicinity, a number of whom came to where the ambulances with the sick were parked, bringing with them many comforts and delicacies.

Next morning, the 10th of October, the column was in motion by three o'clock. At about half-past ten, shortly after passing the picket-post of a Pennsylvania regiment guarding one of the fords of the Potomac, the column was suddenly halted, and word passed from one to another that the rebels were in our rear, had cut our wagon-train in two, capturing the greater part of it, and were working mischief generally. The cavalry went thundering back, followed by one or two pieces of artillery. The Twenty-eighth followed on the double-quick. Half an hour had scarcely elapsed till the entire supply-train was safely within reach, and sent to the front, instead of being kept in the rear. The rebels had no intention of making any special demonstration just then or there, designing to go further, and meet with as little resistance as possible. The rebel column was commanded by Stuart, who made his somewhat noted raid clear round the Army of the Potomac. The division encamped that night on the south side of the Potomac River, opposite Hancock, the intention being to transport the troops from that point to Clarksburg by the Baltimore and Ohio Railroad. Here the troops remained until the evening of Monday, the 13th, when the entire division left for Clarksburg, which point was reached on the morning of the 16th.

The destination of part of the division was the Kanawha Valley, the design being to strike a point at or near Gauley Bridge, so as to coöperate with another force moving up from the Ohio, and intercept the rebels in their retreat either up the Gauley toward Greenbrier, or by New River toward Raleigh and Princeton. Whether some grand strategic combination was going on elsewhere, or whether the military authorities, McClellan to-wit, thought the rebel force in the Kanawha too insignificant for any special effort to be made for its capture or destruction, it would not be easy to say. One thing, however, is certain, that the intercepting column was detained so long at Hancock and elsewhere, that the rebels were duly notified of the trap laid, and, of course, leisurely withdrew from the valley, taking their plunder with them.

While lying at Clarksburg, two new companies—E and I—arrived, under the command of Captains Brown and Staley, respectively. It was at this point, also, that Colonel P. P. Lane, promoted from Captain of Company K, assumed command of the regiment, which, since the death of the lamented Coleman, had been under the command of Major Jackson. At this time, also, Major Jackson resigned, and bade farewell to the regiment and to the army. By a kindly disposition and gentlemanly deportment, as well as his tried bravery, he had gained for himself very general respect and good-will.

Want of Supplies—Blame Somewhere.

It is by no means traveling out of the way, nor is it with the design of finding fault with any one in particular, when reference is made, just at this point, to the condition of the troops sent back into Western Virginia, and, indeed, in the Eastern army generally, after the campaign on the Potomac in the summer and autumn of 1862. Who was to blame it would be assuming too much to say. That some one was at fault somewhere could hardly be denied. Never since that time has there been such wretched management in the Commissary and Quarter-master's departments as then existed. Had there been a well-planned and settled purpose on the part of some high military officials to produce discontent and discouragement in the army, and cause revulsion of feeling toward the

Government, scarcely more could have been done to accomplish such results. As if purely intentional—for it was not necessary in any sense—the troops had not been supplied with clothing. Many of the men were without blouses; large numbers without shoes, socks, or caps, while shirts and drawers were almost an exception. This lack of clothing was rendered all the more disheartening and exasperating from the want of woolen and rubber blankets, and the entire absence of tents, save those which individual ingenuity or good fortune supplied. To all of this, it may be added that we were now amid the bleak, dreary mountains of Western Virginia, with the cold winds and rains of November beating upon us. Efforts were made to attach blame upon officials at Washington, while some army correspondents, seizing the clue given by others, wrote flaming philippics against the Government. For, neglecting to care for the heroes of the nation, to defend himself from the severe criticisms of every loyal journal in the land, General McClellan had officially to complain of the want of supplies. But General Meigs set this at rest when he telegraphed to McClellan, "The railroads are now embarrassed to supply you, and supplies here wait for the return of cars detained while loaded near your position."

Post quarter-masters, who had under their control immense quantities of supplies, could not issue to brigade or regimental quarter-masters, because they had no orders so to do. And thus, while stacks of clothing and thousands of tents were within easy reach, the men, who had endured the perils and privations of a heavy campaign, were shivering around the camp-fires by night, and during the day felt that their manhood was insulted and humiliated by insufficient clothing. If curses were not loud, they were deep enough and bitter enough, truly.

It was under such circumstances that, in November, the Kanawha division took up its line of march for points on the Gauley and Kanawha Rivers, in Western Virginia. Already the bleak hills of that wild country were swept by the cold autumn winds and rains. The various regiments had traversed but half the distance, when a fierce storm of sleet swept down upon them, already wet and shivering with the cold rains that had prevailed for several days. One night, while the sleet and rain was driving in fitful gusts, the men shivering in the cold, the wood too wet to make warm camp-fires, no shelter to be found but under trees, and scarcely any prospect for getting hot coffee, as the fires would not burn, fears were entertained that some of the men would perish. Orders were accordingly issued, at the instance of the medical director, for a small quantity of whisky to be given to each man.

I make this statement here and now, because friends at home have frequently asked whether ardent spirits were not issued to the troops, especially when going into battle—*a thing I never knew or heard of being done.*

CHAPTER XIV.

EXPEDITION TO COLD KNOB—REBELS CAUGHT NAPPING—HEROIC ENDURANCE OF THE UNION SOLDIERS.

Simply as a record of heroic endurance and bravery, as well as to show what sacrifices the soldier makes for his country, the following narrative is here given.

Scarcely had the Kanawha troops been stationed at the various points thought necessary, when orders came to the Eleventh, at Summerville, for an expedition into Greenbrier County.

A rebel cavalry force was reported as stationed near Cold Knob, on the turnpike north of Lewisburg, and the design of the expedition was to capture or break up that force. The Eleventh was to support the Second Virginia Cavalry, which was to move from Camp Piatt by a different road—a junction of the forces being to take place at a designated point. The cavalry force was five hundred strong, and under the command of Colonel Paxton.

The Eleventh left Summerville on the 24th of November, moving south toward Lewisburg. On reaching the Gauley River, it seemed as if an effectual barrier was placed right in the teeth of the expedition; for the clear, cold waters of that mountain-fed river were dashing over their rocky channel, swollen by the late rains. Colonel Lane asked no man to do what he thought dangerous to attempt himself, and he was the first to test both the depth of the river and the strength of the current, and find the safest fording place. In thus plunging into the cold, swollen stream, however, in his effort to secure, by his own personal examination, the best and safest crossing place, he came very near losing his life. The incident was significant, and had a good effect upon all; for it exemplified, by an apparently trifling circumstance, the interest taken in their welfare by their lately-appointed commander. After some little delay, the regiment crossed the river safely, and, leaving the road to the right, took a mountain path known only to the hunters of that wild and desolate region. Captain Ramsey, an old hunter, and familiar with every road and path, acted as guide.

Before noon, a cold rain began to fall, which, toward evening, turned into a driving storm of sleet and snow, which continued, without cessation, for thirty-six hours. The regiment marched seventeen miles the first day, notwithstanding the rough, hilly, broken paths and the inclement weather. The men were in light marching order—very few were supplied with overcoats, each man had but one blanket, and there were no tents. It was under such circumstances that, after a toilsome march, the men, wet and shivering with cold, prepared to bivouac on the mountains. The second day's march was through snow from six to twelve inches deep; and the snow still continuing to fall and partially melt, rendered the mountain path—at the best, rough and rugged—one of the worst imaginable. At times over rough bowlders, then plunging through slush, anon winding round fallen timber and through brush, with the blinding snow-storm beating in their faces, onward the column pressed. Several miles had to be traversed in this manner after darkness had set in. It was also necessary to march in single file, and what with the dense forest and the blinding, driving snow, it was so dark that it was impossible to see further than a few feet. Under these circumstances, orders were given for each man to place his hand on his file-leader, so as to keep the column from being broken. Thus, in pitchy darkness, through a dense forest on a wild mountain pass, and the sleet and snow driving and eddying above and around them, the men wearily, but uncomplainingly, pressed forward. With all the care and precaution used to keep the file from being broken, and to prevent accidents during the pitchy darkness that settled down, an accident did occur. One of the men happened to make a misstep, and fell over a precipice. His comrades stopped to assist him out of his perilous position. This being unknown at the head of the column, the chain—so to speak—was broken, the regiment cut in two, and the rear left without a guide. Colonel Lane, who was at the head of the column, knew nothing of what had occurred until his attention was arrested by a loud halloo from the rear, repeated at short intervals, indicating some one in distress. He immediately halted the column, sent the guide to the rear to learn the difficulty, as he was the only one who could find the way back. He found the lost party, made the connection of the line again, and the column moved forward. The regiment was ordered to make a certain point by the second day, so as to connect with the cavalry force, which was moving by another and more circuitous route—the line pursued by the infantry not being practicable for cavalry. The point indicated was reached at about nine o'clock on the evening of the second day. By this time the cold had increased greatly, and the driving sleet and snow had given place to a severe frost. The men were wet to the skin, and, weary with the day's fatiguing march, they stood shivering in the piercing blast that swept down the mountain gorges. It was desirable to keep the movements concealed from the enemy; hence large fires must be avoided, as they would necessarily attract the notice of pickets, and, no doubt, reveal the whole plan. And, even had it been desirable to make fires, there was nothing to be had but green wood, and there were no axes, even, to cut with, except the hatchets which the men carried in their belts. It was so dark, also, that the men had to go by the sense of feeling rather than by sight. Small fires were finally kindled, however, and the men, scooping away the snow, wrapped their blankets around them—wet as they were—and laid down to sleep. Not all! Ah, no! All can not sleep. The guards—those never-failing attendants of an army—must be posted, whatever may be the circumstances, and faithful watch be kept while comrades are sunk in repose. No matter how long and weary the march may have been, nor how keenly the sleet-laden blast may have driven into his face, nor how cold and hungry he may be, the sentinel must remain at his post, and peer watchfully and anxiously

17

into the dim and dark distance, while with a firm grasp of his musket, loaded and capped, he faithfully keeps watch while his wearied comrades are sleeping.

That was a long, cold, dreary night; but morning came at last. Shaking off the snow, as they arose from their Arctic-like beds, the men came forth like half-buried ghosts. A cup of coffee, and some of the inevitable hard-tack and pork, got up without loss of time and with precious little ceremony, had an enlivening and cheering effect, and neither few nor pointless were the waggish remarks bandied about, relative to sleeping comfortably—whether the sheets were clean, and whether thorough ventilation was not very necessary to health—and whether any one did n't want to be helped to a slice of turkey, or to a dish of delicious ice-cream. The larger majority, however, could not see where either the joke or the laugh came in. Like the minister who, on being told by one of his deacons that he ought to live more on faith, and not be so anxious about his salary, replied that he did live on faith, but that he wanted it pretty well mixed with beef and bread—so these men, shivering in the cold while munching their hard-tack and salt pork, felt that it was all very well, perhaps, to those who had a relish for such a primitive, romantic style of living, but, as for them—well, they "could n't see it!"

As early as possible, the line was advanced a short distance nearer the road on which the cavalry were to come; but hour after hour wore away, and still they came not. So intensely cold had it become, that the men's clothing was freezing on them, and their inactivity, under such circumstances, was having the usual effect. Many of them were rapidly falling into a dozy, stupefied state. In fact, they were freezing. Colonel Lane gave orders for them to be formed into squads, and marched round a circle on the double-quick. So benumbed and stupefied were some of them with cold, that it required force to get them into motion; and two or three had so far yielded to the drowsiness and indifference—the sure precursors of freezing to death—that their comrades had to lay hold on them, and shake and drag and dance them round and round. Had such a plan not been adopted and rigidly enforced by all the officers, some would, doubtless, have frozen to death. As it was, several were severely frost-bitten, and suffered for some months in consequence. Colonel Lane personally examined the arms, to see what condition they were in, and found nearly all of them more or less unserviceable. The rifle-barrels were found full of ice and snow—the rammers frozen tight in their sockets, and the ammunition nearly all damp. This was rather a critical condition to be in. Orders were instantly given for all who could draw their loads to do so, and every preparation was made, which experience and the exigency of the circumstances could suggest, to meet the enemy, should they appear.

About noon the cavalry arrived; but nearly one-third of their horses had given out, and the remainder were nearly useless for any very active, dashing service. Colonel Paxton, in command of the cavalry, declared that the expedition, as such, was a failure, and that he would withdraw his command from that point, as it was useless to go further with his horses in their present broken-down condition. He, being the ranking officer, ordered Colonel Lane to return with his command to Summerville, stating, at the same time, that he would return by the same road he came. Thus, after all the toil, exposure, and privations endured, the expedition was about to be abandoned when within a few miles of where the enemy's camp was supposed to be, and even before finding out whether the enemy were there or not. But for Colonel Lane and Major Powell—now a brigadier-general in Sheridan's army—the expedition would thus have been given up. These officers urged that a reconnoissance at least be made, if nothing more. Major Powell asked permission to take the cavalry to the enemy's camp, some five miles distant, to see whether the enemy were there, and in what force. Leave was granted, and preparations were made accordingly. Major Powell asked the coöperation of Colonel Lane, with his infantry force, which was gladly acceded to. The plan adopted was for the infantry to precede the cavalry and drive in the enemy's pickets, and then, opening right and left, the cavalry were to dash in and take the camp by surprise. This plan was put into operation, and worked to a charm. The infantry had proceeded about three miles, when a party of rebel cavalry was met coming up the mountain road to go on picket. The storm had been so severe for several days, that they had concluded the Yankees, instead of causing any trouble, would very gladly stay at home. Consequently they had allowed their outer pickets on the mountain to be withdrawn, and the movements of the Union troops were scarcely known till they were thundering and clattering right among them. The infantry advance-guard had a brisk skirmish with the inner line of pickets, but the latter, getting sight of the head of the advancing column of infantry, and, concluding there was too much for them, retreated slowly, and rode back toward their camp. As soon as the firing had commenced, the cavalry, with Major Powell at their head, advanced to the front, overtook the retreating pickets, who scattered into the brush, and, without opposition, dashed into the rebel camp, and captured two hundred prisoners, with their horses and equipments, and about five hundred stand of small arms. They also burned their camp, with a large quantity of supplies.

The plan of attack was as novel as it was successful. The idea of infantry preceding cavalry is by no means according to military tactics, as laid down in the books, and yet here was a practical and successful illustration of the fact that, in military as well as in other departments of science, the books do not contain the finality either of theory or practice. The infantry preceding the cavalry—the cavalry being concealed—the rebel scouts or pickets, themselves mounted, were, consequently, in no haste to give the alarm, never dreaming of a cavalry force being so near them. They thought, of course, as they slowly fell back to their camp, that they could arrive in sufficient time to give the alarm, and have every thing in readiness before the infantry could reach them. As it was, the pickets, upon whom the safety of the camp depended, were scattered everywhere, long before they could give any sufficient alarm, and the advancing column dashed in right among them, with the results already stated.

Colonel Lane and others declared it to be one of the neatest little affairs of the kind ever seen, and they voted Major Powell one of the most dashing and adroit of cavalry officers, and attributed the success of the expedition almost entirely to him. His promotion to a star, and to an important command under the brave, dashing Sheridan, shows how he has fought his way up, and how his services have been appreciated.

It may just be added that the Eleventh returned to Summerville by the same route by which it came, arriving there on the evening of the fifth day.

CHAPTER XV.

REGIMENTAL LIBRARY—RELIGIOUS MEETINGS—HOW SOLDIERS PRAY—THE PRODIGAL'S RETURN—A THRILLING SCENE.

"Prayer is the Christian's vital breath,
The Christian's native air;
His watchword at the gates of death,
He enters heaven by prayer.
Prayer is the contrite sinner's voice,
Returning from his ways;
While angels in their songs rejoice,
And say, 'Behold, he prays!'"

WHILE in winter-quarters at Summerville, time passed, on the whole, quite pleasantly; and perhaps it might be said that, considering all the circumstances, it passed not altogether unprofitably. Through the instrumentality of the Christian Commission—that blessed institution which has done, and is still doing, so much for the soldiers in the field, as well as by the kindness of friends generally, among whom may be named Rev. E. Babb, editor of the *Christian Herald*, Cincinnati—our little regimental library, the nucleus of which had been formed by Rev. Mr. Dubois, while chaplain of the regiment for a few months, in 1861, was greatly enlarged. During a trip to Ohio, on official business, opportunities were given me to secure large quantities of reading matter, so that, in addition to a full supply of Testaments, hymn-books, and tracts, we had not less than four hundred volumes in our regimental library. An old but quite comfortable little house was set apart for the chaplain's quarters—one end being used as a library-room, the other for quarters proper and for prayer-meetings. After the quarters for the men had been fitted up, a dismantled church was repaired and made quite comfortable for meetings. For several weeks, religious services were held nearly every night. A writing-school was organized, a Bible-class formed, and, twice a week, lectures on temperance, philosophy, history, etc., were delivered. Some of the most interesting and encouraging meetings, perhaps, ever held, under such circumstances, were held here, and impressions were made which will never be effaced.

True, as a regiment, we were in a very exposed situation, and the utmost vigilance had to be maintained at all times. We were some thirty-five miles from the nearest reinforcements, and did not know the moment when an attack might be made; yet Providence favored us, and, both in regard to moral and material privileges, we were abundantly blessed. And, while these lines are penned, the little, dilapidated house, which was so frequently the scene of richest spiritual enjoyment and social comfort, seems to rise before me. A few of those who came to the services there, and whose voices were often heard in prayer, or in the song of praise, and whose Christian fellowship was so highly prized, now sleep their last sleep. Men who had fought bravely on bloody fields, and faced death at the cannon's mouth, often met together there, and shed tears of holy joy while pouring out their heart's desires at a throne of grace, or singing those hymns which, for ages, have been as the songs of holy joy and the shouts of triumph in the Church of God. How tender and pathetic were the prayers which often went up in behalf of dear wife and children, who, at home, might be feeling lonely and sad! How earnest were the petitions that the everlasting arms might be around them, and that the sheltering wings of Divine love might be over them, and that, if a reunion of the loved and loving at the domestic hearth should never take place on earth, they might all meet in the Father's house on high! How frequently, too, were the dear names of mother and father breathed! and how often—forgetful of all but himself and his own heart's longings—did the individual, engaging in prayer, beseech God to bless "*my* wife" or "*my* children;" and, in some instances, a full-hearted son would, in affectionate simplicity, speak of "*my* father" or "*my* mother!" What an absence of all formality, and what a full, free, outgushing of the heart's holiest sympathies and tenderest emotions were at those meetings! And how fervent, too, were the petitions for an outpouring of God's Spirit on the regiment, that a great and glorious work of saving grace might be experienced—souls saved and God glorified! O, those were precious seasons of social and religious enjoyment—seasons of rich comfort, to be remembered as long as life shall last!

THE PRODIGAL'S RETURN.

On a dark, stormy evening, a scene transpired in my quarters which, for deep interest and touching pathos, I have seldom seen surpassed. As a fitting introduction to this picture of mingled "lights and shadows," the following note is here introduced :

DEAR CHAPLAIN: While listening to you, last evening, delivering your sermon on the subject "Remember Lot's wife," I was, as I have often been of late, thrown into serious meditation. I viewed myself thoroughly, and was surprised that, having held the position I once did, and enjoyed what I once enjoyed, and then being what I now am, I was allowed to live. I am lost, forever lost! I know that God is ever ready to forgive even the greatest sinner, but for me there is no redemption. When but twelve years of age, I gave my heart to God. For more than twelve years I lived a Christian life. I served God, because I loved his service, and was happy. I received license to preach, and, for over a year, engaged in the work of the ministry, and was blessed. To-day, where am I, and what am I? My very frame shakes at the thought! . . .

I know that I have fallen, and that I am responsible; for every man must answer for the sins he commits. I should like, some time, during a private interview, to reveal all to you. My history is without a precedent, and is an example for others to take warning by. . . .

I am, with respect, yours, &c., ——.

On reading the above, I immediately penned the following note :

MY DEAR BROTHER: Don't give up to despair, nor limit the mercy and grace of God. The very fact that you feel as you do, is a proof that there is salvation for you. The Divine Spirit alone can or does bring a sinner to consider his ways, and to remember from whence he has fallen; and the Spirit does this to bring the sinner to Christ. If there were no salvation for you, or if, as you say, you were lost, those feelings of sorrow would not be in your heart. The Lord is dealing with you in mercy. Think over those precious texts of Scripture which have comforted and sustained you in other and brighter days. Get leave of absence for an hour to-night, after roll-call. I will be alone, and will gladly see you. I sympathize deeply with you, and am interested in you; but, better than all, the blessed Savior sympathizes with you, and is infinitely interested in your eternal welfare. May you be enabled to rest your troubled soul upon the all-sufficient Savior!

A few minutes after the drums beat "tattoo," the young man came to my quarters. He was the very picture of sorrow. I spoke kindly and soothingly to him, and tried to get his attention fixed upon one or two points; namely, the infinite value of Christ's atoning sacrifice, and the fatherly character of God. He told me how he had fallen. His mother, long since gone to glory, had led his infant mind to the Savior, and, by her holy example and prayerful teaching, had impressed on his heart lessons of love and faith. In early youth, he had made a public profession of faith in Christ, and for twelve years had enjoyed that peace and happiness which can only be found by walking with God. One deeply cherished desire had taken full possession of his heart, and had only been intensified as time passed on. That desire was to preach the Gospel of Christ to his fellow-men. He prepared for the ministry, was licensed to preach, and became a candidate for ordination. While pursuing his Christian and ministerial course, he imprudently, as some of the fathers in Israel thought, made proposals of marriage to a gay young lady, who, it was thought, loved music and dancing too much to make a good minister's wife. Thinking that he had the first right of deciding the somewhat delicate but very interesting question as to who should be his wife, he rather plainly intimated to those who took a deep interest in the matter, that a minister was just as capable of choosing a wife as any other man, and that, consequently, he would do as he pleased. The brethren, who thought it their duty to show him the error of his ways, in taking unto himself a dancing, music-loving young creature as wife, unfortunately undertook the hazardous work of proving that the young lady in question was totally unfit for any Christian's wife, and finished by calling his attention to her defects. Ministers, especially young ministers, have generally as much human nature as other men, and are as apt to be headstrong and foolish in love affairs as the rest of sinful mankind, and the result was that he cut the whole business short by making the young lady in question his wife. The censure of brethren was dealt out to him, as he thought, unsparingly and unmercifully, to which was added the significant hint that the gates of ordination were now closed against him. In an unguarded moment, when chagrin, disappointment, and blind resentment had driven out or smothered holier feelings, he rashly declared his determination to renounce the Christian ministry! From that moment he fell! In renouncing the sacred work of a life's training and a life's desires, he renounced his Savior! This he felt. He could not pray, he could not read God's Word. Wherever he went, and whatever he did, he was miserable, and only miserable. He plunged headlong into ungodliness, and the deeper he sank, the more deeply and desperately did he drink of sin's poisoned cup, to drown serious thought or quench the awful consuming fire that raged within and scorched his very soul. One day he passed the church in which he had preached, and such were his feelings of horror and despair, that tears trickled down his cheek, and he trembled so that he had to lean for support against a wall. Wretched, miserable, and desperate, he wandered up and down, seeking rest and finding none. The thought that he was abandoned of God—cast off forever—that he was guilty of the "sin which hath never forgiveness"—took possession of his mind, and he settled down into a kind of cold, calm despair! In the mean time, his young wife had been led to the Savior, and made to rejoice in the forgiving mercy of God; and, singular to relate, she became a member of the very church in which he had preached many a Gospel sermon!

One day, while in deep dejection, he enlisted, and, after coming into camp, tried hard to forget the past, and live regardless of the future. He succeeded so far in casting off the last vestige of piety as to indulge a few times in profane swearing, and was, to all intents and purposes, a fearful illustration of a homeless, peaceless, godless wanderer—a prodigal in a far country, sunk in misery and degradation. At times the fearfulness of his state, the terrible nature of the gulf into which he had so madly plunged, would overwhelm him with alarm, and anon he would plunge all the deeper and the more madly into sin. A special letter from his wife—a letter full of love and Christian endearment, and earnest, faithful pleading—reached him, one day, and his heart was touched. The memories of other days—days of peace and hope and joy—days of Christian honor and ministerial usefulness—came rushing like a mighty tide-wave over his heart, and in agony he exclaimed, "I am lost! I am lost!" In this state of mind, he came to one of the meetings which were held nearly every night in camp. The subject of the discourse was, "Lot's wife a warning to backsliders." The following points were made:

She was connected with a pious husband.

She was divinely warned to flee from destruction.

She made a fair start toward the appointed place of safety.

She was almost saved—almost.

She perished within sight of the refuge.

Such is a very brief sketch of the sad narrative this fallen minister gave me, as, in deep distress, he paced up and down my little room.

"Now," said he, as he finished, "do you think there can be mercy for such a sinner as I am? O! can the blood of Christ wash away such dreadful guilt as is lying on my poor soul?"

He burst into tears, and sobbed as if his heart would break, while his whole frame shook convulsively. The storm-blast was howling around the frail cabin in which I had my quarters, and the sleet was driving heavily against the shingles and the window-pane, while the numerous crevices caused the wind to moan sullenly within; but, gloomy and fearful as the tempest was without, it was nothing to the storm of guilt and terror with which an awakened conscience was lashing this poor wanderer. "O God!" I mentally exclaimed, "if these are the sufferings of the unforgiven on this side of the grave, where Mercy still invites, and Hope yet waves her shining wings and points her radiant finger to a Savior's cross and a believer's heaven, what, O what, must they be in the regions of the lost, where remorse and despair shall beat down upon the naked soul in one eternal storm!"

I tried to comfort him with the assurance that God had not cast him off, and that his fearful state of mind was not only caused by felt guilt, but was also the result of a conflict between him and God. "Your Heavenly Father," I said, "whom you have so fearfully forsaken, is striving to bring you into his fold again. He is infinitely interested in you; he loves you dearly, and now waits to be gracious. Struggle no longer in the horrible pit and in the miry clay, but cast yourself, as a helpless, miserable sinner, into the arms of the Savior—

"'Five bleeding wounds he bears,
Received on Calvary:
They pour effectual prayers,
They strongly speak for *thee;*
Forgive him, O forgive! they cry—
Nor let that ransomed sinner die.'"

"Pray for me," said he, "and I will try, through God's help, to give my heart to him—if—if there *can* be mercy for me."

Lieutenant Conklin having come in, we knelt down and had two seasons of prayer. Both of us labored with this poor, crushed, penitent soul, and tried every effort to lead him to realize the infinite fullness of Christ's atoning work.

Next day I had an interview with him, and found him more calm and collected. At the prayer-meeting two nights afterward, he stated that he was a brand plucked from the burning. He confessed how fearfully he had fallen, and that his comrades knew how wicked he had been.

"But now," said he, "I have resolved to return, as a poor, wretched prodigal, to my Heavenly Father, and I humbly trust that, through the merits of Christ's death, I may yet say he has forgiven my sins, and given to me that hope and that love without which I have been miserable so long."

His statements were simple and humble, and told with thrilling effect upon all present.

CHAPTER XVI.

A GOOD MAN'S LAST RESTING-PLACE—REVERIES IN A GRAVEYARD—HOW WE SHOULD THINK OF DEATH—CHRISTIAN TRIUMPHS IN THE LAST HOUR.

"Then while, with visage blank and sear,
  The poor in soul we see,
Let us not think what he is here,
  But what he soon will be;
And look beyond this earthly night,
  To crowns of gold and bowers of light."

"This is where J——, poor fellow, is buried—right here, chaplain."

This was said by a member of the regiment, one day, as I walked through the neglected graveyard, in the vicinity of camp.

"A kind of strange genius, you know; but, a good fellow, a splendid soldier; we all felt sorry when he died," repeated my informant.

True, he was gone! that quiet, unassuming, good man. Like many others in this world of ours, he was not known till he died. He was one of the Savior's humble and childlike followers. Few of us appreciated his character till he was laid in his grave. In appearance he was awkward and ungainly, paid little attention to neatness of person or clothing, which, together with his retiring disposition, served to separate him somewhat from his companions in arms. He frequently came to my tent to talk on religious matters; yet, on such occasions, he said but little. The only time that he ever, with any degree of freeness, spoke of himself or of experimental religion, was a few days after the battle of Antietam. His conversation then was but one blessed, glorious outpouring of a loving, Christian heart, anxious to perform every duty, and yearning for more of the Savior's presence! He told me of his experiences on the several battlefields on which we had been engaged, and how he felt while in the midst of destruction and death. Artless and simple was his little unvarnished tale of Christian experience; but how suggestive, how meek and childlike! Never will I forget the humble, thrilling manner in which he said:

"I wanted to tell you how happy I've been in the love of Jesus!"

Good, patient, brave Christian soldier! thy worth was not known till the angels came near to thy lowly cot, and waited to waft thy patient, Christlike spirit to the bosom of God!

"At midnight came the cry—
'To meet thy God prepare!'
He woke, and caught his Captain's eye,
The strong in faith and prayer.

"His spirit, with a bound,
Left its incumbering clay;
His tent, at sunrise, on the ground
A darkened ruin lay."

Reveries in a Graveyard.

The graveyard referred to as containing the sleeping dust of some of the brave soldiers of the Eleventh, was used also by the Thirty-sixth Ohio as a burying-place during the stay of that regiment at Summerville the previous winter. But, notwithstanding the fact that my attention had been called to the grave of poor J——, and I noticed here and there the plain, homely headboard—the invariable token of a soldier's grave—it was several moments before I could realize the fact that the spot on which I stood was really a graveyard. And yet, that it was such a place, it was soon easy to discover; for, amid the tangled briers and alders and rank yellow grass, there glimmered, here and there, a dilapidated tombstone, the lettering of which was covered with moss or green mold. And, even had no marble or freestone marked the lowly bed of many a peaceful slumberer, the grassy mounds—some but slightly elevated, others nearly level, and some so rounded as to show that the occupants had been but lately laid to rest—would have told the tale of buried, sleeping humanity.

A grave is always to me an object of solemn interest, but I seldom read a tombstone. I can give no reason for this, save that the grave itself—whether covered with the green sod, adorned with summer flowers, or but recently made—is suggestive of interesting and important reflections. Imperceptibly my thoughts revert to the past, or glide onward to the future; and scenes pertaining to life, death, immortality, the resurrection, and Day of Judgment loom up before me, and I think less on the age or name of the silent tenant of the tomb than I do of his relationship to these dread scenes. The lonely character of the place referred to, the neglect everywhere visible, the tangled, withered grass, and rank weeds, and matted briers, and wild shrubs, which seemed to shelter the lowly graves and tottering tombstones from the profane foot of the thoughtless man, or the iron hoof of the war-horse, were all conducive to gloomy reflections. Perhaps, too, the dark clouds overhead, and the wet yellow grass, and the dripping alder and brier bushes, which seemed to drip tears over neglected graves and the desecrated resting-place of a past generation, deepened the gloomy feeling, and it seemed as if some hollow, sepulchral voice reëchoed the words of Gray's dirge-like poem—

> "The Grave—dread thing!
> Men shiver when thou 'rt named. Nature, appalled,
> Shakes off her wonted firmness. Ah! how dark
> Thy long-extended realms and rueful wastes!
> Where naught but silence reigns, and night, dark night!"

On returning to my quarters, I sat down by the rough board which served for table and writing-desk, and was soon absorbed in deep and saddened thought. The lonely, neglected graveyard seemed to be still before me. I could think of nothing else but that desolate place, and all the associations, both of peace and war, with which it was connected. I remembered the soldiers' humble graves there, and thought how appropriate would be the inscription over each sleeper:

"A STRANGER HERE. LITTLE KNOWN OF THE SLUMBERER BENEATH, BUT THIS: HE LOVED HIS COUNTRY, AND IN HER SERVICE AND FOR HER DEFENSE HE DIED! TREAD LIGHTLY O'ER THE SOLDIER'S GRAVE, FOR SACRED TO THE NATION'S HEART ARE THE RESTING-PLACES OF HER FALLEN HEROES."

I thought, too, of the manner in which many graveyards are kept; how the dead are forgotten, and their last resting-places neglected; and that, instead of flowers or evergreens being planted over them as tokens of affection and sweet emblems of the resurrection, the long rank grass, and tangled weeds and briers, are permitted to grow in melancholy luxuriance. All this, thought I, shows that the dead are friendless and forgotten, and that the living are thoughtless and neglectful. The atheist who writes the fearfully wicked words, "There is no God," and the infidel who inscribes the terribly dark and revolting sentence over the gateway to the tomb, "Death is an eternal sleep," may, consistently with their unhallowed creed, forget the dead as they insult the living, and they may tread profanely upon the silent chambers of mortality; but it ill becomes the Christian so to act. Rather let believers in the pure, lovely, hope-inspiring doctrines of the Gospel not only keep the memory of departed friends ever green, but, in token of hope and love, let them beautify, with Nature's own gems and jewels, the lowly resting-places of the sainted dead. Let them make the graveyard itself a scene of quiet and subdued loveliness. Yea, let them make it—like the place where the blessed Savior himself was laid—"A garden, and in the garden a new sepulcher."

Why should not the living desire that the resting-places of the dead should wear, as much as possible, a calm, peaceful look—a look of hope, a look of beauty? Was it not from a childlike faith, and from child-like instincts of repose and beauty, as well as from a shrinking back from the dark, dreary repulsiveness of the neglected and festering graveyard, that the little dying girl exclaimed, "Bury me in the garden, mother! bury me in the garden?" Was it not from the desire that in the early spring the apple-blossoms might fall upon her little grave, and that the flowers might bloom, and the birds sing, and the sunshine fall all around where she peacefully slept? And was it not the same instinct that prompted the dying boy to ask whether his little sister would n't come and plant favorite flowers on his grave, and whether she and mother would n't come, in the long summer evenings, and sit and sing by his resting-place? And did not the same feelings animate the bosom of Wilson, the great ornithologist, when he breathed the wish to be buried where the birds might sing over his grave?—a wish that has been literally fulfilled. We can not make graveyards cheerful; neither can we dissociate from them solemn feelings and sad, painful reflections. It is not desirable we should do so; but we can make them beautiful, lovely, ay, sweet and inviting, to the stricken, bereaved mourner, and fitting places for calm meditation and serious thought.

The above reflections, suggested as already noted, brought up others related to the same subject, but invested with more importance and interest. I thought about death, as well as the grave; and wondered whether our feelings as Christians, concerning both, were not entirely too gloomy. In sermons and books and obituaries, do we not speak of Death as that grim and ghastly tyrant that has waved his black scepter over all the generations of men, and made the march from lisping infancy to hoary age but a dark and dismal procession, under funeral banners and gloomy badges? Do we not represent Death as an angel of darkness, whose visage is terrible, and whose touch is cold and remorseless as the grave? Or as a skeleton specter, whose teeth rattle in the fleshless skull, and whose bony fingers grasp a keen-bladed scythe and ominous sand-glass? Or as a dull-eyed, unfeeling potentate, arrayed in garments of gloom, and whose symbol of power is his dark and shadowy foot, placed remorselessly on the bosom of helpless humanity? That a busy, thoughtless world, sunk in sin, and feverishly grasping the gilded bauble of sensual pleasure, should, when it does think of death, have such a grim, gloomy specter rise up before it, and point threateningly to the dreary shades of the silent land from whose dark shores no voyager ever returns, is but in keeping with the fearful forebodings of a guilty conscience.

But why may not the Christian, happy in a Savior's love, and rejoicing in hope of the glory of God, think of Death rather as a white-robed angel, radiant with the splendors of the City of God, and having at his azure girdle the golden keys of life, ready to open the mysterious gates of the glorious future, and admit the weary pilgrim of earth to all the unimagined splendors of the home of the redeemed? Even the ancient heathen represented Death as a celestial messenger, who, with smiling face and folded wings quietly extinguished the light of life. O! let us take the Bible, with its holy teachings, its sure promises, its blessed comforts, and its beautiful pictures of the believer's life and death and immortality, and we shall be enabled to feel that, however varied the figures adopted to represent the last scene, we shall be able to say—

"O, 'tis a peaceful rest;
Who should deplore it?
Trance of the pure and blest,
Angels watch o'er it!
Sleep of a mortal night,
Sorrow can't break it;
Heaven's own morning light
Alone shall wake it."

While in quietude and meditation I sat there, after our usual evening services—all quiet around save the heavy, measured tread of the sentinel—other scenes were brought vividly before me. The thought that death, to the believer, is not terrific, but welcome; not a hideous monster, but an angel of brightness; not the grim, ghastly specter of fate, but a white-robed messenger from the skies, sent to gather, here and there, in the Lord's garden of grace, sweet flowers and buds and blossoms, that they may be planted in the garden of glory, led me to think of glorious death-bed scenes I had been privileged to see in the quiet walks of pastoral life, in the military hospitals, and on the field of battle. I thought of the death of one who, through weary months of suffering, patiently waited for his summons to the shining shore. How calmly he could talk of death! How strong his faith in Christ! How sweet his enjoyments were, when, a night or two before he died, he partook of the Lord's Supper! And how sweetly, at the last, he fell asleep in Jesus!

And I thought, too, of another room, into which Death came, but cast no shadows. We had watched the dying one during the night, and when the summer's sun poured his morning beams through the branches of the trees, and in at the open window, we gathered more closely around the bed to witness the calm triumphs of a redeemed spirit. Save that the loving young wife held the cold hands of the sufferer, while the holy tears of woman's love and sympathy trickled over her cheek, and a sigh of anguish involuntarily burst from her lips, no one could have imagined that any thing like grief or gloom was there. That room was not on the brink of the dark stream where mortals shiver, and from which they shrink aghast; but it was quite on the verge of heaven, and we felt like as if we might almost hear the rustling of angels' wings.

"It is sweet to die in Jesus!" whispered the dying one, while a smile of joy irradiated his pale countenance. "Happy day, happy day, when Jesus washed my sins away!" were faintly murmured, as, like a wearied infant, he gently fell asleep.

Months rolled away, and, while loving hearts yet mourned in the solitude of bereavement, strength was gained so as to have the mastery over feelings of undue grief. Again sweet music was heard in that dwelling, and songs such as angels may sing—songs of hope for stricken hearts—songs of rest to the weary, tempest-tossed soul—songs of joy in anticipation of the triumphal odes of heaven were sung, and—Death came to that household again. This time he came to one over whose pathway a dark cloud had hovered, and whose young heart, years ago, had been crushed "nigh unto death" by bitter and cruel grief. Plighted vows had been broken by him who stood up before God's minister and promised to love and cherish her. The fair flowers and priceless jewels of woman's pure and noble love he had ruthlessly torn in pieces and flung from him as if worthless—a crime, O, reader, which is, perhaps, seldom if ever forgiven; and he had—But enough! Years of silent, secret grief had written premature lines on that fair brow, and dimmed the luster of that bright eye. But now Death had come to take her away to her heavenly home, and surely to her the messenger was one of light, for her countenance was radiant with joy, and so calm that

"We thought her dying when she slept,
And sleeping when she died!"

How sweet that death-bed was, only those could know who were privileged to behold it. So near heaven did it seem, that our hearts felt unutterably full of sacred joy, and some of us, at least, felt a mysterious heart-longing—a kind of home-sickness for the heavenly home. Death, in this instance again, was assuredly an angel of light; and the wearied one whom he came to release, saw only the messenger of her Savior, sent to take her to the shores of glory.

A cloud lay cradled near the setting sun;
  A gleam of crimson tinged its braided snow;
Long had I watched the glory moving on
  O'er the still radiance of the lake below;
Tranquil its spirit seemed, and floated slow,
  E'en in its very motion there was rest;
While every breath of eve that chanced to blow,
  Wafted the traveler to the beauteous west.
Emblem, methought, of the departed soul,
  To whose white robe the gleam of bliss is giv'n,
And, by the breath of mercy, made to roll
  Right onward to the golden gates of heaven;—
Where, to the eye of faith, it peaceful lies,
  And tells the man his glorious destinies.

WILSON

CHAPTER XVII.

LITTLE SHADY—THE BEAUTIES OF SLAVERY.

ONE morning, toward the close of 1862, a little fellow, not quite as black as coal, but a genuine specimen of what official orders distinguished as persons of "African descent," made his appearance within our lines, and within the special limits of our camp. He had been everywhere among the men, knew almost every command, could dance "Juba" with such earnest good will, and introduce such comical variations and facial contortions, that his "culled bredren" seemed to be in imminent danger of getting "clar done gone" into convulsions or something else equally serious; could whistle any bugle-call, and drum any tune ever heard in camp—and some that nobody in camp or out of it ever heard—could kick the cap off his head with his heels, and roll his eyes in his round, black face with such a serio-comic expression, that one scarcely knew whether he was the impersonation of drollery or an imp of mischief. My first special acquaintance with this little fellow, who was, by the way, a perfect *facsimile* of Topsy or Tom-tit, was in this wise:

One cold morning, just after reveillé, I had tucked my blanket snugly around me for another half hour's "little more sleep and little more slumber," which good old Dr. Watts reprehends so much. I was just getting into that calm, dreamy, pleasant kind of repose which lazy second sleepers are apt to fall into, when a tremendous racket at my cabin-door brought me up in a hurry. It seemed as if the battering and kicking were sufficient to waken the Seven Sleepers, and as if intended to give warning that the gray-backs were right upon us.

Rat, tap, tap! rub-a-dub, dub!

"What's wanted?" I shouted.

"Please, Massa Chap'in, I'se come to make yer fire."

Of course I opened the door and admitted the author of the noisy demonstrations, and there stood before me the very impersonation of mischief, native shrewdness, and demure humility. The little fellow had his feet encased in army shoes of about number seven, and dressed in a cast-off uniform which was large enough for him to be buried in. The wool on the top of his head was kinky and matted enough to be impervious to any thing in the shape of a comb, and would have driven good Miss Ophelia, with her New England ideas of thrift and neatness, into a fit of hysterics. He was seemingly about twelve years of age, had a peculiar confidential air about him, and a merry, roguish twinkle of the eye that told of fire and fun and mischief. After he had got the fire roaring and blazing, and tumbled every thing upside down in his frantic efforts to put things in order, and kicked up such a dust in flourishing a hickory broom over the floor, that I was nearly strangled, he subsided into a corner and surveyed his labors with the air of a hero.

"Would you like to stay with me?" I asked.

"Yes, sah," he replied, quickly, while his eye twinkled with a pleased, roguish expression, and his ivories gleamed in striking contrast with his jolly black face. Forthwith little Shady was regularly installed into office, and went to work accordingly.

One evening I got into conversation with him as follows:

"How old are you, Shady?"

"Dunno, massa; neber knowed how old I is."

"Have you any brothers or sisters?"

"Yes, sah."

"How many have you got?" I asked.

"Dunno how many I'se got—got some."

"You don't know how many you've got! Why, what do you mean?"

"White folks count one, two, three—dis nigga can't count more'n one, two, three. I'se got one, two, three brudders; den dar's de gals, more'n one, two, three."

"Do you remember their names?" I asked.

"Yes—dar's Jim, was sold to Massa Green, and dar's Sal in de big house, and dar's Luce that massa sold to gen'lman in Baltimore, and dar's Sam and Pete and Sue—and den dar's de baby and t'other baby and me—how many dat ar, chap'in?"

"Nine," I replied. He then named them all over again, pronouncing each name as he touched his fingers.

"Why did you run away?" I asked. "Did your mother know that you were going off with the soldiers?"

"Yes, sah," he replied, in a low, confidential tone. "Mother told me I oughter go wid dem Yankee soldiers, for massa had sold me to anoder gen'lman, an' she would neber see me again, jest like poor Luce in Baltimore. How far to Baltimore, chap'in? I'se gwine dar sometime—I want ter see Luce—she 's good gal."

"Do you know who made you, Shady?"

The little fellow looked up into my face with such a comical, quizzical expression on his round, black face, that I did not know what to make of it. He seemed to wonder at such an abstruse, perhaps to him absurd, question. I asked again, "Do you know who made you?"

"Dunno who made me; neber hearn tell 'bout sich things."

"Did no one ever tell you about God, who made all things?"

"Old Uncle Pete sometimes spoke 'bout de Lord—but dunno nothin' 'bout sich things."

"Did you ever hear about a good man called Jesus Christ, that wicked men nailed on a tree called a cross?"

"Neber hearn tell 'bout um. Who was Jesus, chap'in? Did you eber see um?"

I then told him, in simple language, the Story of the Cross, and, when I spoke of Jesus by the name of *Savior*, the little fellow interrupted me, saying:

"Now I 'member mother talkin' to Sal 'bout de Savior. Is Jesus de Savior?"

Talk about the heathen in Africa and India and the South Sea Islands! Talk about the divine, patriarchal institution of slavery, and the eminently Christianizing spirit which it has manifested! No wonder that slaveholders and their miserable, servile apologists in the North have sought for years to cover up the iniquitous system! But how terrible the thought that ministers of the Gospel have stood forth before heaven and earth, and baptized the vile thing in the name of the God of truth and love, and thrown around it the sacred protection of the Divine Word, and received it into the Church of Jesus Christ! But slavery is dead! Thank God, it is dead! What an emasculated Gospel, in the hands of corrupt ministers, failed to do for the South, the bayonet, in the strong hands of brave soldiers, has, in the providence of God, most signally and gloriously accomplished.

CHAPTER XVIII.

THE ARMY OF THE CUMBERLAND—EFFORTS OF NORTHERN TRAITORS—FEELINGS OF THE SOLDIERS.

On the morning of the 24th of January, 1863, the Eleventh, Thirty-sixth, Eighty-ninth, and Ninety-second Ohio Regiments, under General Crook, left the Kanawha Valley to join the Army of the Cumberland, under Major-General Rosecrans. The division, on arriving at Nashville, was further reinforced by Stokes's regiment of East Tennessee Cavalry and the Nineteenth Indiana Battery. On the 22d of February, the division left Nashville for Carthage, on the Cumberland River, and reached that point on the 26th instant.

We encamped on the south side of the river; but, being some forty-five miles from the nearest support, and as Bragg had made this point a favorite crossing place, General Crook was induced to seek a more defensible position on the north side of the river. The division, accordingly, fell back to a more commanding position on the north and east of the village. The position, strong by nature, was further strengthened by extensive lines of earth-works and rifle-pits, commanding the river and turnpike, and which were so constructed that, in case of necessity, guns could be mounted *en barbette*.

REBELS IN FRONT—MEANER REBELS IN THE REAR.

It does a great amount of good, sometimes, to look to the past. In the light of experience, as well as with the logic of events, individuals and nations may not only recognize their own failings, but they may, also, see how an overruling and All-wise Providence has directed, sustained, and protected in the most difficult, depressing, and dangerous circumstances. Were it within the scope of this work, which it is not, it might be both interesting and profitable to trace some of the darker and more concealed lines of history connected with the opening of the year 1863. But, as it is, it seems as if at least a passing reference should be made, just at this point, to some of the desperate schemes of rebel sympathizers in the North at the time referred to. Well-laid plans had been formed by Northern traitors to demoralize the army in the field, as well as to neutralize efforts at home to crush the rebellion. They put forth every effort, directly and indirectly, in public and in private, by newspapers and letters, to induce discontent and despondency, and even insubordination, both among officers and men. Private letters, artfully worded, but too plain to be misunderstood, were sent to the soldiers by those shameless traitors every day. The writers affected to admire the devotion and bravery of the army, expressed pity for each individual soldier who was suffering so much in the camp and in the field, but—but—yes, it was a great pity—a great pity, indeed, that he was deceived by designing Abolitionists; for it was quite evident, to far-seeing people of the Democratic persuasion, that this war was not for the Union, but for "negro equality." Then the letters were usually closed with a piece of information to the effect that, so numerous were the friends of the poor deceived soldier, every facility would be given him to leave the army, and that, if necessary, citizen's clothing, and money, also, would be furnished in abundance to aid him in getting away from the "Abolitionist hordes." Newspapers, also, like the *Cincinnati Enquirer*, *Dayton Empire*, *New York Herald*, and *World*, were circulated as much as possible, and no one needs to be informed of the atrociously false and traitorous character of those papers at the time referred to, nor of the unscrupulous and persistent efforts they made to seduce the people into a wicked and dishonorable peace with traitors. By means of mail facilities, some of the more vile of the papers named were circulated in the army, which, had they been published within the army lines, would have caused the arrest of the editors as traitors. Like all pro-slavery sheets that have ever been published in the interest of human oppression, the papers referred to were full of unblushing falsehoods, filthy inuendoes regarding the motives of the friends of freedom, forged correspondence from the army, asserting that the President's Proclamation of Emancipation was fiercely denounced by the soldiers; that the national finances were in a ruinous condition; that, instead of gold and silver being at a premium, as many people supposed, government "greenbacks" were, in reality, at a discount, and so on. The same papers, also, asserted that the army everywhere was becoming demoralized, that the soldiers would not fight in such an Abolition war, and that, instead of the Emancipation policy being received with favor, it was unsparingly denounced both by officers and men. It was added, also, that the families of soldiers were neglected by those who had pledged to see their wants supplied, while it was distinctly affirmed that domestic ruin had already overtaken many of those whose purity and integrity of character had ever been above suspicion, and that the ruin which had thus been wrought was hardly so much a crime as a misfortune, and almost a necessity.

A private letter was sent to the regiment, at this time, by one who had formerly been an officer in the army, which expressed great regret, on the part of the writer, for being instrumental in recruiting for the army, and stating that he would be exceedingly glad could he only get out of the clutches of Abolitionist-military despotism those whom he had induced to enlist. He further declared that the people at home were so tired of the war, that Indiana, Illinois, and New York were about to recall their troops then in the field; that the National treasury was so depleted, that if the troops were paid off for the few months due them, it would be the last they would ever get, and that the war was neither for the Constitution nor the Union, but for the freeing of the "niggers." The letter closed with an exhortation to all who possibly could to desert from the regiment and come home, assuring them that ample protection would be afforded them in the event of any attempt being made for their arrest.

So much for efforts in the rear of the army.

There were matters intimately connected with the army itself, also, at this time, that had a tendency to deepen any feeling of discouragement that might result from such treasonable efforts. Officers decorated with stars, and officers of lesser note, whose ideas of war were merely professional, instead of being patriotic, and who looked to no results but such only as tended to individual and selfish gratification, played into the hands of home traitors, by insinuating that the rebellion would never be subdued. Officers of various grades—from the staff down to company commanders—could be heard, not unfrequently, repeating the vile epithets of the Copperhead press against the Administration, and even insinuating that if they had known that the war would have been conducted to anti-slavery issues and results, they would have drawn their sword in defense of the South. Having so little sympathy with the work of subduing the rebellion, it is not a matter of wonder that many of these professionally military gentlemen should be found acting in such a manner as to discourage or irritate those placed under their command. Not a few of them, mere fops in blue and gold, acted as all such are apt to do, played the petty tyrant toward their subordinates, and the cringing, cowardly sycophant toward their superiors.

Some of them vexed and annoyed the rank and file by unnecessary and unreasonable exactions, while, at the same time, they involved company and regimental commanders in serious misunderstanding with their commands. The policy of guarding rebel property, inaugurated by McClellan in the East, and rigidly enforced by Buell in the West, had by no means ceased to exist, especially in isolated commands. Instances were too well known of sick soldiers being compelled to lie on the ground, without even straw under them, while the boards, fences, out-houses, and barns of well-known rebels were sacredly guarded by Federal bayonets. In some instances, surgeons were the undesigning causes of severe complaints against the order and discipline of their respective regiments, because they appropriated rebel property for hospital purposes. There were several instances of regiments being gravely censured, and even of degrading punishment being inflicted, because rails had been taken from the fences to keep the loose corn-husks under the sick and dying soldier! Regimental and company commanders had to enforce orders that could not possibly fail to irritate and exasperate their men ; for military orders are never to be explained, defended or excused, much less criticised, by subordinate officers, but simply enforced by them. It was frequently the case, therefore, that they had to bear that odium which ought to have fallen upon others.

Take these facts, with the Copperhead influences which existed at home, and one can see, at a glance, that the aspect of affairs was none of the brightest at the time referred to. And yet any discontent or discouragement which might thus have been in the army was but partial and momentary. Like the finely-tempered, keen-edged Damascus blade, that yields to the test-pressure only to spring back again with a ringing twang that tells its strength, and which, perhaps, pierces the hand of him who tampers with it, so did the noble army of the Union when tampered with by Copperhead traitors. If it did bend for an instant, under such untoward circumstances, it was but to rebound again, with such a startling energy and with such fierce determination as rung out a death-knell for armed traitors in the front, derision and contempt for meaner, because more sneaking and cowardly, traitors in the rear. Generals Grant, Burnside, and Rosecrans, in the West, and Generals Hooker and Meade, in the East, soon put a quietus on Copperhead intrigues *with* the army; and, by a wholesome application of purifying measures *in* the army, backed by the resolute and unbending integrity and lofty patriotism of officers and men, the blade, which for a moment had been severely tried and tested, sprung again ready for action, and flashed defiance upon all, whether rebels in the front or rebels in the rear. What the feelings and determinations of the soldiers in the field were, the following extracts from a series of resolutions, adopted while at Carthage, by the Ohio troops, will abundantly show:

"We, the officers and soldiers of General Crook's Division, comprising the Eleventh, Thirty-sixth, Eighty-ninth, and Ninety-second Regiments of the Ohio Volunteer Infantry, being all the Ohio troops in his command, having, in common with our comrades in arms, cheerfully periled our lives, and every earthly interest, to secure to ourselves and to our posterity a country and a government—the same which in historic times were bought with blood, and established by that quality of wisdom which, though human, seems divine; and, whereas, a number of intriguing demagogues at home have recently, by word and act, sought to create dissatisfaction among us, block the wheels of wise legislation, excite discontent in the public mind, and in every way to baffle all effort to conquer the rebels; therefore,

"*Resolved*, That, in the name of our God, we will still defend our flag, and, with an abiding faith in the justness of our cause, we will still go forth to meet the foe, with unshaken confidence that He who led our patriot fathers to victory, will crown our arms with success, and preserve to us our glorious heritage of 'civil and religious liberty,' and preserve it for our children after us, until Time's latest hour.

"*Resolved*, That we hold in utter detestation that clique of miscreants known as the 'Vallandigham Democracy,' or 'Anti-war and Pro-peace Party,' thereby disgracing the time-honored name of Democrat—they being, in our opinion, but a band of traitors and national assassins, who have no censure save for the officers of our government — no complaint save that energetic measures are employed to crush out the rebellion—no aspiration save to embarrass our executive and legislative departments, and engender mutinies in our armies—that we spurn, with unfeigned contempt, the shameful lie, circulated by them, that we are tired of fighting, and willing to compromise with the Southern hordes now in arms against the Union.

"*Resolved*, That we look with satisfaction and pride upon the unalloyed patriotism, wisdom, earnestness, and moderation of our Chief Executive, feeling that we have in him a man of unswerving integrity; and we also approve and fully indorse all the acts of our late Congress, being satisfied the grand majority of its members are men of devotion to the Union and purity of purpose.

"*Resolved*, That, despite the frenzied efforts of our foe before us, and the *despicable intrigues of our other foe behind us*, we will abate not one jot of faith or hope; but, believing that the maintenance of our government is worth all the cost expended in its establishment, we emphatically assure all traitors at home, that not until we have undergone a *seven years' struggle*, if need be, will we cease this contest, and not until we have experienced such suffering as was endured at Valley Forge, will we begin to murmur." . . . .

It was then as now, in this year of grace 1865. The friends of the country, the friends of righteousness and truth, required to be strengthened, and to-day the struggle is by no means doubtful. It will be seen in this, as in other great events in the world's history, that God will defeat all the plans and purposes of the wicked, and show that the potsherds of earth may strive with the potsherds of earth; but "woe be to him who striveth with his Maker!" Slavery, the sum of all villainies, the cause of this wicked rebellion, the corner-stone of the so-called Confederate Government, and the cause of all the misery and wretchedness and bloodshed arising out of war, is doomed to die. It must, it shall perish! And in its final and complete overthrow, God's government among the nations shall be vindicated, his benevolent purposes concerning the children of men more fully understood, the doctrine of Divine Providence more devoutly believed in, the day of Christ's kingly reign upon earth hastened on apace, and man's temporal and spiritual happiness increased. This is a transition period in the world's history. Amid political convulsions, civil wars, and general upheavings among the nations, let us hold with a firm grasp the promises of God!

As a fitting conclusion to this chapter, the following patriotic lines, written by an eminent statesman, are here inserted. They were written in reply to a question which was asked by a lady, Whether he was for peace?

Am I for Peace? Yes!

For the peace which rings out from the cannon's throat,
  And the suasion of shot and shell,
Till rebellion's spirit is trampled down
  To the depths of its kindred hell.

For the peace which shall follow the squadrons' tramp,
  Where the brazen trumpets bray,
And, drunk with the fury of storm and strife,
  The blood-red chargers neigh.

For the peace which shall wash out the leprous stain
  Of our slavery, foul and grim,
And shall sunder the fetters which creak and clank
  On the down-trodden dark man's limb.

I will curse him as traitor, and false of heart,
  Who would shrink from the conflict now,
And will stamp it, with blistering, burning brand,
  On his hideous, Cain-like brow.

Out! out of the way! with your spurious peace,
  Which would make us rebellion's slaves!
We will rescue our land from the traitorous grasp,
  Or cover it over with graves.

Out! out of the way! with your knavish schemes,
You trembling and trading pack!
Crouch away in the dark, like a sneaking hound
That its master has beaten back.

You would barter the fruit of our father's blood,
And sell out the Stripes and Stars,
To purchase a place with rebellion's votes,
Or escape from rebellion's scars.

By the widow's wail, by the mother's tears,
By the orphans who cry for bread,
By our sons who fell, we will never yield
Till rebellion's soul is dead.

CHAPTER XIX.

A KIDNAPPER FRUSTRATED—A SURGEON'S ANTI-SLAVERY TALK—A SHARP TRICK; REBELS SOLD—SICKNESS AND MORTALITY—DEATH OF A CHRISTIAN SOLDIER—REV. T. SHAIN.

It is said that "murder will out." So will nature. Former habits, still loved and longed for, will manifest themselves, in spite of all assumed traits, which *are* assumed merely because they are popular, remunerative, or conducive to personal safety. An unconverted, impenitent slaveholder or slave-trader can no more help showing his mean, treacherous, man-stealing propensities than the feline tribes, however tamed and domesticated, can help pouncing on their prey. He may invest himself in the robes of loyalty; he may amass wealth from the profits of rich government contracts; he may even have stars on his shoulders, and he may be placed in confidential and important positions; but the unchanged character and disposition will be manifested, and the insatiable lust for power and riches will devour as remorselessly as ever. There were polished desperadoes and smooth-tongued villains hanging around the army, or, in one way or another, connected with it, not a few of whom had figured in the slave-markets of the South, and their palms still itched for the gains of the vile system.

When about to leave the regiment for a few days, on one occasion, I charged little "Shady" not to straggle away, lest he might be picked up, at the same time requesting my friend Dr. Hartman to see that he was kept out of trouble. When the troops debarked on the Cumberland River, it was found that Shady had been sold to the captain of the temporary transport—or, to speak more correctly, that the said captain paid a heartless fellow twenty dollars to keep the friendless boy on board, so he might get him. When the hospital corps left the boat, Shady accompanied them, and was immediately ordered by the captain, who was on the hurricane-deck, to come on board.

"What do you want him on board for?" asked one of the hospital nurses, whose suspicions had been awakened by what he had seen.

"He is mine," replied the captain, with a fearful oath. "Send him on board here, instantly. Come on board, darkey, or I'll kill you!"

"You stop your nonsense," replied Jacob, getting thoroughly aroused, "or I'll come up there and squeeze your windpipe for you."

"You mind your own business and put off—that darkey 's mine. Come on board, you little black cuss you, or I'll whale you to death."

The whole affair beginning to assume a serious aspect, Jacob sent for the surgeon, Dr. McCurdy, to come down. In a very short time he made his appearance, and was informed at once of what had taken place. The doctor—a little, wiry, energetic man, sharp as a steel-trap and quick as a hair-trigger, and as generous as he was impulsive—ordered Shady up to the regiment, which was the signal for the captain to storm and swear again. But he had met his match. The boys who stood by say the doctor opened on him such a torrent of invective, and heaped upon his head such maledictions, half religious and half rather otherwise, that if the air didn't get blue and sulphurous it ought to. The captain seemed as if in a tight place; for, if the doctor was a small man, he had a big soul in him, and tongue enough for a preacher and lawyer combined. However, he put a bold face on the whole matter, and demanded again:

"Send that cussed little darkey aboard, or I'll know the reason why!"

"You contemptible, child-stealing old villain you," said the doctor, getting the steam up considerably above common high-pressure, "if you don't shut up, I'll have the regiment marched down, and blow you and your confounded old boat to blue blazes, before you have time to——! Come, boys, what's the use talking to such a miserable excuse for a man—confound the kidnapping whelp!"

Perhaps there never was such a withering, sarcastic anti-slavery lecture delivered as that short one on the bank of the Cumberland River—certainly there never had been such another heard in Tennessee.

The stay of the division at Carthage was but for a short time, and nothing of any special import took place while there. An occasional reconnoissance on the south side of the river, toward Alexandria or McMinnville, varied the routine of camp life somewhat, and an occasional rumor that a large force was on its way to attack the post, would give some little variety and zest to camp conversation.

One afternoon, Colonel Lane took the Eleventh out toward Rome, on a scouting expedition. The intention was to reach a certain point after dark, and early in the morning to make a dash on a rebel force reported to be in that vicinity. The regiment reached the point indicated about ten o'clock. The colonel was not satisfied by merely fulfilling the letter of his instructions, however; but, in order to find out what was going on in the neighborhood, he shortly after detailed several scouting parties, who were to move cautiously and secretly in various directions. One of these, under command of Captain Jordan, made a descent on a happy company of the chivalry, in a manner which was both adroit and amusing. The captain, seeing a bright light in a house, marched his party to within a short distance of it, and, leaving them in a concealed place, with instructions to be on the alert, he proceeded by himself to reconnoiter the position. On approaching the house, he discovered that the light was from a blazing fire, showing that there must be some people there who were trying to make themselves comfortable at that late hour. Walking boldly up to the house, but keeping away from the glare of light, so as to conceal his uniform, he accosted a Confederate soldier, who at that moment opened the door and looked out.

"Any of our men there?" asked the captain.

"Wall, yes."

"Have n't you room for more in *thar?*" said the captain, imitating the pronunciation of the chivalry.

"Not much—tho' I reckon we'll make room for another. Come in an' get warmed—you must be a'most froze."

"How many of ye's in thar?" asked Jordan.

"Dunno—house chuck-full—reckon you'll find a corner, tho'. Come in."

"Wait till I go to the fence and hitch my horse," said the captain. "I'll be back in a moment."

The captain went, *and did hitch his horse;* at the same time he brought up his men, who were concealed within a few rods of the spot. With hardly the cracking of a twig, it was not three minutes till trusty bayonets were closed around the house, and Captain Jordan, with revolver in hand, sprang into the midst of the rebel soldiers, ordering them, in a voice of thunder, and with no very complimentary terms as to themselves or antecedents, to surrender instantly. A rifle or two were raised toward him, but, as if for pure mischief, he sneered at them—

"Git eout! Why, I ve men enough to chaw ye up, ye ——. Surrender!"

A file of blue-coated boys, with rifles in hand, crowding in at the door, and the decidedly dangerous proximity of the Union bayonets, had a very persuasive influence, and down went rebel rifles and up went rebel hands in token of surrender.

"Purty well done, cap'n," said the officer in charge of the picket-post, as this turned out to be.

"Yes," said Jordan, "we always do things pretty well. Fall in here! and keep pretty quiet, if you know what's good for you."

If Captain Jordan's squad could have "chawed up"

the rebel gang, their numbers assuredly would hardly have guaranteed such work. So thought the rebels while they were being marched off, for some of them could not help muttering, "Sold again!"

Sickness and Mortality.

The sickness and mortality among the troops at Carthage were very great. The Ninety-second Ohio suffered terribly; and it seemed as if nothing but change of location could save it from serious depletion. Before that regiment had even been in a skirmish, it had lost more men, by disease alone, than the Eleventh had during the time that had elapsed since its organization. At one time, the Eleventh had fully one-sixth of its entire strength reported on the sick-list! The Thirty-sixth and Eighty-ninth suffered also very severely. The entire division was suffering for want of proper diet, and it seemed, at one time, that unless those in authority, especially in the medical departments, did not take more interest in the welfare of the men, as splendid and as brave an army as ever went forth would melt away through sickness and death. Diarrhea, of a most obstinate character, and very fatal withal, together with scurvy, was thinning our ranks, while abundance of fruits and vegetables could be brought by railroad to within thirty miles of the post! What made the whole matter so distressing, was the fact that deaths were invariably sudden and unexpected. And, O, it was a very mournful sight to see one funeral escort enter the graveyard while another was performing the last sad rites at the grave of some other comrade! I was sometimes so overwhelmed with sorrow at the daily scenes of weary wasting away, and the kind of calm, despairing resignation to surrounding circumstances, on the part of the sick, that many a time, when I returned from the hospital or graveyard, I could not refrain from tears. Forgive me, dear reader, for this acknowledgment of what might be deemed a weakness; perhaps it was weakness, but I could not help it. A chaplain in the army hears many a sad and weary sigh from brave and stricken hearts, and listens to many a little tale of silent, weary, wasting grief, and he has to comfort many a mourner, and place himself in the position and speak the words which wife or mother would say if near the sufferer.*

Among those who died at Carthage, Tennessee, and whose dust quietly reposes in the burial-ground on the beautiful banks of the Cumberland, was Sergeant

---

*While at Carthage, the following-named members of the Eleventh Regiment died, and were buried in the graveyard there, namely :

James Melaney, of Company D, March 12.

Perry Carter, of Company D, April 19.

Sergeant J. B. Dixon, Company G, April 12. His remains were sent home.

Jesse Bartholomew, Company H, April 22.

Frederick Lucke, Company B, May 22.

Charles Segur, Company D, May 18.

George Anderson, Company D, May 29.

Thomas H. Fall, Company I, May 17.

Rensselaer Carson, Company K, May 25.

J. F. Colther, Company E, June 3.

E. A. Morrow, Company F, June 2.

J. T. Kemper, Company I, June 5.

Sergeant T. Shain, Company I, June 22.

Shain, or, as he was known at home, Rev. Thomas Shain, minister of the United Brethren Church, and pastor of a congregation in Dayton at the time he entered the army. I desire to place on record here a tribute of more than common respect to the memory of this most excellent man.

He was one of the most humble, unassuming, godly men with whom I was ever acquainted. His piety was genial, loving, and Christlike. Many an hour he spent in my tent, conversing on personal piety and the work of God in the army. The Thirty-sixth Ohio Regiment had no chaplain, and many a sermon he preached and many a prayer-meeting he held in behalf of that regiment. Not a few were converted through his instrumentality, and claimed him as their spiritual father. Good brother Shain! How closely he walked with his God! With what child-like confidence and thrilling earnestness he could unite in the services at our prayer and fellowship meetings! And how refreshing, consequently, were his Christian conversations! With Thomas Fall, his friend and comrade, at whose grave he spoke of Christ and immortality, and with others of the dear, noble men of the Eleventh, Thirty-sixth, Eighty-ninth, and Ninety-second, he sleeps his last sleep, far from kindred dust. But he and they fill honored graves, and their memory will ever be green.

And speaking of the graves of our honored dead—the graves of our patriot soldiers—reminds me here of the fields of graves at Nashville and Murfreesbor' and Chattanooga, and elsewhere—on the Potomac and the Mississippi, amid the swamps of the Chickahominy and the bayous and the swamps of the far South. I used to look with sad emotions upon many of the places set apart for burying the dead, and I used to wonder whether those sad-looking, desolate spots would ever be beautified, and their mournful yet sacred associations be held with hallowed remembrances by coming generations? Let us talk a little of these things, dear reader, in the next paragraph:

"Gottesacker"—God's Field.

That is a happy and, withal, a poetic idea, expressed by the Germans in their own "Faderland," who, when speaking of the graveyard, call it "God's Acre," or God's Field. However thoughtlessly it may be uttered, like many other precious words in this busy, thoughtless world of ours, and however familiar and common-place it may have become, it surely must have originated from a beautiful and happy view of death and the grave, based upon a loving and living trust in Christ, as the Resurrection and the Life. God's Acre—furrowed all over with green graves—receptacles of precious seed—some smaller, some larger, some more recently formed, and others covered with green sod and cypress and flowers, and over which the white tombstones stand like the labels which careful florists set up over the spot where they have sown the seeds of favorite flowers! God's Acre—the Lord's garden, where precious seeds of humanity have been sown amid the blinding tears of sorrow and the fitful sunshine of hope, and where, perhaps, angel watchers keep holy guard over that which is precious in the sight of the Lord! God's Acre—where restless, worldly man sees no beauty, and from which he turns hastily and shudderingly away, but in which, perhaps, for aught we know, are going on silent, mysterious forces, which for long ages have been working, and for long ages will continue to work, until the dawning of the bright and glorious day of the world's eternal Summer, when the long-buried, forgotten seed, sown in corruption and dishonor and weakness, shall bloom forth in incorruption and glory and power! Yes, let us call the graveyard a garden! Let us beautify it with flowers and evergreens, which will be frail but beautiful emblems of hope concerning those over whose grave they bloom, and fade, and die, and bloom again! Let us listen more with the ear of the soul than of the body to the plaintive music of the evening breeze, as it sweeps gently amid tombstones and trees and flowers, and green, grassy mounds, and if our spirits are sad and weary, we shall hear, as if it were the melody of some far-distant harp, breathing out sweetly—

"There is no death! What seems so is transition.
This life of mortal breath
Is but the suburb of the life elysian,
Whose portal we call death."

There is but one drawback to this hopeful, encouraging view of man's last resting-place, and, alas! it is a sad one. Not all who die, die in Christ. Not all who sleep in God's Acre will awake and come forth to everlasting life. Living, God was not in all their thoughts; they desired none of his ways. Dying, they flung from them, in despair or impenitence, the last offers of pardon, and rejected the last but loving invitations of an all-sufficient Savior. There are graveyards, too, the sight of which awakens in our hearts only the saddest and gloomiest emotions. Enter, dear reader, the quiet, peaceful graveyard near your own village, and which, perhaps, to-day seems so beautiful with its green covering of grass, and tufts of flowers, and snowy tombstones, and where, perhaps, you have laid your own heart's treasures, and where, too, it may be, you often go to meditate and to water some little grave with your tears. Enter that quiet resting-place of the dead, and call it GOD'S ACRE, and speak of it, too, as beautiful, hopeful, peaceful, and bear away with you soothing reflections and hopeful memories! But come, now, with me, and walk amid the thousands of fresh graves, in those portions of our land, to-day, where the fierce storm of war has been roaring and raging; and if your soul is not stirred to its deepest depths, it is because you can not see, or, seeing, you can not feel. Imagine yourself at any one of the military burying-places. Just look upon this field, for example, several acres in extent, without flower or shrub, or one green blade to relieve the eye, but bare and brown, and all cast up into thousands of little ridges, each one marked off with mathematical precision, and all so close together you can scarcely put your foot down between them; and remember that this bare, brown field has been furrowed by the grave-digger's mattock and spade, that each little ridge is itself a grave, where some loved one sleeps his last sleep, far from home and kindred dust! Remember, too, that, in this doleful inclosure, so saddening to look upon, the dead are crowded so closely, but so regularly together, that it seems like a field just planted, and that the headboards are only so many labels, to tell the names of the seed sown! ALAS! THE FIELD IS SOWN WITH HUMANITY! Tell me now, dear reader, whether it does not cause your heart to thrill with strangely solemn and saddened emotions? How many hearts are wrung with anguish to-day, because of these fields of graves! How many once happy homes are desolate to-day, because these, at present, dreary, repulsive fields are crowded with stranger dead! How long, O, how long, do you ask, is this carnival of death to continue? And do you pray, in agony, "Come, blessed Jesus! come and speak into calmness and rest the dark and heaving waves of human passion, which surge to and fro in our land, and which threaten to swallow up all that is dear to man and precious to thyself?"

Fear not, dear reader, although your own heart may be stricken, because your noble son or brother or husband is sleeping his last sleep far from you, and because his life's blood crimsoned the dark land of slavery. The sacrifice has not, will not be in vain! the country will be sanctified by the fearful baptism of blood now upon us; the hideous institutions of wrong be forever swept away, and the glories of the millennial day hastened on apace. Our God is a wonder-working God. He has his own gracious plans and purposes, and however mysterious they may seem to frail man, they will all be unfolded for the wonder and admiration of all created intelligences in time and in eternity.

How will Posterity look upon those Military Burial-Places?

There is another and brighter view to be taken of this otherwise dark and terrible scene. Those graves—the sight of which, so numerous, and looking so forsaken and desolate, have often awakened in my heart painfully sad emotions—are, nevertheless, THE GRAVES OF HEROES—THE RESTING-PLACES OF FREEDOM'S NOBLE DEFENDERS! And, in the brighter and better days yet to come—for come they will—every one of these fields of graves, so sad and solemn and forsaken now, so brown and bare, like some deserted "Potter's Field," will be a Necropolis—a city of buried heroes. They will be adorned with the richest treasures of art, and the more beautiful but less imposing ornaments of nature. Coming generations will hold as sacred trusts these halls of death, where a nation's heroes are sleeping; and they will tell to their children, and children's children, the story of Freedom's struggle with Oppression, and how that, in the final victory, not only America, but the shores of every continent and island of earth, were blessed with the advancing tide-wave of love and liberty.

"We never can be deathless till we die.
It is the dead win battles. And the breath
Of those who through the world drive like a wedge,
Tearing earth's empires up, nears Death so close
It dims his well-worn scythe. But no! the brave
Die never. Being deathless, they but change
Their country's arms for more—their country's heart.
Give, then, the dead their due; it is they who saved us."

CHAPTER XX.

> If God hath made this world so fair
> Where sin and death abound,
> How beautiful beyond compare
> Will Paradise be found!
>
> MONTGOMERY.

"WILL you give us that sermon which you said was preached to you and your regiment, by some falling waters, once, when on a march?" asked a friend, who knew that these "Lights and Shadows of Army Life" were being put into book form.

I came pretty near saying "No!" People don't like sermons in army books. It wasn't a sermon, at all, dear reader; it was only a beautiful picture of Nature's own drawing, and I just spoke a little about it— that was all. But would you like to hear about the picture? Very well. I will give it to you, roughly drawn, it may be.

Let me tell you how the picture was seen. It was on this wise. The column had been marching from early morn, along dusty roads and literally in a dry and thirsty land, where there was no water. It was now a little past the hour of noon, and the blazing sun shone out fiercely in a cloudless sky. Many a strong-hearted soldier had fainted by the wayside—

for his canteen was empty, his lips were dry and parched, and he was foot-sore and weary. "Water! water!" was the great cry. "Water! any thing for water, and some shady place in which to rest!" More and more intensely did the sun shine out from the brazen sky, while the earth seemed to glow like a furnace. The dry, hot dust, flung up by thousands of feet, irritated the throat and lungs, at the same time increasing the intolerable thirst under which all were suffering. Onward and still onward pressed the men, wearily and in pain, while the dust, increasing in heat and quantity, threatened to suffocate them at every step. Not a breath of air seemed to be stirring. The very leaves on the low shrubs, and the grass by the wayside seemed to partake of the general depression and suffering, and looked drooping and dying. Thus, mile after mile of the weary way was traversed, and hour succeeded hour, as if each one was an age, and impressions of suffering and utter exhaustion were made so deeply on the minds of all, that time will never efface them. Suddenly we entered a narrow defile, through which the road wound, and, as if by magic, or like the creations of some fairy tale, a cool and fragrant breeze began to fan our cheeks.

Presently the bugle, at the head of the column, sounded the welcome "Halt!" followed immediately by the still more welcome "Rest!" On riding forward a few paces, to where there was a general and frantic rush, I beheld a scene of such beauty and interest that I will never forget it till my dying day. We had entered a somewhat rocky pass, or gap, shaded on one side by hemlocks and cedars, "arrayed," literally, "in living green." On the left was a cool, shady glen, or grotto, scooped out deep in the mountain-side—semicircular in form, or shaped somewhat like a horseshoe. The face of this grotto, composed of solid rock, rose like a massive wall sixty or eighty feet high, and terminated in an evergreen crown of cedars and hemlocks. The wall itself was literally covered from base to summit with moss and flowers and evergreens, among which bloomed, in rich profusion, the beautiful wild honeysuckle, which hung in gay festoons from every crag and crevice. This was a grotto which the hand of man had never made, and these were flowers and shrubs which he had never planted. Ages ago, God himself had scooped it out of the solid rock, and clothed its granite walls with fragrant flowers, which bloomed and faded, and bloomed again, as successive seasons rolled on, long before the foot of man had disturbed its quiet solitudes. But there were other charms, and, if possible, richer beauties still. At the further end of this lovely scene, and from an elevation of perhaps thirty or forty feet, there issued a stream of cool, pure water, clear as crystal. As it descended from "the cleft of the rock," which was nearly concealed by the overhanging flowers and shrubs, it divided into a number of little rivulets, which, in contrast with the green foliage around, looked like so many rills of liquid silver. At each one of these silvery "shady rills" stood, or kneeled, or lay groups of weary, thirsty soldiers, eagerly quaffing the precious beverage, as if determined never to be thirsty again.

A murmur of intense satisfaction and delight was

heard on every side. It seemed as if all felt that that sublimely beautiful scene had in it more of heaven than earth; and so strong, seemingly, were the feelings awakened in each bosom that a kind of holy awe, a subdued, sacred admiration, filled each heart. O, how welcome to those exhausted, thirsty men was that "shadow of a great rock in a weary land!" How refreshing those cool and sparkling waters, which gushed forth so full, free, and abundant from that flower-festooned rock! And how impressive the scene, too, when those exhausted, thirsty soldiers reached forth with such feverish eagerness to drink, and drink, and drink again! How they bathed their hot, fevered brows, or stooped under the shelving rocks, and allowed the cooling waters to fall upon them! How it seemed as if every leaf and spray and flower were in sympathy with the gladsome scene, while the dancing sunbeams looked like rays of glory streaming down through the leafy openings above, and the songs of the birds, far away in the cool green-wood, seemed to be the sweet melodies of the better land!

And as I looked upon that scene of thrilling interest, I thought of that loving ONE who, a weary and thirsty traveler, once sat, at the noontide hour, by the well of Jacob, and asked drink of a woman of Samaria. And it seemed as if he might almost be seen again, standing in the midst of those groups of thirsty men, with pity in every look and love in every word, saying, with compassionate tenderness and entreaty, "Whosoever drinketh of this water shall thirst again; but whosoever drinketh of the water that

I shall give him, shall never thirst; but the water that I shall give him shall be in him a well of water springing up into everlasting life." And it seemed, also, as if that scene of intense interest could be more fully understood, where it is said that, to the multitudes who hovered near him on the last great day of the feast, Jesus cried, so earnestly and so lovingly, "If any man thirst, let him come unto me and drink."

I thought, too, of the fullness and freeness of the living streams of salvation which flow from the great fountain of life and love, to which weary man may go and drink, and live forever. And I felt that man, though a stricken, sin-burdened sinner, groaning in the bitterness of helpless misery, estranged from God and heaven, traveling, a weary pilgrim, on life's high-way, and suffering from that soul-thirst which no earthly streams can ever quench, had not been abandoned by God, nor given over to hopeless despair. No! no! That very scene before me—that flower-festooned rock, from which gushed forth so plentifully those cool, refreshing waters—those groups of exhausted men, reaching forth so eagerly to drink and quench their burning thirst—all seemed to speak of the glorious plan of God, whereby the healing streams of salvation had been opened up in the moral desert, and of which all were invited to drink, without money and without price. Thank God! the Savior has come into the world and suffered and died, that whosoever believeth in him might not perish, but have everlasting life! He is the hiding-place from the storm, a covert from the heat, and as the shadow of a great rock in a weary land! He is the sinner's

Friend, the soul's Physician, the sin-atoning Lamb of God, from whose wounded side flow those healing streams that have washed and purified and saved a countless multitude in earth and heaven! And just as those refreshing waters which flowed forth so freely in that beautiful flowery recess, and of which the thirsty soldiers drank so eagerly and gladly, were free for all—just as every flower and leaf and spray, and dancing sunbeam and crystal stream, which made up the beauty and gladness of this precious scene, seemed to say, "Drink, ye weary, thirsty ones! Drink freely! Drink abundantly! Drink, one and all! Drink without limit and without fear! Drink, for all are welcome!"—so, in like manner, the waters of salvation are free for all; and the great work of the Spirit and the Bride is to say to every sinner, "Whosoever will, let him take the water of life freely!" But, alas! alas! just as any of those soldiers might have framed excuses, found fault, procrastinated, or refused to drink of the cool and abundant streams before them, and thereby suffered pain, and perhaps death, in like manner do many sinners, in their madness and folly, refuse to drink of the waters of salvation—die in their sins, and perish forever, while the gurglings of the healing streams are sounding in their ears!

I thought, again, that this was no temporary fountain to which these men had come—that those were no transient waters of which they drank, and which gushed forth in such strength and fullness. Their source was deep in the heart of the mountain—so deep that it would never be dried by summer's hottest sun, nor frozen by winter's coldest blast. Flowing on, flowing ever, by night and by day, through summer and winter, in sunshine and storm—O, what a type of God's unchanging love! Earthly friends change, and the happiest homes change, and the scenes of our mortal life change, till our eyes are dim with tears, and our hearts are crushed with sorrow; but, O, the warm sympathies and the outgushing love of the Infinite Father are ever full, ever free, and ever constant! "I, the Lord, change not." "For the mountains shall depart, and the hills be removed; but my kindness shall not depart from thee, neither shall the covenant of my peace be removed, saith the Lord that hath mercy on thee."

Such, in brief, were some of the reflections suggested by the beautiful and impressive scene described. I thought, too, of the happy time, when, in the radiant home on high, God would wipe away the tears from all faces, and crown his redeemed ones with crowns of dazzling splendor, and array them in garments of unfading beauty. I thought, also, how that the blessed Savior, once "A poor, wayfaring man of grief," asking a cup of water at the well of Jacob, would lead forth his white-robed followers, amid the immortal splendors of that heavenly country to where the fountains of glory play perpetually, and the streams of joy flow on forever. And as I stooped and bathed my own fevered brow, I could not refrain from praying that every one there might be refreshed with living waters, and that when the great work and conflict of life were ended, we might at last all drink of the streams of joy in the home of God.

After a brief rest—very brief it seemed—the bugle

sounded—"Forward!" and again the column was in motion. While we halted, the booming of cannon and the sharp rattle of musketry were heard on our right, which told us, in unmistakable language, that the battle had been renewed. It was not till evening had set in that we reached the scene of action—merely a skirmish—and in the mean time the enemy had been driven back. We lay down and slept soundly on that ground on which, a few hours before, the tide of battle had surged to and fro.

Such is life in the army. Such, indeed, is the life of man upon earth. Happy he who has the hope that when he sleeps his last sleep, having fought his last battle, it will be to awaken in that land where the sword of the spiritual conflict will be exchanged for the palm of victory, and the helmet of salvation will be exchanged for the crown of glory.

CHAPTER XXI.

HOOVER'S GAP — TULLAHOMA — WATER-CURE — WILL IT DO IN THE ARMY — A GREAT CHAPLAIN.

FORWARD—HOOVER'S GAP.

SHORTLY after three o'clock, on the morning of the 24th of June, hundreds of bugles sounded out far and near, through woods and valleys, and over hill and dale, on the east and west and north and south of Murfreesboro, the sweet but not always welcome notes of reveillé. It was a dull, cloudy morning—the sky, seemingly, all the more dusky and somber from the reflected glare of a thousand camp-fires. Toward five o'clock, the scenes that everywhere met the eye, and the sounds that everywhere fell upon the ear, were of the most intensely interesting and thrilling character. Dense, moving columns on every road, bristling bayonets gleaming everywhere, gay battle-flags streaming out on the morning breeze, or glancing amid the green foliage, as regiment after regiment deployed on the various roads—staff officers and orderlies galloping here and there—the sharp rattle of drums and the shrill sounds of the fife, the confused clangor of countless bugles, and the softer, sweeter, but no less confused notes of brigade bands beating off at the heads of the various columns—made both scenes and sounds not soon to be forgotten. This was the first move in the great campaign that drove Bragg out of Tennessee, in 1863, and, for the time being, was the poetry of war, soon to be followed by war's stern realities.

By five o'clock, Thomas's corps, occupying the center, was in motion, moving on the Manchester road. General Wilder's brigade of Reynolds's division, consisting of mounted infantry, armed with Spencer rifles, was in the advance, followed closely by Crook's brigade and the rest of the division. General McCook moved on the right by the Shelbyville road, his part of the work being a feint on Bragg's left, while the great work was really to be done by the forces moving against his left and center. By nine o'clock, the rain began to fall, and a regular storm set in, notwithstanding which the troops pushed on with great rapidity. General Wilder drove in the rebel pickets near Hoover's Gap, and pushed on, with daring energy and skill, so as to take the gap—a position very strong in itself, and rendered still more so by works commanding the approaches. In thus pushing on with such rapidity and dash, and securing the works before the enemy, seemingly, was aware of any movement, not only did Wilder gain an important point, but, as was acknowledged by all, thousands of lives were saved. He pushed forward so as to gain the southern extremity of the gap; but the enemy fought desperately, and, but for the deadly Spencer in the hands of his well-tried troops, he might have been seriously worsted before the infantry got up. The fighting for the possession of the gap was very stubborn, but gradually the rebels were driven back, with considerable loss. In the mean time communication had been opened with McCook, on the right, who was reported as in possession of Shelbyville.

Rain was falling heavily and darkness had set in, but still desultory firing, both of musketry and artillery, was kept up till eight or nine o'clock. Between sixty and seventy of the division were killed and wounded—nearly all belonging to Wilder's command. A log-house on the right of the road was selected as field hospital, and, shortly after dark, several tents were put up, and the wounded cared for as well as possible. The arrangements for so doing were most admirable. Several hospital wagons were driven up, and the good things furnished both by the Government and the Sanitary Commission were quickly in use for the comfort and relief of the wounded. The rebels had suffered considerably, and, as they were steadily pushed back, the greater part of their wounded fell into our hands. During that afternoon and night, and the following day, the field hospital, established at the point indicated, was soon full. Those, however, who were able to be removed, were sent back to Murfreesboro, thus giving greater facilities for the care of those still on the field, and insuring more comfort to those removed. And just at this point, let it be stated, that not very often are matters more forbidding, disagreeable, and in every way discouraging for the wounded, than they were at Hoover's Gap for the two or three days it was held by our advance. The rain fell incessantly, night and day. Every one was soaked through, and covered with mud, and all around the various field hospitals every thing was, to a mere beholder, of the most dreary and forbidding aspect. But—and to their praise be it spoken—the surgeons of the division worked like men in earnest. It would be invidious to mention names where all did so well, and those who might be most deserving would much rather let their deeds praise them, than any mere record, either official or otherwise. But let this much be said, that this first step of the great campaign of 1863, in Tennessee and Georgia, augured well for the comfort and care of the patriot soldier.

At the request of the medical director I attended to getting food for the wounded, and hence had opportunities of seeing how matters were conducted, and can, therefore, here and now give my cheerful testimony to the kindness, promptness, and efficiency of the medical staff.

The skirmishing was kept up briskly next day, the design being, apparently, not to drive the enemy too fast, nor to show a very heavy force just at this point. McCook on the right, however, was driving heavily, and the booming of his guns told that he was fighting in earnest. The struggle was for the possession of Liberty Gap, which was finally gained, and this, with the possession of Hoover's Gap in the center, gave Rosecrans the command of the position, and Bragg was compelled to fall back. It was reported that the mass of the rebel army was in and about Tullahoma, which had been strongly fortified. Rebel papers asserted that Rosecrans would come to grief the moment he moved from his intrenchments at Murfreesboro, and attempted to touch the intrenched position of

Bragg. But, as Rosecrans moved rapidly down by the gaps named, upon Manchester and Winchester, he flanked Bragg at Tullahoma. This was effectually done on the 27th by Reynolds's division taking possession of Manchester, Crook's brigade entering that place about ten o'clock, and bivouacking on the southwest of the town. A general halt was made here, the troops resting during Saturday and Sabbath.

Early on Monday morning, the army was again in motion, moving forward as rapidly as the incessant rain and the miry roads would permit. And it did rain, too, as if another deluge were about to come on this part of the earth. Night and day it was either a drizzling, misty shower for an hour or two, or a genuine thunder-storm; and it was hard to tell, sometimes, whether the rumbling noises which accompanied the heavier rains were the artillery of earth or heaven, for sometimes both were at work simultaneously. Soaked with the continual rain, and covered with mud from head to heels, there was decidedly more of the practical than the poetical seen among the columns as they pushed wearily but cheerfully along—some of the more light-hearted and waggish of the men cracking jokes at the general appearance of each other. One day, and nearly the whole of one night, however, there were precious few jokes. Waggish remarks were voted a nuisance. Jokers themselves were silent—completely collapsed. Haversacks were half filled with odd mixtures of hardtack, fat bacon, coffee, sugar, salt, and pepper—perhaps an iron spoon or a case-knife, and other simple odds and ends which make up a soldier's commissary—

all in one mixed up, undistinguishable, water-soaked mass! Not a very savory breakfast had been eaten before starting. Lunch consisted of a piece of the mixture indicated, washed down by a mouthful of muddy water, and supper was about the same, with the exception that the contents of the haversack were considerably softer. It was just in such remarkably romantic and eminently hygienic circumstances that we pushed on—men, horses, artillery, ammunition and supply-wagons plunging and floundering through the mud. Onward, through the deep mire and bridgeless streams, swollen by the incessant rains, over the hills, through the dense woods, out on the open, swampy plain, we pushed, if in no very poetic mood, yet having a very realizing sense of the intensely actual of military life. One gets the sentimental starch pretty well soaked out of him by a week or ten days' experience, as we had then. Don't talk empty sentimentalism to an old soldier. He knows better. If you doubt it, my non-military readers, just ask any of the heroes of the Cumberland if they have any recollections of the march from Murfreesboro to Tullahoma, in June, 1863.

A person is very apt to remember getting up in the morning, feeling as if he had been sleeping on the furrows of a potato-patch, or on the ridges and angles of a "corduroy" bridge, and having a very strong impression that his garments were decidedly damp, and had a strong odor of decayed leaves, wet grass, and fresh earth. To make one's toilet out of doors, under such circumstances, and eat breakfast by the glare of the camp-fire, are both sufficiently rustic and simple to satisfy the most enthusiastic poet that ever sighed for the return of the good old days of sylvan shades, moonlight musings, love in a cottage, or a romantic retreat in some vast wilderness, and other nice, pretty, innocent nonsense. My word for it, if the most enthusiastic poet that ever wrote heart-rending sonnets to dear Augusta Matilda, and devoutly envied the wanton breeze that toyed with her auburn ringlets, and raved to the moon about something he called his heart—just as if the moon knew any thing about anatomy—and who felt so superior to the common experiences of this practical world of ours, that he could only live in dream-land, and subsist on sentimental moonshine—if such a simpleton had marched by day and slept by night alongside some of us during those days and nights—got up long before day, floundered about in the mud, and eaten his breakfast while the rain threatened to weaken his coffee and soften his bread, the starch of sentimentalism would have been completely taken out of him, and he would have been as limp as a rag. And, for myself, I frankly confess that there was precious little starch of any kind left in me, after a few nights of such experience. The army is a fine place to get different kinds and qualities of starch taken out of people; and if they have nothing to keep them perpendicular, either in a moral or physical sense, but what is external and circumstantial, the soft spots in their general stamina will soon be discovered, and they will learn at least one lesson of life—*to know themselves*—

a lesson, by the way, which seldom injures any one to learn correctly. But to return.

Moving on the left of Tullahoma, and on a line nearly parallel with the railroad, Thomas proceeded so as to strike Bragg, said to be retreating east. On the first of July, part of the column entered Tullahoma, from the east—fairly flanking that place—Bragg having taken the alarm, barely getting clear, before our cavalry had dashed upon his rear-guard. According to all reports which had been made by scouts and prisoners, it was generally expected that a long and bloody battle would be fought for the possession of Tullahoma, where, it was asserted, the rebels had strong fortifications, mounted with heavy artillery, and where, it was also said, they had abundance of resources. The scene which presented itself on entering Tullahoma, told how precipitate Bragg's flight had been. Whole fields of wall-tents, of the best quality, were left standing just as they had been in use; and around them, as well as in them, were trunks, mess-chests, clothing, etc. We captured some thirty thousand pounds of corn-meal, five sixty-four-pounder siege-guns, and other military equipments. Every thing indicated that the flight was sudden, unexpected, and precipitate. All along the by-paths, in the woods as well as on the highways, over which the fleeing army had gone, were strewed clothing, wagons, blacksmith's tools, and corn-meal. Even in the soft places of the roads, where their artillery and wagons had mired, they had thrown whole sacks of corn-meal and beans, in order to fill up the ruts, and thus make a bridge, not of trees or rails, but of bread! Under all these circumstances, judge of our surprise when, on picking up a copy of the *Chattanooga Rebel*, of June 30—the day previous—we read that "General Rosecrans's army was in full retreat toward Nashville, closely pursued by the victorious army of Bragg!" Still onward, although it continued to rain almost without intermission, and although new roads had frequently to be cut for the artillery and trains—the old ones, in many places, being impassable—still onward pressed the columns, so as to intercept Bragg, rapidly retreating eastward, and endeavoring to reach Chattanooga on the south of the Tennessee River. Before Bragg could reach the mountain ranges, he had to cross Elk River, a rapid stream, now swollen by the rains. The intention was to strike his army at or near this river while in the act of crossing. Thomas's advance reached a point not far from Estelle Springs, just as the rear of the army had got across and taken up a position on the opposite side—a high bluff, on which were constructed two or three stockades, and some rifle-pits, commanding the bridge. They had attempted to burn the bridge, but it was so little injured that a few hours' work rendered it passable by the infantry, while the cavalry and artillery crossed at several points above and below. In the mean time, Crittenden, on the left, had moved up toward Tracy City, thus taking possession of the best and most direct route to Chattanooga. This turned Bragg's right, and compelled him to move almost due south, and through a rough, mountainous country.

On the 8th of July, the forces generally halted, forming a front from Tracy City almost to Huntsville, the center resting in front of the mountain ranges opposite Winchester. The command of General Reynolds lay near Big Springs—General Crook's command being encamped close by the Springs and within two and a half miles of Dechard Station, on the Nashville and Chattanooga Railroad.

THOUGHTS AND INCIDENTS.

No doubt the reader has already discovered that the pen which jots these army items, or, if you will, traces these Lights and Shadows of Army Life, is a very erratic and uncertain pen. Here is another evidence of that fact.

Imagine yourself just resting under a tree, or, if you like it better, come into one of our "shelter tents;" that, dear reader, is the polite and official name of what the boys call "dorg tents;" but, no matter, let us have a little talk. And, first of all, let me ask a plain question. Were you ever hungry? I don't mean to ask, Did you ever have a good appetite? for, of course, you have. Neither do I mean to inquire whether you ever felt a certain keen, healthful commotion in the gastric region when by your watch it lacked precisely fifteen minutes and ten seconds of the dinner hour, and which—not your watch, but your stomach—induced you to believe you could eat like a New Zealander. Neither do I ask whether you ever felt somewhat dissatisfied and considered yourself as entitled to the honor of martyrdom, because your better half (perhaps your better half all to nothing) set before you a cold lunch on some day of general domestic tribulation and soapsuds, and which caused you to pray that the millennium might speedily come, when the miserably abused lords of creation, yourself included, would be saved from the weekly crucifixion of stomach and temper. No, no! I don't mean any such healthful, hopeful hunger as that; but I mean a real, genuine, hopeless, prostrating hunger, the result, for instance, of thirty-six hours' pretty general fasting, followed by two hours' sleep at the foot of a tree, in rain and mud and wretchedness generally. That is the kind of hunger to which reference is made. If you have ever been in such circumstances, then you deserve to be pitied; if you never have, then be thankful, and pray that you never may.

During the time indicated in the previous chapter, and, indeed, during the whole of my army experience, I have, in common with others, known what is included in that comprehensive term "a campaign;" and one of the lessons learned was this—namely, that the history of this war will never be written. The history of no war has ever been written, and for this reason, that it is an utter impossibility. A sketch may be given; brilliant generalities may be recorded by the pen of the historian after the dust and smoke of battle have cleared away; rhetorical flourishes, and rounded periods, musical expressions strung together and sounding like silver bells, and pet military phrases placed at proper distances on the page, like general officers on a review, may all be brought into play in the production of some grandly pretentious history of any given campaign; but the history, as such, will be a failure. War, as written on the page of history, is vastly different from war as written on the long, weary march, the bivouac, and the battlefield. It is vastly different as seen from the cozy parlor fireside, through the page of a book or the columns of the daily paper, and seen from amid the smoke and din of the conflict itself, the groans of the wounded and the dying, and scenes of horror that the beholder never can forget. And, then, there are elements of individual privation and suffering that never enter into the sum total of the historian's grand estimate of war, and which "special correspondents," enjoying special privileges, sometimes never know, or, if known, are seldom referred to in their communications. And those very sufferings and privations, endured by the patriot soldiers during this wicked rebellion, only show how devoted they have been to the good cause in which they have been engaged, and what a debt of gratitude the country will owe them when the rebellion is crushed. Owing to circumstances, which it is needless to relate, on more occasions than one did the brave men composing the Army of the Cumberland suffer from absolute hunger. During the advance into Southern Tennessee and Northern Alabama and Georgia, amid the cheerful feelings caused by a victorious entrance into Bragg's strongholds, and the driving of his army before us continually, there were times when it needed both patience and patriotism to bear up in the midst of severe privations. I remember, and ever will remember, one particular time, during that campaign, when the Eleventh, Thirty-sixth, and other Ohio regiments, neither rested, slept, nor ate any thing, save crackers, for forty-eight hours, standing up or lying down, their muskets never out of their hands, skirmishing with the enemy the whole time, while shell and shot were passing over and around them—all this, too, in rain and mud, and after long and fatiguing marches. The utter wretchedness of that weary time will never be forgotten. There was no place to rest, unless one chose either to lie down in the mud, or take two or three rails and place them so as to form an inclined plane, or search for some root-prongs above water and mud, and lie down in the easiest position possible.

I am a great admirer of the water-cure system, if you will allow me to regulate the *water* part of the cure, and not mix it too much with *mud;* but I acknowledge that forty-eight hours in rain above and mire beneath, two hours' sleep at the foot of a tree, with one of the root-prongs for a pillow, a cracker or two for the inner man, and a "wet pack" for the outer, is taking the starch out a little too rapidly for comfort, and seems sufficiently convincing of the powerful effects of cold water and *plain* diet to suit the most rabid Grahamite. Do you suppose, dear reader, that it would savor much of the carnal mind if one were frankly to confess that he felt hungry and faint and miserable after such rough experiences? Or do you think that one's conscience would be much troubled about transmogrifying a stray sheep into mutton—especially if its bleating was constructively disloyal—and partaking of a savory slice, asking no questions, for the stomach's sake and often infirmities? I don't want you to understand, for a moment, dear reader, that any sheep ever came to an untimely end, or was accidentally changed into mutton-chops through my instrumentality; but I will just acknowledge that one of the sweetest morsels I have ever eaten was given me, one miserable, wet evening, by "Shorty"—may his shadow never grow less! Where he got it I didn't ask, but assuredly he hadn't time to go to market for it!

Apropos to speaking of long fasts, rain, mud, fence-rail beds, and pine-root couches, let me state a fact, which I most humbly commend to the notice of the more metaphysical of my readers. It is this: I have noticed that, after a long fast, or a three or four weeks' diet of hard crackers and muddy coffee, a good, substantial meal has a most wonderful effect on one's religious enjoyments. Why, I have felt pious all over, after a good dinner or supper under such circumstances, and my heart, or stomach, perhaps, was so full of good feeling that I loved everybody, and thought every thing looked brighter and more beautiful generally. Even the rebel chivalry, in dirt and rags and general squalidness, seemed to be somewhat improved, and to look less lean, lank, cadaverous, and loose-jointed. The very leaves seemed to quiver in sympathy with my good feeling, and the few birds that had not been driven off by the incessant noise and confusion, seemed to chirp more musically and cheerfully; while at night, even the doleful "Whip-poor-will" seemed to sing cheerily, "Mutton's good! Mutton's good!" O, you needn't contract your pious brows into a sanctimonious frown, my good Brother Skinflint! It's all true, and if you don't believe it, just make the experiment. If you do, perhaps your own experience with the lights and shadows—especially the shadows—of life in general will lead you to ask, as I have often done, How much religion is there in good living? How much do our "frames of mind," especially of the exuberant, comfortable kind, depend upon juicy roast beef, savory potatoes, and good things generally! What connection is there, after all, between the state of our digestive organs and the nature of our religious emotions? To what an extent do our fervency of devotion, or strength of zeal, or power of faith, or brilliancy of hope depend on whether we have made our dinner or supper from an abundance of good things, and with keen relish, or whether we have had to snatch an unpalatable morsel from under the dark shadow of Want? Do the luxurious apartments and soft couches and well-loaded tables of wealthy Christians have any thing to do with their self-satisfaction and easy spiritual victories—freedom from harassing cares and general hopefulness? Or do the continual struggles with poverty, and the anxious cares and the want of many things that are craved both by bodily and mental appetites, from which the pious poor have to suffer, have any connection with their inward conflicts, their seasons of darkness, and their deep, earnest longings after other and brighter days? And should there not be more Christ-like tenderness and sympathy felt in dealing with the sad and suffering of earth? Should there not be more attention paid to the physical wants of the poor, while their spiritual necessities are by no means neglected? Might not a loaf of bread, or any little delicacy from the hand of some Christian lady, do more good to the soul as well as the body of poor Widow Brown, over the way—bring her nearer to Christ and heaven—than an eight-page tract, containing a thin, meager, metaphysical homily on the "Duty of Contentment," handed to her, with all due formality, by the Rev. Jonathan Creamcheese?

Speaking of the Rev. Jonathan Creamcheese, reminds me of one of his eminent brethren, who flourished somewhat during the campaign of 1863. Let me introduce the reader to

A Brave Military Chaplain.

During the continual skirmishing with Bragg's retreating army, there were several occasions when severe and serious fighting took place. On one of the occasions referred to, when the casualties were unusually numerous, and when there was ample work for all to do in ministering to the wants of the wounded, my attention was frequently attracted by a portly-looking, fresh-faced gentleman, who carried a very nice walking-cane, and was invariably seen with a cigar in his mouth, from which he blew a continuous and quite fashionable cloud of smoke. He seemed to be in very good humor with every one in general, and with himself in particular. He had a jovial, hail-fellow-well-met kind of air about him, and seemed to be so full of general good humor and camp *abandon*, that he was perfectly indifferent to the very sad scenes by which we were then and there surrounded. Who could he be? He could not be a surgeon, for there was too much work to be done, just then, for any of the medical staff to be idle. Perhaps a special correspondent of some daily paper, thought I, and, therefore, he is looking on with that air of *nonchalance* peculiar to professional coolness and long intimacy with sad scenes. But he had no note-book nor pencil in hand, and he was too robust and well-dressed for a genuine quill-driver for the newspaper press. And then, too, I had noticed that correspondents were invariably busy, in one way or another, where there were any wounded. No, no; he could not be a correspondent. Perhaps a visitor, then—one following the army to satisfy his curiosity. But even that did not seem to suit, and so I gave up my guessing. One thing was certain—he had not, as I noticed, spoken a word to one of the wounded—he had rendered no assistance where help was so much needed, but only flourished his cane and smoked his cigar. However, the mystery was solved at last, and my curiosity satisfied. He finally spoke to me. This of itself was a favor for which one ought to have been profoundly thankful—that is, considering the circumstances. I had torn my coat the day before, in a frantic attempt to overload the pockets with hard-tack and two or three numbers of the "Atlantic." From the crown of a dilapidated felt hat, knocked into all conceivable shapes, to the toes of a pair of coarse cavalry boots, I was well covered with mud. Add to this, I had spent the previous night in the driest corner of a leaky wagon-shed, with my saddle for a mattress, and a cracker-box for a pillow; had been liberally supplied with water from above, and thin mire from below, and, therefore, felt decidedly cheap.

"Hospital nurse or steward, eh?" said he, condescendingly, as I straightened myself up, after having finished supplying the wounded with hot coffee and dry rusk.

"Here, chaplain—my pardner, here, says he wants some more coffee. I'll take some, too—blamed if I'm going to miss my rations for this scratch. The ball came purty near knocking out my chunk, though—it's a fact!"

The "pardner" and his friend were duly supplied—and again the gentleman of the cane and cigar addressed me:

"You're a chaplain, eh? What regiment do you belong to?" he inquired, most majestically, as he blew the tobacco-smoke into curling wreaths.

I informed him, with becoming deference, at the same time scraping some mud off my coat, and trying to straighten out my hat, which had been jammed and softened out of all shape.

"I am chaplain, too," said he, with becoming gravity, and with that self-importance becoming so great a personage. "I am chaplain of the —— regiment," he continued, between the puffs—"have been at home sick for some time, but, in all the engagements which we have been in, I have always occupied my official position, namely, six paces in the rear of my regiment."

Bah! thought I—your true position would be a few score of miles in the rear of the army. Sick! Was there ever such a jolly, ruddy, plump, ponderous burlesque on sickness! And that shining cane, too, and those everlasting cigars! Six paces in the rear of the regiment during battle! How brave! No wonder he could not condescend to such small matters as to speak a word of comfort to the sufferers, nor give one of them a cup of cold water!

In striking contrast with the conduct of the above-mentioned gentleman, was that of Chaplain Grimes, of the Ninety-second Ohio. Although in feeble health himself, he worked everywhere, and at all times, for the good of his own men as well as for those of other commands. He persevered for months in his arduous labors, seeking the welfare of all with whom he came into contact, till, at last, he had to yield to stern necessity and ask to be relieved from duty. When he left the army it was with the respect and esteem of all who knew his labors and his self-sacrificing spirit. Of him, however, it might be said, that his very anxiety to labor, and his nervous energy in all he undertook, especially in visiting the hospitals, so exhausted his already weak frame, that he was all the sooner and all the more completely incapacitated for army labor. I thus record my appreciation of a good man and an efficient chaplain.

CHAPTER XXII.

ROSECRANS'S ADVANCE—CROSSING LOOKOUT—PERILOUS POSITION OF THE ARMY.

TOWARD the middle of August, the railroad from Murfreesboro to Chattanooga had been repaired as far as Cowan, and materials had been collected at different points, from Tullahoma to Dechard, to continue repairs as the army advanced. Supplies had been collected, the troops were rested and refreshed, and every thing was promising and cheerful. On the 16th and 17th a general advance of the whole line took place. General Reynolds's division had already advanced to University, a point of some note on the Cumberland range, so that while part of the corps was moving from Dechard, our division was already well advanced. The line pursued by Thomas's corps was nearly parallel with the Nashville and Chattanooga Railroad—the third division (Reynolds's) being considerably east of that road. General McCook, still on the right, moved on a line a little west of south, so as to strike the Tennessee River west of Stevenson. On the 23d of August our troops occupied Jasper, at which point our division lay till the 1st of September. On that and the succeeding days, the entire force in the Sequatchie Valley crossed the river, at

Shellmound, while other portions of the corps crossed at different points below, while McCook, at about the same time, crossed at points at and below Bridgeport. Meanwhile, Crittenden was moving more to the east, threatening Chattanooga, whither, it was stated, Bragg had retreated and was fortifying for the final struggle in the "last ditch." Thus, it will be seen that the line of battle formed by the various columns of the Army of the Cumberland, at the time referred to—say from the 28th of August till the 4th of September—was not less than forty-five miles, and facing nearly south, or a little east of south. The intention of Rosecrans was to get Bragg out of Chattanooga—not by fighting, but by strategy. To accomplish this, part of Crittenden's corps, as already stated, moved up on the north side of the Tennessee toward that place. Proceeding a short distance above the city, they made demonstrations as if about to cross the river. The troops flapped and pounded boards, cut down trees, sawed off the ends of planks and logs, designedly made chips and coarse shavings, and threw them into the current, which, floating past Bragg's camps below, intimated that the Yankee invaders were making pontoon bridges, in order to cross above the city. Wilder suddenly showed himself on the bluffs north of the town, unlimbered his artillery almost under Bragg's nose, and sent a few shells and round shot into the city and the rebel camps. While Bragg's attention was thus diverted near Chattanooga, and Crittenden was seemingly working with the utmost energy to effect a crossing above the city and turn his right, the pontoon bridges at Caperton's Ferry, three miles from Stevenson, and the one at Bridgeport, twelve miles above, were successfully finished, and the troops under Thomas and McCook safely across. As soon as the army was fairly across the river, the right was pushed rapidly forward, which changed the line of battle from nearly due south to south-east. The cavalry on the extreme right swung round, so as to avoid the immense mountain ranges, and threatened the extensive net-work of railroads in Bragg's rear, and upon which he had to depend for supplies. Thus, by the peculiar nature of the country, the long sweep which the railroads have to make in order to avoid the northern extremity of Mission Ridge, Crittenden threatened Bragg's lines of communication on the north and east, while Thomas and McCook, sweeping around or over Lookout and the mountain ranges below, threatened them on the south and west. Any one, who will take a map and trace these movements, will admire the military strategy displayed by General Rosecrans on this occasion, and which was so successful.

On the afternoon of the 3d, we crossed over the high range of hills known as Raccoon Mountain, our division taking a commanding position in the Trenton Valley, shortly after dark. A rebel cavalry force evacuated the north-east point of the mountain as our advance swept round. The rebel signal-lights could be distinctly seen working on Lookout Mountain. Our camp-fires, however, were kindled on the west side of some low hills at the foot of the mountain, so that the movements were partially concealed. Two pieces of artillery were wheeled into position so as to command the Trenton and Chattanooga roads, while several pieces were placed in position and masked in the woods overlooking the valley. General Crittenden, with the remainder of his corps, was cautiously moving up on our left toward the great pivot on which both armies were at this time swinging—namely, Chattanooga.

Crossing Lookout.

The crossing of Lookout Mountain by the Army of the Cumberland equaled, and, in some respects, excelled, the celebrated crossing of the Alps by Napoleon—aside, entirely, from the fact that it had to be crossed in the face of the enemy, and that there were but two passes or gaps by which an army, with its artillery and wagon-trains, could possibly proceed with any reference to safety. On Wednesday, the 9th of September, Thomas's corps commenced the difficult work of crossing the mountain by the central pass, about eight miles south of Trenton, known as Cooper's and Stevens's Gaps. McCook's corps crossed by the pass known as Winston's Gap, about twenty miles south of Trenton. Crittenden swept around the northern extremity of Lookout Mountain, where it terminates close by the Tennessee River, and within five miles of Chattanooga. Before the crossing of the central column had commenced, intelligence was received that Bragg had evacuated Chattanooga, and Crittenden had taken possession of the town. So well planned and so well executed, so far, were the movements of Rosecrans, that Bragg was compelled to fall back from Chattanooga, or permit himself to be shut up in that nook on the Tennessee between two mountain ranges. By moving across Lookout by Stevens's Gap, Thomas's corps threatened Bragg's rear at Lafayette, and McCook's cavalry were threatening Rome still further south, a detachment of which, under Colonel Brownlow, having advanced to within five miles of that place.

On the evening of the 10th, after a toilsome march through the steep, rough, rocky, mountain pass, the advance, under General Turchin, of Reynolds's division, reached the southern base of Lookout, a little after dark. The Thirty-sixth Ohio was in the advance of the brigade, and their skirmishers drove in the enemy's pickets. A force sufficiently heavy was advanced in order to drive back the enemy sufficiently to permit us to get room enough to camp, and reach a supply of water. No sooner were the enemy's pickets driven in, than hundreds of camp-fires were speedily blazing all along the foot of the mountain and through the gap, just as if there had been twenty thousand of us, when, in reality, there were not then three thousand fairly over the mountain and facing the enemy! During the darkness we had to grope our way in search for ground sufficiently level upon which to spread our blankets, while the immense trains had to be huddled into the closest possible position. A heavy picket line was thrown out, and we held ourselves in readiness for battle any moment. As troops with their artillery and wagon-trains were pushing close behind, and in the darkness objects wrapped in rubber blankets could not be distinctly seen among the pine and laurel bushes, there was not much hope of a comfortable night's rest—even granting that the rebels should not make an attack during the night. Colonel Lane and the chaplain entered into a joint-stock partnership in the matter of blankets and saddles, and, with the assistance of the ever-faithful Mike, prepared to spend the night with a due regard to comfort. By dint of groping with hands and feet, and aided somewhat by the glare of the camp-fires, we discovered two immense logs, lying nearly parallel, and about five feet apart. Here were double breastworks—or *side*-works, rather—which would prevent us from being unduly disturbed either by stray mules or their drivers, floundering about in the darkness. After a sweet—not literally, but ideally sweet—cup of robust coffee, and an equally sweet allowance of hard-tack, we lay down in our rural retreat. O, ye love-sick noodles, who sigh for sylvan shades, wouldn't ye have been in transports there! Mike, who was always exact in military etiquette to the colonel, and exhibited all due respect for his "riverence," treated both of us, in the matter of going to bed, much as if he thought us a couple of spalpeens that were under his special care. The colonel might be equal to Alexander the Great, and the chaplain—"barring he was a heretic, bad scran to him for that!"—might be next-door neighbor to the "howly praist of Ballyshannon," but neither of them knew enough to make an orthodox bed!

"Sure, an isn't it meself knows how to fix yees right?" he would say, as he tucked the blankets round us, and gave our saddle-pillows a finishing touch.

It is a matter of doubt whether he did not give the colonel the worst side of the rough, rocky bed that night. I have an indistinct impression that he was inclined to roll down hill, and, but for the log, there is no saying where he might have gone. We were just beginning to doze sweetly and dreamily, when a teamster, thinking it would be a good place to feed his mules at, pitched an armful of green cornstalks over us, and began leading up his mules—using the colonel and the chaplain as the bottom of his feeding-trough! This was a little too much of the romantic all at once, and the teamster was informed that we were not anxious to cultivate such a close acquaintance with his mules, just at that time. Again we were trying to sleep amid the hum and bustle of the troops, when a weary soldier, putting his gun close by our heads, stretched himself on the log above us. I began to calculate his possible weight in pounds, and the laws of gravitation which would operate, should he begin to roll in his sleep, and formed a rough estimate of the number of ribs which I might require set in the event of his rolling on *my* side of the log. He finally moved away. Now for sleep. *Midnight.*—There is more quiet. But no!

"Colonel! Colonel Lane!" Aroused again. It is Captain Price, of General Turchin's staff.

"The general desires me to say that you will send out two companies, under Major Higgins, at three o'clock, to strengthen the picket line. The enemy's pickets are to be driven in, and our own pickets advanced half a mile beyond where theirs now are."

The necessary orders are given, and again Colonel Lane lies down. But we may as well give it up. *One o'clock.*—No sleep. *Two o'clock.*—The men, wearied with the toilsome march of the previous day, are sleeping soundly on their rocky beds and under the starry canopy of heaven, and must be aroused. We expect the roar of battle any moment, and listen for the boom of the first gun. *Three o'clock.*—The companies detailed for the picket line have had a cup of coffee, and have started with the major.

And so the morning wears away. At seven o'clock the lines are advanced cautiously. Negley has been fighting already, and the enemy is showing strength. The column moved forward cautiously till the 14th, when the battle lines were formed in the valley lying between Pigeon and Lookout Mountains, known as McLemore's Cove. General Reynolds's division was opposite Catlet's Gap, a deep gorge in Pigeon Mountain. Turchin's brigade was pushed close to the gap, and engaged Hood's division more or less during the whole day. The Eleventh Ohio, at this time, was on duty for forty-eight hours, and constantly under fire. The regiment was relieved on the evening of the 16th, a few hours after having repelled a determined assault of the enemy.

CHICKAMAUGA.

The strategic movements of Rosecrans, sketched so briefly in the foregoing pages, not only bewildered Bragg, but alarmed the whole Southern Confederacy, as was evidenced by the strenuous efforts put forth to arrest the further progress of the Union army. It was but a few days after Rosecrans had fairly crossed Lookout Mountain, when accumulating evidence was given that Bragg was being reinforced, and that now a stand would be made, and, perhaps, a battle fought for the final possession of Chattanooga. While Thomas's corps was feeling the strength of the enemy holding the gaps of Pigeon Mountain, Crittenden had advanced on the left as far as Ringgold, on the railroad leading to Atlanta. He soon ascertained that Bragg was at Lafayette, and was in position. Seeing this, he fell back toward Lookout, crossed the Chickamauga at Gordon's Mills, and so disposed of his forces as to be within reach of Thomas, and yet not uncover Chattanooga. All the gaps in Pigeon Mountain were held by Bragg, and it was now ascertained beyond a doubt that he had been largely reinforced, and was marching back so as to fight Rosecrans's scattered army, and regain the point from which he had been driven by strategic movements. Then came the hours of anxiety for generals, and the days and nights of forced marches for brave but weary soldiers, over the mountains and through the valleys. McCook, who was seventeen miles further down the valley, was ordered to close up on Thomas with all possible haste, which he did after a toilsome march of forty-six miles—he having made a detour around and across Lookout, instead of marching by a road on its crest. He reached Catlett's Gap on the evening of the 17th—having, by a mistake he made in believing the reports of refugees that there was no road on the mountain, occupied four days in marching a distance which should have been accomplished in a day and a half.

On the evening of the 18th, the great movements, designed to concentrate the Union army at a point nearer Chattanooga, were commenced. McCook's corps relieved Thomas at Catlett's Gap, who immediately began to close up on Crittenden, who was seriously threatened by Bragg's right. Already three days of precious time had been lost waiting for the troops under McCook to reach the valley—days employed to great advantage by Bragg, for whose reinforcement troops had been hurried from every part of the Confederacy. In one week's time he had received Longstreet's veteran troops from Lee's army, several brigades from Mobile and Charleston, ten thousand, under Buckner, from East Tennessee, a portion of Johnston's army, from the Mississippi, together with thousands of those whom Grant had paroled at Vicksburg. Bragg's army was thus swelled to eighty thousand—some statements make it as high as one hundred thousand—effective troops.

CHAPTER XXIII.

BATTLE OF CHICKAMAUGA—PREPARATIONS—RELIGIOUS SERVICES ON THE FIELD—REYNOLDS'S DIVISION—HEROIC CONDUCT OF THE UNION ARMY.

At five o'clock on the evening of the 18th, Thomas's corps was fairly in motion. Although in the month of September, and in a warm climate, it was very cold, and was more like a night in November in more northern regions than a September evening in the sunny South. The point aimed at was the junction of the roads in the Chickamauga Valley leading into Chattanooga, toward which the enemy was moving in great force, in order to crush Crittenden and get between the river and the Union army. Our way, the entire distance of about twelve miles, was lighted by burning fences, all of which, on each side of the road, were in a blaze. Not a single fence the entire distance but was blazing, and no human power could possibly have extinguished the immense conflagration. The mountains on either side could occasionally be seen illuminated as the cold, eddying wind, now and again, lifted up the heavy, dark cloud of smoke which hung above us, and the stars seemed to shine with a pale, ghastly hue from out the reddish sky, lighted up with the lurid glare from below. This was in keeping with War's stern, gloomy visage, a fitting accompaniment to the fearful scenes of the morrow. The remorseless fire by night was in stern keeping with the devouring sword by day.

About four o'clock in the morning, we halted for a short rest. Our division had been engaging the enemy during several days and nights preceding, and not one of us had enjoyed the comfort of a night's rest for nearly a week. Men more weary or exhausted, perhaps, never lay down to rest upon the cold ground, than did those composing the Eleventh Ohio on that eventful morning. Our eyes and nostrils were smarting with pain, caused by the dense clouds of smoke from the burning woods and fences, and we shivered in the cold night-wind that swept down the valley as if from some icy region. Soon after, sitting down under a tree, near which a fire was burning, exhausted nature yielded to sleep's gentle wooings, and I became oblivious to the weary tramp, tramp, the blinding smoke, and the choking dust. My sleep was sweet, although a fence-rail was my only pillow, and the bleak night-wind chilled my weary frame, and the dreams of that hour's repose were of other and brighter scenes than those of a long and weary night-march. We had rested thus for about an hour, when "Fall in!—Forward!" fell gruffly on the ear of many a dreamer who would, ere another night, be sleeping his last sleep on the field of battle. Day was just dawning as we resumed our rapid march, and at seven o'clock we halted near Gordon's Mills. A short time was allowed the troops to make coffee, and, in the straits of military exigencies, the colonel and chaplain were glad to share with each other the contents of their haversacks.

Scarcely had we finished our frugal breakfast, when the heavy booming of cannon told that the conflict had begun. Preparations were needed for the dark and terrible hours which were impending. Not only does the body require nourishment, but the soul requires strength. If this be so in the hours of peace and conscious security, how much more in the dread hour of battle, and in the consciousness of danger and death! And then how necessary to have grace to speak words of encouragement, words of sympathy, words of warning to dear comrades who may fall bleeding and dying on the field of strife! And where can needed strength for soul and body be secured but at a throne of grace? There are "stones of memorial" which faith and gratitude have reared at Bull Run and South Mountain—at Antietam and Hoover's Gap; and there is one, too, under a tree on the southern slopes of Mission Ridge, overlooking bloody Chickamauga, where heavenly voices seemed to whisper, in the ear of a weak, trembling servant of God, those precious words: "For in the time of trouble He shall hide me in his pavilion; in the secret of his tabernacle he shall hide me."

Preparations for Battle—An Impressive Scene.

At eight o'clock our regiment formed in line of battle, and took position on the brow of a hill, about two miles north of Gordon's Mills, and near the Chattanooga road. By this time the engagement had become general, and troops were rushing forward rapidly. Feeling anxious to have one more opportunity of speaking a word of encouragement to the patriot soldiers who were about to enter into the very jaws of death, and many of whom, perhaps, would never hear words of prayer upon earth again, I rode up to Colonel Lane, and asked just five minutes' time to pray with them before going into action. "Certainly," was his instant reply. "I wish you would have services; I think there will be time."

Another pen must describe the scene as witnessed by others on the morning of that eventful day. Says a correspondent:

"General Turchin's brigade of Reynolds's division, Thomas's corps, consisting of the Eleventh Ohio, Colonel Lane; the Thirty-sixth Ohio, Colonel Jones; the Ninety-second Ohio, Colonel Fearing, and the Eighteenth Kentucky, Colonel ——, took position on a low spur of the ridge near the Chattanooga road, and in the rear of the tannery already spoken of. Before the skirmishers were deployed, a scene occurred with the Eleventh, which, for sublimity and moving power, has been seldom surpassed. The chaplain rode up in front of the line, and the colonel gave an order which, on being executed, formed the regiment in two divisions, with the chaplain in the center. Without dismounting, he addressed the troops in a clear, loud voice, that sounded strangely amid the loud explosions of the artillery and the rattle of musketry. He spoke about the holy cause for which they were to fight that day; that it was not for territory or revenge or military glory; but for home and country, for liberty and truth, for GOD AND HUMANITY!

"'It is but little I can do for you,' said he, 'in the hour of battle; but there is one thing I will do—I will pray for you. And there are thousands all over the land praying for you this morning, and God will hear them. You must now pray, too; for God is a hearer of prayer. And if this is the last time I shall ever speak to you, or if these are the last words of Christian comfort you will ever hear, I want to tell you, dear comrades, that GOD LOVES YOU. I pray God to cover your heads to-day in the battle-storm. I pray that he may give you brave hearts and strong hands to-day. Be brave—be manly! Remember the dear old flag, and what it covers. And if any of you feel uncertain as to your future, O look to the Savior who died for you; and, if any of you fall this day in battle, may you not only die as brave soldiers for your country, but die as soldiers of the Lord Jesus Christ! Let us pray.'

"Instantly every head was uncovered and bowed in reverence, while hands were clasped on the rifles, the bayonets on which were gleaming in the morning sun. The flag, pierced and rent on a dozen battlefields, was drooped, and, strange but glorious sound on a battlefield, the voice of prayer was heard. The blessings of the Almighty were invoked upon the army, upon the generals, upon regimental officers, on our bleeding country, and upon the issues of that day. Loved ones at home were remembered, and God's blessing invoked upon all who might fall in battle. When the chaplain closed, he raised himself in his saddle, waved his hat two or three times around his head, exclaiming, 'God bless you to-day, dear comrades, and make you strong and brave! Strike for Liberty and Union! strike for God and Humanity! and may our battle-torn flag lead to victory this day! God's presence be with you, comrades!'

"A low, murmuring Amen was heard from the ranks as the chaplain closed. Major-General Reynolds and staff passed along the lines during the services, but halted when they came to the Eleventh. With uncovered head, the General rode up close to the regiment, and remained till the conclusion of the brief services. At the moment they were concluded, he uttered a hearty Amen, which had a thrilling effect. Grasping the chaplain's hand and shaking it warmly, while a tear glistened on his manly cheek, he was heard to exclaim, 'Sir, I am glad I was here to join with you!' and instantly rode off, followed by his staff. This acknowledgment of religious principle, on the part of General Reynolds, had a very happy effect." . . .

Scarcely five minutes elapsed till the entire brigade moved forward and engaged the enemy.

When the battle opened on the morning of the 19th, the lines extended nearly three miles, and the fierce, fiery conflict raged through valleys and ravines, along hill-sides and amid dense forests, over plowed fields and dead clearings.

In many places the battle-lines could be distinguished only by dense clouds of dust that rose up in long, reddish lines, and by white, vapory smoke that rolled in great clouds through the woods, or rose above the forest trees, and rolled along the sharp ridges and sweeping hill-sides. Sometimes, the long lines of dust and the wreathing, rolling smoke from artillery would recede or advance, be thrown suddenly into sharp angles, or formed gradually into swelling curves, indicating the ebb and flow of the fearful, mighty tide-wave of battle. I had heard the roar of battle at Bull Run, had felt the earth quiver under the fierce conflicts of South Mountain and Antietam, but the incessant roar of artillery and musketry on this terrible day seemed to exceed all three battlefields combined. The musketry was neither in distinct shots nor in repeated volleys, but for hours it was one mighty, fearful, continuous roll, which, added to the shouts of the combatants, as they charged to and fro like the surging tide-waves on the shore, together with the loud, deep booming and crashing of the artillery, seemed more like the mighty roar of a dozen Niagaras than any thing merely human.

From all the indications during the forenoon of this day, and even till late in the afternoon, it was evident that the great struggle was for the roads leading into Chattanooga. On the preceding evening, the 18th, Crittenden was on the left, menaced by the right of the rebel army. Bragg was massing his forces at that point, so as to crush Crittenden and get possession of the roads, and with them Chattanooga. But, during the previous night, Thomas had swept his corps past Crittenden's rear, and formed on the extreme left, thus throwing Crittenden in the center. By this memorable night march, and swift secret movements, he covered all the roads and gaps, so that when Bragg began to move his massed columns, on the morning of the 19th, he was confronted by the veteran troops of Thomas, already in position. Hence the opening of the battle so fiercely on the left, and hence the continual edging away of the line of battle in that direction. Bragg brought up column after column, and hurled them in rapid succession, and with reckless desperation, against the extreme left. It was Chattanooga or nothing. About twelve o'clock, he hurled a massed column on Thomas's right, where Reynolds's division was in position, and followed this up by successive attacks at various points till the battle raged along the entire line. And thus the conflict was waged during the whole day, every evidence being given not only of a hotly contested field, but of greatly superior numbers being in front of the Union army.

A Close Place—A Two-forty Gallop.

While following the regiment, in company with the surgeons, a rebel sharp-shooter, concealed in the trees, sent a ball whizzing among us—whether aimed at Dr. McCurdy or myself, I do not know; but it passed uncomfortably close to my head. An inch or two, more or less, and these "Lights and Shadows" would not have troubled any one. It is said that "a miss is as good as a mile." It may be so—but if a Minié ball misses one's head just by about an inch, the sensation produced is not quite as comfortable as if it was a mile further off. At this juncture an entire change took place in the relative position of the several regiments. The Eleventh made a sudden movement to the left, and took position in the woods. It moved again to the right, to relieve a regiment whose ammunition was exhausted, and we got so bewildered with the rapid changes going on, that we found it impossible to find it, or even to follow. Taking another direction, toward where the firing was heaviest, we were soon made aware of the fact that the rear is not always the place of safety. To say that the bullets whistled around us like hail, might seem extravagant, but I can compare it to nothing else. The incessant roll and rattle and crash were fearful. The peculiar hum, whiz, and shriek of rifle-balls, which give one the idea of fiery arrows cutting the air, grew louder and louder, while the chipping of leaves and twigs told better than words can do of the thickly flying missiles of death. My horse gave a plunge and a snort—poetic enough in a painting, perhaps, but very startling and practical just then. Whether a spent ball or a piece of gravel thrown up by the shot struck him or not, I do not know; but he gave a jump as if he would fly from under me, and, but for a military bit, would doubtless have become unmanageable. Hitherto he had stood fire well—did not seem to pay much attention to the artillery or musketry—but at this moment he became almost wild. It was little wonder. There was a strange surging to and fro of the combatants, while the rattle of musketry and the explosions of artillery made the very earth tremble. What with the noise of battle in front, and the noise of rushing troops coming up behind, it was enough to bewilder and try the nerves of either man or horse. In a few minutes there was that advancing, wavy sound that tells of movements the wrong way! Our troops were being driven! The surgeons became somewhat bewildered, and rode almost at right angles to the line of fire, and toward the point of greatest danger. Giving one glance at what seemed the only outlet, I gave my horse an unusually vigorous touch with the spur, by way of bringing him to his senses, and, holding a tight rein, dashed out on the open field. There was a deep ditch and a rail fence right ahead. Could my noble gray leap both? Leap he must, or break his own neck, and mine, too, perhaps. He nerved himself for the leap, cleared the ditch handsomely—a few more steps, and he bounded over the fence like a deer. Then came the trying moment. The enemy had partially broken our lines, and came tearing down like demons, sweeping the open field with grape and canister, and, as I rode through it, it was plowed up by the shot, which, as it fell, threw up clouds of dust. By the protecting care of a merciful God we passed through the fiery ordeal unscathed; but nothing else than his Almighty arm saved us. Some of our men, who saw the whole affair, expressed their wonder at the escape, and made free to insinuate, by way of friendly advice, that the chaplain had better "keep out of the muss."

The whole thing seemed to occupy but a moment, so rapid were the changes. But it was a critical moment. The balance seemed poised. Our lines had been partially broken by the massing of the enemy's troops, and they were following up their advantage by a deadly and destructive fire. But regiment after regiment of our brave boys rushed forward, with loud cheers and streaming banners, toward the breach, and, in a short time, sent the foe reeling back. As I write these lines, I can hardly imagine the fact mentioned to have been any thing like a living reality—an actual occurrence—but rather some wild dream, the remembrance of which still haunts me.

Turchin's Brigade.

Meanwhile our entire brigade, under the gallant Turchin, was hotly engaged. The Thirty-sixth and Ninety-second Ohio were on the left, as well as the Eighteenth Kentucky. The Eleventh was on the right. The rebel force was so sheltered by dense woods that they could make attacks almost with impunity; as they had their sharp-shooters, armed with long-range rifles, posted in the trees, they picked off both officers and men with great rapidity. The Eleventh lay for some time exposed to the galling fire of rebel skirmishers and sharp-shooters, till at last they could stand it no longer, and begged permission to clear the woods with the bayonet. Colonel Lane finally gave the order, when the men sprang forward with a cheer, and charged upon the rebels as they lay under cover of the woods, driving them half a mile, and capturing, at the same time, a number of prisoners. In this charge the color-bearer, Sergeant Peck, was wounded. His brother, Lieutenant Peck, instantly seized the colors, and led the line in the most gallant manner. In a short time the rebels attempted to drive in the right of the division, but, by a brilliant movement, they were again driven back at the point of the bayonet. In this charge, Colonel Jones, of the Thirty-sixth Ohio, was killed, and Colonel Fearing, of the Ninety-second, and Major Adney, of the Thirty-sixth Ohio, severely wounded. Another attempt was made to break our lines just about dark, but the enemy failed to gain any advantage, although the attacks were made by greatly superior numbers.

And so the day of battle wore on, till the shadows of evening began to fall upon the wooded slopes and deep ravines of Chickamauga and Mission Ridge, revealing, in more startling vividness, the sharp flash of the musket, and the dull, red glare of the cannon. Thousands of the good and brave and noble had fallen, and were bleeding, fainting, dying, on that field of fierce, fiery strife. Human bosoms had been bared to the incessant storm of shot and shell that had been howling and crashing from early morn till the shadows of night hid the combatants from each other! Many a noble-hearted boy, upon whose head a mother's hand had been placed in blessing, as she gave him up, tremblingly and tearfully, for her country and humanity, had fallen that day, whose last thoughts of earth were of mother and home, and whose last whisper, let us hope, was a whisper of Christ and heaven. Many a loving husband and father, as he lay there, mangled and dying, thought of dear wife and children, and home, sweet home, and mingled their names with that of the Savior as he closed his eyes in death! But, alas! alas! painful thoughts crowd upon the mind when contemplating the sad scenes of the battlefield, and the question arises—How many went into that conflict thoughtless and godless—without the peace and joy of salvation or the hopes of heaven? Alas! the answer to such a question is one which is painful in the extreme to him who looks upon human destiny in the light of revealed truth, and in reference to the eternity of moral character.

Night on the Field.

Night, chilly and disagreeable, drew on apace, and the dark shadows came down alike on friend and foe. The wounded were taken to the rear as rapidly as possible, and during the entire night lanterns glimmered over the field, showing where the work of relieving sufferers was going on, while, at the same time, the train of ambulances was kept going to and fro, continually. As I walked among the wounded and dying, trying to relieve where relief was available, and comfort the dying where death was inevitable, I felt unutterably sad. The confusion, dust, and noise, the trampling of horses, the rumbling of heavy artillery, the groaning of the wounded and dying, the camp-fires burning dimly, all made a scene never to be forgotten. It was a bleak, cold night. The poor sufferers, as they lay covered with dust and blood, shivered in the cold night-wind which swept over the field, and my very heart ached for many of the poor fellows, who shook as if in an ague fit, while having their wounds dressed. Many of them were so chilled with the cold wind, and from loss of blood, that their teeth rattled against the tin cups from which they drank the warm coffee with which they were supplied.

The hospital arrangements were somewhat imperfect, so far as supplies were concerned; and blankets or coverings of any kind (aside from what some of the men had themselves), could not be found to cover the cold and bleeding soldiers. As the night advanced, large fires were kindled at every field hospital, warm tea and coffee prepared, and every one made as comfortable as possible under the circumstances. When I had worked as long as it was possible to do, and exhausted nature could stand it no longer, I lay down myself to rest, surrounded by the groaning wounded and by the silent dead! I passed a night of misery. Cold and weary, as I had never been before, crushed in spirit by the terrible scenes of wounding and death among which I had moved that day, and by which I was yet surrounded, no covering with which to keep warm, nor a quiet place in which to rest, I could only think of the thousands and tens of thousands who were in agony all around me, and I thanked God fervently for the blessings and mercies of the day; and, taking some precious texts as the best of pillows for a weary head and aching heart, fell asleep.

SABBATH AT CHICKAMAUGA.

An anxious council of war was held at "Widow Glen's" house on Saturday night. "Each corps commander reported that every brigade had been in that day's fight, that the troops had acted finely; but all agreed that, in every severe attack made upon us, we had been invariably outnumbered. It was plain that the next day's contest must be for the preservation of the army, and the holding of Chattanooga."* The general plan adopted for the second day's battle was read to the assembled corps commanders, and the orders connected therewith were issued to the army at one o'clock on Sabbath morning. At early dawn, General Rosecrans rode along the front, inspecting the lines and so disposing of the troops as to resist the combined efforts that would be made to destroy the Union army. Second only to this, Bragg's great aim was to gain Chattanooga.

The Sabbath's sun finally shone out clear and beautiful above the smoke that lay like a pall over the valley. It was expected the enemy would attack as soon as day dawned, but, with the exception of occasional picket firing, it was eight o'clock before the battle was renewed. The conflict of the day opened, as was expected, on the extreme left, and the determination of the rebels to overwhelm Thomas, who was holding the approaches to Chattanooga, was soon apparent, for they hurled their massed columns against him with the greatest fury and desperation. During the night, our troops had thrown up temporary breastworks of logs and stones, and, as they kept behind these, or lay on the ground, rising up only to pour their volleys into the attacking columns, the rebel loss was very great. By ten o'clock, the fierce roar of battle was at its hight, and the conflict raged with terrible fury along the whole lines, but on the left and left center the contest was the fiercest and most determined. Longstreet's men, as they came up in solid columns, flushed

* Rosecrans's Report.

with the hope of crushing the Western troops, would exultingly shout, "We are not conscripts!" to which the reply was given:

"You are not fighting Eastern store-clerks."

"We are Longstreet's troops!" shouted some of them, in front of the Eleventh and Thirty-sixth—to which our men replied, with a derisive yell:

"Who drove you at South Mountain? We are the boys that drove you there, and we'll do it again!"

At about midday, matters were so serious on the left and center, that division after division had to be sent to succor Thomas, who was contending against fearful odds. Indeed, the army at large, in order to meet the massed columns of the enemy, which were being rapidly concentrated against Thomas, had to be continually closed up on the left. It was during one of those movements that a mistake occurred which came nigh resulting in the ruin of the Union army. "Orders were dispatched," says Rosecrans, in his clear report, "to General Wood to close up on Reynolds, and word was sent to General Thomas that he should be supported, even if it took away the whole corps of Crittenden and McCook." General Wood, overlooking the orders to close up on General Reynolds, passed to the rear of General Brannan, who was somewhat in the rear of Reynolds, which left a gap in the battle line between Thomas and McCook. The right flank of Reynolds's division was thus exposed, as was, also, McCook's left. Through this open gap the rebels poured with deafening cheers, carrying all before them. The writer was close by at the time this scene occurred, and, assuredly, it looked forbidding enough.

The first intimation that Reynolds had of the state of affairs, was a destructive cross-fire from the right, and, finally, solid shot and shell from the rear. All seemed to be lost; for the enemy, taking advantage of the gap made in the battle-front, had not only crushed Crittenden, and swept back the few brigades that were sent in to stay the torrent of disaster, but they were massing in the rear of Reynolds. The entire corps held its own bravely, but it could hardly be expected to continue to do so for any length of time, for the whole rebel army was now hurled fiercely and exultantly against it. Prompt, fearless, decided action was now necessary, or disaster would be inevitable. The ammunition and supply-trains were exposed, two of the gaps in the ridge were open to the Chattanooga road, on which our trains were now moving, and the rebel torrent must be stayed, at whatever cost. Reynolds was ordered to disperse the force massing in the rear. Their artillery was already in position, and was rapidly thinning our ranks. The sharp-shooters in the trees were picking off our men with impunity, insomuch that nearly one half of Company D, of the Eleventh, were killed or wounded in the space of half an hour. General Turchin's brigade, consisting of the Eleventh, Thirty-sixth, and Ninty-second Ohio, and Eighteenth Kentucky, was formed for a charge on the massed forces in the rear, the infantry and cavalry of which could be distinctly seen advancing. The order was given to march by the rear rank—"about face"—and the brigade, starting on the double-quick, was hurled in a bayonet-charge against the enemy with almost as much precision and order as if it had been on dress parade, and all this, too, while the very air seemed darkened with the missiles of death, the ground shaking as if in the throes of an earthquake from the incessant roar and crash of artillery and the rolling rattle of musketry. As Colonel Lane remarked, it seemed as if the explosions "raised the hats off our heads." The concussion of the air was painful, the noise so deafening that orders could not be heard, and the smoke and dust in such dense clouds that objects at a distance could hardly be seen. General Reynolds, waving his sword, led the charge in person. Calm, reverent, and happy as a Christian, he joined us in our devotions on the morning the battle opened. A tear of religious emotion trickled down his weather-beaten cheek, while a fervent Amen! that thrilled every heart, burst from his lips, and now, bravely as a Christian soldier, he led his troops in that desperate charge—the most desperate made on that bloody field. On the left and front and rear the enemy was in massed line of battle; but away went the Ohio boys, charging bayonet back on the massed columns of the enemy, which had closed around them. Onward they rushed, like a resistless wave of gleaming steel, cheering and yelling as they charged on the dense masses of traitors who hoped to stay them. Their charge was irresistible—so thought the rebels—as onward and onward they rushed through one line of battle, a second, a third, and a part of a fourth, till they pierced the entire battle-line of seven deep, brought off a number of prisoners, charged on two batteries on their way out, brought off one gun, and gained a position on Mission Ridge.

But the work was not yet accomplished. In the

terrible noise, and amid the smoke and dust, orders could not be heard, and, before reaching one of the spurs of Mission Ridge, the brigade got divided—one part following Turchin on the left, and the other Reynolds on the right, neither party being aware of the fate of the other. On coming to a halt, the party under Reynolds, comprising portions of the Eleventh, Thirth-sixth, and Ninety-second Ohio Regiments, was re-formed, and measures taken to reach the main body of the army. On marching forward—it was now nearly dusk—the junction of Ringgold and Rossville roads was reached. There was, at this point, a dense forest of heavy timber, rendered still more dense by a heavy undergrowth, which rendered any further movement very critical. General Reynolds, accompanied by two orderlies, went forward himself and reconnoitered the ground. He discovered a heavy force of the enemy in position there, and any further progress in that direction had to be abandoned. This portion of the brigade was marched back a little distance, to a log-house, which had been used as a hospital, and General Reynolds and Colonel Lane held a consultation, the result of which was, that it was thought better to halt a short time there and wait further developments. While performing the movements indicated, artillery had been frequently firing upon our brigade from the left, and it was thought that these being rebel guns, we were still surrounded.

The smoke was hanging heavily over the valley, and now the shades of evening were drawing on, and distant objects were getting more and more obscured. Presently, amid the rifted smoke, and away on a higher ridge, a flag is seen streaming in the wind, but its color can hardly be made out. A man is seen cautiously approaching, gun in hand. He is one of our men; for his uniform, although dusty and soiled, is "Union blue."

"Whose lines are those?"

"Ours!" is the welcome answer, which makes a hundred hearts leap with joy and pride.

In a few minutes the weary but dauntless band reach the outer picket-line, and there, clear, beautiful, glorious in the evening breeze, and amid the smoke and dust, floats the dear old flag! Here is the rest of the division, thought to have been captured! Cheer after cheer goes up, in welcome to the smaller band just come in, and who were also thought to have been either killed or captured. What a hearty shaking of hands! What a trickling of joyous tears over weather-beaten, powder-stained cheeks! What expressions of joy and gladness burst from manly bosoms! O, that was a moment and those were scenes that will never be forgotten!

Here were Granger's troops, that had come up to stay the rebel torrent, and prevent the enemy from overwhelming Thomas's right. The lines were again formed, Thomas presented an unbroken and defiant front, McCook and Crittenden had swept around between Mission Ridge and Lookout—McCook's troops, or part of them, had been thrown across the narrow valley to protect our trains sweeping around into Chattanooga—signal rockets were going up through and above the heavy clouds of smoke and dust, the last gun from Granger's batteries growled a fiercely defiant salute, and night—silent, solemn night—came down upon that battle-swept field, on which were lying twenty thousand bleeding men!

And so ended the battle of Chickamauga.

The rebel army had possession of the field, they largely outnumbered the Union forces, they fought upon ground of their own choosing, they had the advantage of a serious mistake on the part of a division commander, but, to all intents and purposes, they lost the objects for which they fought so desperately—the destruction of the Army of the Cumberland, and the possession of Chattanooga. Neither of these they gained; for Thomas, with his veteran troops, held the rebels in check, and, like a lion at bay, fought them, without giving an inch, till, on the Tuesday following, he fell back to the rest of the army, to an intrenched position around Chattanooga.

CHAPTER XXIV.

WILDER'S BRIGADE AND LONGSTREET'S VETERANS—WAR IS TERRIBLE—HAPPY MEETINGS AFTER THE BATTLE.

WILDER'S BRIGADE—A TERRIBLE SCENE.

WILDER'S mounted brigade was stationed in a strip of woods near to the open field spoken of in a former chapter, and which will be ever fresh in the writer's memory as a scene of personal exposure and deliverance on that fearful battlefield. At the time when the line was temporarily broken, Longstreet's men were seen tearing along through this open field, yelping and yelling—it was always easy to distinguish the loud, prolonged cheer of the Union boys from the short, sharp yelp of the rebels—as they came up in solid column. Wilder threw volley after volley into their very faces, which was continued without interruption—his men being armed with the Spencer rifle, or seven-shooter. He also opened his battery upon them, every gun being double-shotted with deadly canister and grape. The effect was terrific. The head of the massed column wavered and fell like the grass before the mower's scythe, and seemed to melt away or sink into the ground. The reader may form an idea of the fearful slaughter, when it is stated that, although the columns kept moving on across the open field, those in front being pushed on by those behind, yet the head of the constantly advancing column came no nearer. It seemed to dwindle, as if the breath of the destroying angel continually swept it away!

Across the field ran a deep ditch or gully about five feet wide, and toward this the rebels rushed as a ready means for protection from the incessant storm of bullets and canister that drove remorselessly into their very faces, and which would form, also, a rifle-pit, from which they might, with more safety, return the fire. In a few minutes this deep ditch was crowded full, and from it began to come sheets of flame and showers of lead. Quicker than it can be described in writing, Wilder wheeled two pieces of artillery, double-shotted with the deadly canister, to the mouth or entrance of the ditch, and poured volley after volley along its entire length. The missiles of death swept through the struggling mass from end to end. The effect of this was terrible! Comparatively few—it has been said not more than a dozen—escaped from that slaughter-pen alive.

A rebel sergeant, who, with his entire relief-squad of a dozen men, came into our lines, stated, as a well-known fact, that Longstreet took into battle on Saturday twenty-five thousand men, and came out on Sunday with eleven thousand. This shows how greatly the rebels suffered.

Nothing but the majesty of law, the necessity of defending righteous government from the assaults of traitors, and the securing of God-honored and God-honoring peace to ourselves and posterity, as well as freeing our land from the foul misrule of slavery—nothing but these could ever reconcile any humane heart to such fearful scenes of wholesale destruction and death.

Happy Meetings.

None but those in the army know how thrillingly tender, yet manly and noble, are the meetings of comrades after a battle. Some have fallen, to rise no more till the judgment of the Great Day. Some are wounded; others are missing. I will never forget the impressive meeting of the survivors of the Eleventh, after those two days of terrible fighting. It had been reported that the chaplain was captured. This came twice being pretty near the truth. It was also stated that he had been seen on the field wounded—his face bleeding. This last was true, but not serious enough for even this hint. It may just be added that the colonel and chaplain had quite a happy reunion; for each had been informed of the other's being killed or captured on Sabbath evening, and, of course, they were rejoiced to meet each other again, through God's blessing, safe and sound. And the brave men—dearer to me, seemingly, than ever—for whose safety I could only pray while they fought for home and liberty on that dread field, grasped my hand, as they clustered round me, with a fervor that could not be mistaken. And with what quiet, enthusiastic earnestness the men spoke of the noble manner in which they had been led by their brave and skillful commander, and how that he had earned a soldier's name and a patriot's honor during those two terrible days! And I make this record here, and now, of the great gratification it afforded me to hear such eulogies from those who had nothing to gain or lose by making them. They were spontaneous, earnest expressions of confidence in one whom they had learned to esteem and honor—the opinions they had formed of one who had not only shown himself an unswerving patriot, but had done all he could to promote the moral and religious welfare of the regiment. And such expressions were mutual. Members of the different companies spoke of their company officers with the highest admiration, while company commanders did the same of their men. Very frequently did Colonel Lane make reference, in the warmest terms of commendation, to the heroic conduct of every man in the regiment. Lieutenant-colonel Street, a brave and efficient officer, was too ill to be on the field; but, although scarcely able to sit up, he made his way to the front on Wednesday. He had to return, however, being too feeble for duty. Colonel Lane spoke frequently, also, of the cool bravery of Major Higgins, and of the daring deeds performed by several of the commissioned officers. To hear such expressions of mutual respect and esteem from those who had stood side by side in the fierce conflict, was both gratifying and impressive.

Frightened and False Correspondents.

Nothing so much surprised and chagrined the army who fought so nobly at Chickamauga, as the glaringly false statements, made by some army correspondents, to the effect that Rosecrans was defeated. The sinner above all sinners, in this particular, was the swift-footed, evil-omened correspondent of the *New York Herald*. At the time when the lines were broken, and the effort was made to concentrate on Chattanooga, there was, as might be expected, not only confusion, but even somewhat of a panic, among those of the troops belonging to Crittenden and McCook that had been so badly crushed by the solid rebel columns pouring in on the right of Reynolds, and there was also a great panic among some of the teamsters. This was of very short duration, however, for the various trains were got into good order, and conducted rapidly toward Chattanooga. As the whole aspect of a battle-field may change in a few minutes, causing corresponding changes in the disposition of the immense and valuable wagon-trains of an army, it will be seen at once that, where prompt, energetic, and rapid movements are necessary, among some seven or eight hundred wagons and three or four hundred ambulances, it is the easiest thing in the world to get up a panic. The fact that the immense trains were in some danger of being captured, when the lines were broken, and the no less important fact that rapid movements of troops might be prevented by their being in the way, called for quick work on the part of all connected with them. Of course, at the first it was a rush and crush and jam—a helter-skelter race, as if each teamster was a "Tam o' Shanter," with a witch, or the de'il himself—horns and hoofs and all—hanging on by the tail of each individual mule. This state of things lasted about an hour, and might have led to serious results, but one of General Rosecrans's aids rode up to a teamster, and, drawing his revolver, ordered him to stop, or he would shoot him as dead as a herring. This brought the stampede to a close, and in a short time the entire mass was moving as orderly, though not as quietly, as a procession of Quakers.

But, on seeing the first advance of the retreating teamsters, it seems that the *Herald's* correspondent hastened away from the rear—not the field proper, for no one on the field, unless very badly frightened, could have written such dispatches—composed, as they were, of mingled truth and error, misrepresentation and contradiction—as he did for the edification and especial delight of hungry Copperheads and lynx-eyed speculators—away he hastened and telegraphed that Rosecrans was virtually defeated, and, in a word, that every thing had gone to "smash," even the government dispatches, for they "were, in the main, totally false!" Such were the doleful tidings that this panic-stricken, swift-footed correspondent telegraphed to New York, taking care, in the mean time, to have his effusions published simultaneously in the Louisville and Cincinnati papers! He got his news of disaster and defeat from a dozen or two frightened teamsters, perhaps a few negroes, who were probably as demented as himself, and possibly from those who were cut off from their commands. But even this was enough for a willing messenger of evil tidings. Elections were coming off—Vallandighamers in Ohio were somewhat crest-fallen, Copperheadism had evidently gone down in the political market, the Peace-at-any-price men were getting out of date, the pro-slavery philippics of the *Herald* and *World* were getting considerably neutralized by the logic of events; and, as dying men are said to grasp at straws, this correspondent, with feverish eagerness, grasped at the disaster on the right—not knowing or caring to know that the heroic Thomas was holding the rebels at bay—and kindly offered it as a life-buoy to save the sinking wreck of Copperhead treason.

I will just state here that, although I was engaged attending to the wounded on that part of the field where our lines were broken, and where there was the greatest apparent panic, I acknowledge that there was nothing to give any countenance to the terribly gloomy picture drawn by this army correspondent. True, I came pretty near paying dearly for my temerity in remaining so long at that point. I had left but a few minutes, when that part of the field was swept by the left wing of the rebel army, and it was only after I had crossed a ravine that I saw the rapid change that had taken place, for I was scarcely inside our own lines. Several surgeons were taken prisoners at this point, and quite a number of the wounded fell into the hands of the enemy; but there were no such terrible things as represented by the correspondent in question.

God's Providence in the Battle of Chickamauga.

If ever there was a time when the Almighty Ruler of earth and heaven manifested his providential dealings on the field of battle, that time was Sabbath, the 20th of September, when the slaveholding Confederacy hurled nearly its whole military strength on the

Army of the Cumberland, and made the most desperate of efforts to crush it at one blow. That the plan of the rebel leaders was so to mass their troops in overwhelming numbers, and strike Rosecrans before he could either contract his lines or receive reinforcements, and, by mere force of numbers, either annihilate his army or compel him to surrender, is too obvious now for any one to doubt. If the Lord had not favored the cause of Truth and Freedom at that time, humanly speaking, Rosecrans's army would have been so seriously crippled, if not destroyed, as to have made that campaign but one grand disaster. The greater part of Lee's army, under Longstreet and Hill, together with the fragments of Pemberton's Vicksburg army, under Johnston, Buckner's troops, from East Tennessee, and thousands of the prisoners paroled by Grant, were all brought together to reinforce Bragg, so as to make the battle of Sabbath decisive. The intention was to render failure an impossibility. But, although Rosecrans's slender battle-lines had to receive the shock of columns of regiments and brigades, and, in some instances, even of whole divisions, and so continuous and terrible were the onsets that defeat seemed inevitable, yet, essentially, the little army of Freedom's champions was victorious—victorious to a degree that struck terror still deeper into the hearts of the rebels. It is not necessary to repeat here what has already become history; but there is one item of history not generally known. When it is considered what an immensely superior force Bragg had to hurl against the Union army, it is a matter of wonder why he did not open the battle at an earlier hour on Sabbath morning. All expected the attack to commence by daylight; but hour after hour elapsed before he moved, and it was nearly nine o'clock before the battle fairly opened. Why was this? Major-General Bishop Polk, who was in command of the extreme rebel right, was ordered to attack our extreme left at daylight on Sabbath morning. Before giving the orders to move, he discovered that his troops were not in a proper position, and that, through some mistake, a whole division *overlapped the battle-line, and that, if the battle opened, that entire division must be inevitably slaughtered.* It took several hours for the rebels to rectify this mistake, but they were precious hours for the Union army.

CHAPTER XXV.

WAR IS DREADFUL—BRIGHTER DAYS FOR OUR NATION AND THE WORLD—SLAVERY'S CURSE.

Do you say, dear reader, that war is dreadful? It is dreadful; so much so that no humane heart can love it for its own sake. And it is not a pleasant task to write about war, especially to those who have seen it in all its grim, ghastly realities. As I have been penning these few simple sketches of army scenes and incidents, it has often been with very sad and solemn feelings. Especially has this been the case when writing about the battles themselves, and the scenes connected with them. It was with no love for war's dark records that this work was undertaken; neither was it from a love of describing the sad scenes of the battlefield. Other, and it is humbly hoped higher, motives have prevailed in the sketching of these LIGHTS AND SHADOWS OF ARMY LIFE.

It is rather a sad task than otherwise to write about what one has seen of suffering and death. It is enough for me that I have seen the stern, the fearfully stern visage of War; that while with steady hand, perhaps, but with throbbing heart, I have bound up the torn and mangled limbs of the fallen brave, or spoken of Christ and salvation to those whose eyes were growing dim in death; it is enough that I have been amid the horrid crash and rush and roar of battle, as the gleaming columns surged to and fro like the angry waves of ocean—it is enough for me, without attempting to portray the whole on paper, or enter into minute details which properly belong to the historian! Rather, much rather, would I try to paint any stray sunbeam of hope and comfort, Christ and heaven, which may have glimmered forth from amid the dark and angry clouds, and lighted up, here and there, with the light of Christian hope and joy, some sad and gloomy scene of bivouac and battle! And yet, I would by no means have it understood that I have looked upon the battlefield, with all its tragic accompaniments and consequences, with the eye of a mere sentimentalist, or with the feelings of one who only hears the cry of the patient, instead of seeing the deeply-seated cancer which the surgeon's knife is removing. We ought to look upon every American battlefield as the arena on which—not men, but ideas; not physical forces, but great moral principles—have been, and still are, contending for supremacy. We ought to realize that, beyond and above the angry clouds, and the lurid lightnings, and the ghastly features of the mere material scenery, the eye of faith can behold the bow of peace spanning the heavens of a redeemed and sanctified country—a country redeemed from the withering curse of human bondage, and sanctified by the blood of Freedom's martyrs. But, with all of this to nerve the hand and strengthen the heart, I envy not the feelings of that man who can behold, with stolid indifference or philosophic calmness, the dread carnage of the battlefield. The bursting shell scatters death and destruction just as surely, and the solid shot and grape and canister sweep the ranks of living men into one great livid mass of quivering, mangled humanity just as remorselessly, and the saber and bayonet cut and thrust just as keenly and mortally, in a holy as in an unholy cause. It is war; and war is dreadful, view it as we may. But, O, if God himself, as the great and righteous Ruler of the Universe, is bringing about a great and glorious revolution in our suffering country, and in the world at large, by which the tide-wave of human progress, human liberty, and human happiness shall roll onward with majestic sweep, and carry upon its bosom blessings to every shore, and the peaceful banner of the Cross shall be unfurled in every land, and wars and tumults shall forever cease, then we can feel that our national tribulation has not been in vain, and that a nation's heroes have not bled and died for nought!

Dark Scenes—Nameless Crimes.

Man may commit crimes that man dare not describe; and society may become so corrupt that only an inspired pen may safely expose and reprove its moral hideousness. There may be such a state of morals existing in communities, that it may even be "a shame to speak of those things which are done of them in secret." Sometimes very salutary lessons may be gained by simply looking at the sad wrecks of humanity which cluster around the purlieus of vice, while it might be morally dangerous to enter such dens of iniquity, and explore their dark, mysterious chambers of vice, which are reeking with moral foulness, and which pour out on society the virus of physical and moral leprosy.

A statement of the fearful results of what the fashionable world calls "an intrigue—an affair of the heart"—but which the law of God denounces in plain, unmistakable language, and threatens with fearful penalties, may have a decidedly good effect, while to open the secret chambers and expose the sensual imagery of the libertine would be pernicious in the extreme. For these reasons, and for others, the history of slavery will never be written; its darkest pictures will never be painted; its more fearful and hideous secrets will never be revealed. Not only is it utterly impossible to describe slavery as it is, but, perhaps, it is wise not to make the attempt. A better reason could not be given than that contained in the remark made by Lieutenant McAbee to a couple of slaveholding ladies. With much hauteur of manner, mock delicacy, and seeming surprise at the ignorance and audacity of a Federal officer daring to speak against the pet institution of rebeldom, one of them said:

"It is only because of your low Yankee breeding and ignorance of Southern institutions, that you talk against slavery. You have given a number of reasons for denouncing what you do n't know any thing about. Have you nothing better to say?"

"Madam," said the lieutenant, who had been most polite but firm in his remarks, "Madam, the one other great reason I would urge against slavery is one which no gentleman will name in the presence of ladies—one which every Southern lady of true womanly feeling should blush to think of; but which she must know is part of the institution itself, and which has undermined domestic honor, purity, and peace. My respect for woman forbids me saying more."

The shaft went home. The ladies blushed, then grew pale, and blushed again. A hint was enough; they felt it was too true, and they instantly dropped the subject.

Wesley's definition of slavery is at once brief, truthful, and expressive; it requires no addition, it can not be improved: "THE SUM OF ALL VILLAINIES." There, you have it in a nutshell.

As a mere matter of policy, the slaveholding oligarchy of the South could not have done a more foolish act than to rebel against the Federal Government. It is as if a band of assassins, robbers, counterfeiters, and swindlers were to throw open the doors of their secret dens, and, with insolent sneer, invite the world to walk in, with lighted torch, and scrutinize every nook and corner, examine every blood-stained weapon of death and every implement of robbery, and drag forth into the light of day such evidences of crime as would excite at once the wonder and loathing of all coming ages.

The Church of Christ, assuredly, fell fearfully in the snare of Satan when she took to her bosom, and protected by the broad shield of her good name, the slave-owner whose merchandise was slaves and souls of men! Away with all cant about Christian slaveholders! Christian slaveholders! As well talk about honest thieves, benevolent murderers, loyal traitors, and pious devils. The one is no more absurd and self-contradictory than the other; and had it not been for a time-serving ministry, corrupt political platforms, and a venal press, the absurdity would never have been palmed on the Christian world as a Bible truth.

One good result of this war, however, is, that like a mighty plowshare, it has been driving remorselessly into and under the very foundations of slavery, and laying bare its ramifications of unheard-of and indescribable wickedness, its fiendish malignity, its lust and brutality, that the world might see the vile system as it is, and execrate it as it deserves. The work is not accomplished yet; it is but fairly commenced—scarcely more. But if the few furrows already turned up have made such revelations of the substratum, what will be the sum total when the whole field of Southern society, with its habits, customs, plans, and purposes, shall be plowed up and laid bare? What fearful revelations will then be made! How dark the records of crime that will then be exposed to the gaze of an astonished world! What a ghastly caricature of civilization, refinement, and religion will then be uncovered! And until a complete overturning of Southern society is accomplished, and a full revelation of the mysteries of its habits and customs are made, the history of this rebellion, in the full sense of the term, can not be written. Until then such efforts are comparatively premature. The keenest observers can not see clearly; the profoundest thinkers are waiting for more light. Not only must the smoke of battle be cleared away, the passions of conflicting interests be subdued, and the bias of political opinion be corrected;

but from the dark and secret chambers of rebeldom itself must be dragged forth the fearful records of fraud, falsehood, perjury, and treason, which for long years have been accumulating, and which will form the blackest page of history the world has ever read. The plowshare must be driven deeper yet, the entire social system of the South overturned and exposed; then, and not till then, may the historian seize his pen for a full and complete history of the "Great Rebellion."

Impenitence

In my efforts to minister to the physical wants of the suffering, I came to a rebel soldier mortally wounded. His countenance wore that ashy pallor peculiar to those who are wounded in the bowels. He was shivering with cold and loss of blood. His garments were soaking wet, but with that humanity which I am proud to record concerning our army, a heavy, double United States blanket was thrown over him.

"Would you like something to eat?" I said to him—"a warm drink, such as a little beef soup or hot coffee?"

"I would like something warm to drink," said he, shivering as he spoke, "for I am cold."

I brought some nice hot coffee to him, but, after taking a sip or two, he declined it, saying he was very sick, and in much pain. I asked where his home was. He replied, "In Pike County, Georgia." After examining his wound, I told him, as kindly as possible, that there was little or no hope of his recovery, and that it was his duty to look to God in this the hour of his extremity. Notwithstanding I tried to be as kind and soothing as possible, he seemed to resist my well-meant endeavors in behalf of his spiritual state. To my statement that he could not possibly live but for a short time—that even now he was dying, and that I spoke to him not as an enemy to insult him, but as a friend to warn him—he replied, "He would not die, but if he did, he reckoned 't would be all right." Dying as he was, he seemed to take special pains to show his hatred. He ordered me, in a surly manner, to place some water near him—it was all he wanted. I got a cup of water, drew the blanket closer around him, and asked if I could do any thing more for him, but he only answered me with a growl, and treated me much as he might have done a dog. Near him lay two other wounded rebel soldiers, one of whom was too weak to say much, but the other spoke kindly, but reprovingly, to his dying comrade. Every thing I did for them they accepted kindly, and expressed their thankfulness in a way not to be misunderstood. One of them—the weakest—in answer to my inquiry as to whether he would not wish something to eat, replied "He was very cold, and would be glad of some hot coffee." On presenting it to him, his looks, more than his words, told his surprise and gratitude.

And here I wish to record a fact against all the malicious reports and complaints of rebels in arms, as well as their sympathizers everywhere, that, during all my experiences on the battlefield and in the hospital, both East and South-west—in the Army of the Potomac, in the Kanawha Valley, and in the Army of the

Cumberland—I have never seen or known a single wounded rebel soldier insulted or injured after falling into the hands of the Union soldiers. I noticed but one instance where a rebel prisoner was insulted—at least he thought so. It was on the Saturday of the Chickamauga battle, and was on this wise:

Close by a little clump of bushes, and sheltered from the missiles thrown by their own army, were clustered a few rebel prisoners. Among them was a short, dumpy fellow, whose physiognomy was decidedly Hibernian. Even his gray uniform and unkempt hair could not make him one of the chivalry.

"Whose division do you belong to," asked our surgeon, as we passed the group.

"Faith an' I belong to Gineral Johnston's divasion—an' he's a gintleman, too."

"What part of Ireland are you from?'

"Bedad, an' I came from Tipperary, so I did."

"How long since?"

"I left owld Ireland in April—yes"—scratching his head—"faith, an' I can hardly tell yez."

"What are you fighting against the United States Government for?" demanded the doctor, getting a little emphatic.

"Why, an' to be sure, aint I fighting for liberty? Haven't the Yankees been staling the nagurs, an' haven't—"

"Confound you, you Irish renegade! You can't get potatoes and salt herring enough in your own country to keep you from starvation, and a lot of you Catholic hounds—of course you're a Catholic—growl about your oppressions in Ireland, and come over here to fight for slavery! Confound you! the meanest negro in the South is better than you are! Shucks! I can stand a Southern rebel, but an Irish renegade and a home traitor would make a preacher swear. Would n't it, chaplain?"

The doctor's own Irish was up, for he had first seen the light of day somewhere between Bantry Bay and Inneshone—was an ardent Presbyterian of the Scotch school, and, like Luther, had a standing grudge against the Pope and the Devil.

"In de Cane-brake, dar."

A day or two after crossing Lookout Mountain, our division encamped, or rather bivouacked, on a rebel slaveholder's plantation. It was well stocked, apparently, with every thing necessary for a Georgia planter's ease and comfort, including slaves, black and white. There were immense fields of corn in a beautiful valley, sweet potatoes and yams in abundance, which tasted most deliciously when varied with hard-tack, as *we* can testify. The corn was excellent for succotash—so thought the soldiers, as they luxuriated in that celebrated dish. The corn was good for army mules, too, as, no doubt, they thought—that is to say, if mules do think. Shortly after we were fairly encamped, a stalwart negro came within the regimental lines, and seemed much interested in "Massa Linkum's sogers."

"Look ye'ah, boss," said he, bringing the words seemingly from the bottom of some empty hogshead, "look ye'ah—want ter know whar massa's mules are gone? Massa dun' no nuffin 'bout 'em, when sogers ober dar—but I know! Massa says dey is clar done gone ter *our* army; but I know whar dey clar done gone. Dey is in de cane-brake 'way ober dar, an' I'se sot on gwine dar wid you, ef you want 'em. Mighty peart mules, boss! Golly, won't ole massa swar when de mules clar done gone ter Linkum's army! But say, boss, dar 's a sick woman—she 's one of dem poor whites—chil'en sick, too; she 'most dyin'. 'Pears like 't would be better she *would* die; she 's a poor critter, boss—a poor critter—she came from ober Sand—her ole man 'scripted inter secesh army! Wall, yer see dat ar patch ob corn ober dar? Dat b'longs ter dat poor woman—she 's worked an' worked! Whew, how dat ar critter's worked on dat patch ob corn! Now, boss, 'pears like ef it would be mighty bad ter tech dat ar corn. Take massa's corn an' de mules, too, down in de cane-brake, but 'member dat ar poor critter. She lives in dat cabin ober dar."

By a somewhat circuitous route " de cane-brake ober dar" was reached, and a fine lot of sleek mules were confiscated to Massa Linkum. Not a single blade of the poor woman's corn was touched; but if the lordly slaveholder gleaned a few bushels on his immense plantation after our army foragers had passed over it, it was merely accidental. It may just be added that Dr. McCurdy and myself visited this poor family whose cause had been so ably pleaded by the noble-hearted negro, and we saw a scene of such abject poverty and misery that no language could do it justice. As a tribute to the humanity and benevolence of the Union soldiers, let me state here that, during the fifteen or twenty minutes we remained there, at least a dozen came in with coffee, sugar, bread, and salt—all out of their own rations—and before next morning enough was sent from our commissary to keep the family a month. The soldiers, whenever they killed beef, invariably sent a piece to the poor, pinched, poverty-stricken children. The Union soldier has no conscientious scruples in regard to slaveholders and their property. He has benevolent feelings, however, toward the poor, and scorns to touch the little property of the helpless and needy, and is ever ready to share the contents of his haversack with the destitute and afflicted.

Before we moved forward, the surgeon sent some medicines for the sick woman, and a few delicacies from our hospital supplies.

CHAPTER XXVI.

INCIDENTS ON THE FIELD—THE OLD FLAG YET—INDIVIDUAL FEELINGS AND EXPERIENCES—THE ARMY AT CHATTANOOGA—YANKEE DASH AND ENERGY—BROWN'S FERRY

AN AFFECTING SIGHT—"THE OLD FLAG YET."

ON Saturday, while our regiment was charging up a hill, an incident occurred which, for tragic pathos, has seldom been surpassed. At the foot of a tree, and among a large number of the dead and wounded of both armies, lay, or rather reclined against the tree, a wounded man in rebel uniform. He was seen to wave his hat as the regiment advanced, and it so happened that, as he lay in the direction of the center of the regiment, he was opposite our colors, which were floating in the breeze. As our regiment came up to where he lay, he shouted, feebly:

"Hurrah for the old flag yet!—the old flag yet!"

He was seen to be severely if not mortally wounded; his garments were soaked with blood, his face covered with dust, and his lips dry and parched.

"Hurrah for the old flag yet!" he again feebly shouted, and, as if by an instinctive impulse, Lieutenant Peck, who, at that moment, was carrying the flag, drooped it over the dying man, and as its battle-worn stripes and stars flashed before him, he muttered again:

"The old flag yet! the old flag yet!"

He grasped its silken folds, for a moment, as it swept over him; his lips were seen to move, but his words could not be heard. A sad, melancholy smile lit up his pale and haggard face, and, exhausted with the effort, he sank down, perhaps never to rise again. It was the work of a moment—one of the rapidly-shifting scenes in the horrid drama of war—but it was a scene never to be forgotten.

Individual Feelings and Experiences.

Through the kindness of the Rev. W. M. Cheever, of Troy, Ohio, the following letter was put into the author's hands. It was written by a brave, worthy young man, who was a member of Mr. Cheever's Church, and an officer in the Eleventh Ohio Regiment. It is inserted here for the purpose of showing what religious faith can do in the hour of danger and death.

"Chattanooga, Tenn., *October* 7, 1863.

"Rev. W. M. Cheever:

"*Dear Sir*—After a long interval that has elapsed since I last wrote, I again address you a few lines, that you may know that I have not entirely forgotten you, and to tell you of God's providence to me during the late battles. Although, perhaps, by this late date, you have become tired of listening to the many and varied and conflicting reports that have reached you, through the press and otherwise, yet there is much that transpires, through the long and tedious hours of the contest, that 'history and the world never know,' and which is only known and felt by individuals who take part in the engagement.

"On the evening of Friday, September 18, just as the sun had sunk behind the hills, our brigade was ordered on the march. To one accustomed to watch the movements of an army, the circumstances connected with this movement would have told what was in prospect; yet every one seemed cheerful, and appeared, apparently, unconscious and indifferent in regard to what the morrow might bring forth. A soldier never anticipates danger until near at hand. However, night and darkness soon enveloped our division within its murky folds, and the dust and smoke from burning fences thickened the atmosphere around us. These, together with a chilling wind, and the utter want of water, rendered our sufferings very severe. Yet we toiled on, step after step, until the gray of morn lightened the eastern horizon, when we came to a stand-still. The men, overcome with fatigue, sat down on the road, and were soon fast asleep. Stretched at full length in the dust, with a fence-rail or a stone for a pillow, we slept sweetly. An hour and a half thus passed, and the road was once more cleared. The command, 'Fall in!' brought the men again to their feet, and we moved forward feeling somewhat refreshed from our sleep. Every one began now to feel that we were nearing '*hallowed ground.*' Many long columns could be seen winding over hills, through woods and meadows, filling every road, as far as the eye could reach. At nine o'clock we halted in a field, that the men might shake the dust from their clothes and enjoy a moment's rest, as that was all that could be done, under the circumstances. Not a drop of water could be procured either to quench our thirst or bathe our faces, so we resolved to reconcile ourselves to the same fare for breakfast that we had for supper—that is, wait until the next meal. While halted here, we were warned by the thunder of a cannon that the 'ball' had opened for certain. After sending a detail, with the canteens, in search of water, we were soon on the march for the field of action. In a few minutes, we were formed in the edge of a wood, close by the battle-line, awaiting orders as to which part of the line we were to occupy. Here we could distinctly hear the incessant roar of small arms, and the deep booming of artillery, that told too well how fiercely the enemy contested our advance. Being halted a moment, oui brave and worthy chaplain, W. W. Lyle, rode to the front of our regiment, and spoke a few words of encouragement and cheer, that sent a thrill of joy and comfort vibrating through every heart, and which nerved and strengthened many a noble lad, whose cheek there paled at the thought of the conflict, to stand the shock in the fiercest of the fight, as the records of that hard-fought field will show. Never did I witness a scene more impressive than the services of that morning before going into action. Our regiment was drawn up in 'double columns, companies closed in mass;' our old colors, which had been through several battles, were unfurled to the breeze, and waved over the heads of a phalanx of tried men. Silence reigned in our ranks. Every one seemed to commune with his own heart—perhaps thinking of home and friends.

"As I looked down the line of faces, I could see firmness and determination depicted on each countenance. As our eyes met in silence, we could read each other's thoughts, and gather courage from their glance. While the chaplain lifted up his voice in prayer, a thousand heads bowed in reverence, and a thousand hearts mentally offered up an anxious and earnest appeal to their God for his guidance through the ordeal that awaited them. At a time like this, man thinks in earnest, not in jest. General Reynolds, our brave and gallant commander, happened to be present, and, after Brother Lyle closed the services, he rode up to him, and, with a tear in his eye, grasped his hand and shook it warmly. That hearty grasp of the hand and that earnest look expressed more there than tongue could tell.

"That scene, so simple but so sacred, so full of all that can move the heart, was often referred to during the battle. That a major-general, while busy posting his troops, and while the battle is already raging, should be seen pausing, for a moment, beside a portion of his troops engaged in prayer, joining with them himself, being so deeply affected as to shed a manly, Christian tear—shaking hands with the chaplain who led the devotions, thus acknowledging his own religious principles before the men he was about to lead in battle—had an effect that may be imagined, but can not be described. We always had confidence in the cool bravery of General Reynolds, but we had more at that moment than ever before. We would have followed him anywhere. But now we are off to the front to fight, and the chaplain, as usual, to care for our wounded. But a few moments, and we are mixed up, midst the noise and confusion, 'the hurrying to and fro,' with the horrid din that is usually found behind a battle-line. Passing through, we reach the front, form quickly into position, and advance, under fire of the enemy, to the assistance of our friends, and are just in time to save a regiment that has run out of ammunition. We pass over them, and can see the long lines of rebels advancing slowly and steadily, and, by this time, pouring a destructive fire into our ranks. 'FORWARD—DOUBLE-QUICK—CHARGE BAYONET! was shouted, when off darted the old Eleventh, with our battle-worn colors flung to the breeze. A 'Hurrah!' was shouted by hundreds of voices, that made the woods around us ring, and curdled the blood in the enemy's veins. The glittering steel was too much—it had its effect. The enemy wavers—they break, they run like sheep—they try to rally again, but fly as before! Dismay and terror seize them. Many fall by the unerring aim of our rifles—a complete rout ensues—the field is ours, and another star is added to our battle-flag! New lines are immediately formed, and the enemy appears again upon our front and left, more desperate than before. Again they are driven by the bayonet, and a second victory is won. So closed the day with us of Saturday's fight. Fresh troops are brought forward, and we retire, worn completely out. The water that was sent for in the morning comes up at this late hour, and is seized by famished men, and used with moderation in making coffee. This, together with a cracker, roasted or parched on a stick, formed the basis of our first meal in nearly thirty-six hours. God has, however, protected and favored us much. Only a *score* wounded and one killed from out our regiment! O, what fortitude God gave me in this hour to bear up under the fatigues and hardships of that night, with the prospects of a renewal of the terrible scenes in the morning! But, thanking him, with my whole heart, for his favors of to-day, and knowing in whom to trust on the morrow, I laid down on the battle-ground to rest my weary limbs—to sleep and dream—not of WAR, but of HOME. Saturday night passed as has many other nights of bivouac, and Sabbath morning came, at last, bright and glorious. Yes, the holy Sabbath came—but not with its cheering Sabbath bells—not with its happy rest and sacred privileges—but with scenes of horror, fields of carnage and blood; with the thunder of war, the groans of the wounded and dying, and with all that could be heaped in a day of fierce, deadly conflict! Buoyed up by the excitement, we again face the enemy—hold our position under a shower of Minié balls, grape, and canister. Many of our brave boys fall, yet we stand firm through the long and weary hours that pass so slowly. Our left and right are driven back time after time, until, finally, our flanks are entirely exposed; but we still hold our ground. Late in the afternoon, when we are surrounded, cut off, orders reach us, '*Cut through or surrender!*' We re-form, in a new position, while the enemy close in on all sides. The order is given by General Reynolds to move by the rear rank, and the startling words ring out, above the noise of battle, 'FORWARD—DOUBLE-QUICK—MARCH! CHARGE BAYONET!' Our men are falling at every step. Grape and canister are rained upon us—the very air seems black. 'Forward, 't is life or death! Forward! forward!' is the cry. The enemy give way before us. We are soon up to them. They cry for mercy, or attempt to escape, but we cut them down before us, and they give way in utter rout. 'Forward! forward!' driving them still, until we pass line after line, and we see our own men, and the Stars and Stripes, through the smoke and dust, to our left, and we bear off toward them. We are soon under the protection of their guns; and, with three hundred prisoners we have captured during our terrible dash through the rebel battle-lines, night thus closed our last great effort in the battle of Chickamauga. Our casualities are heavy; yet, through all this, God has spared our regiment very remarkably in comparison with others. O, how my heart goes out to Him, in humble gratitude, for bringing me safely through the terrors of this dreadful day without the slightest injury! . . .

"Yours, for God and our country, A. L. C."

The Army at Chattanooga—An Adroit Movement.

Although occupying what might be called an impregnable position, the Army of the Cumberland, as it lay at Chattanooga immediately after the battle of Chickamauga, was by no means in an enviable condition. Chattanooga is situated in a bend of the Tennessee River, and the army lay in intrenched positions across this bend, both flanks resting on the river—the left above, and the right below the town. The right flank rested on the Chattanooga Creek, near the base of Lookout Mountain, and where it empties into the Tennessee. The left rested on the Citico, above the city. The rebels held Lookout Mountain and Mission Ridge—their left resting on the Tennessee River, and their right on the ridge. They held all on the south side of the river, from Lookout to Bridgeport, and not only had possession of all the roads on that side of the river, but their sharp-shooters commanded the road on the north side also.

We had the gratification of watching the rebel engineers at work, day after day, busy constructing their works on both mountains, but especially on the northeastern face of Lookout. When they endeavored to push their works a little too close to Chattanooga Creek, our rifled thirty-two-pounders usually gave them a hint that we did not wish to cultivate any closer acquaintance. We had several strong works erected on our front, all of which were connected by a heavy line of rifle-pits, in addition to which were continuous lines of earth-works still further in front. The bulk of the army lay within these intrenchments, while strong picket-lines were maintained outside. The position was the strongest possible, while the facilities for still further adding to its strength were unlimited. There were not the slightest fears, therefore, so far as the mere holding of the place was concerned, if the army could only be supplied. This was the most serious feature of the whole, and caused the greatest anxiety in the army. If supplies could be thrown into Chattanooga, the Army of the Cumberland could defy the whole Confederacy. Toward the close of October, however, matters began to assume a very serious aspect so far as supplies were concerned. It was evident that a crisis was at hand, and something must be done to avert impending difficulties of the most serious nature.

The base of supplies was at Bridgeport and Stevenson, but the rebels had possession of the roads on the south side of the river, while their sharp-shooters commanded the road on the north side leading to Bridgeport, so that no supplies could be brought from below on either road. The supply-trains, therefore, had to be brought from Bridgeport round by way of Jasper and Dunlap, in the Sequatchie Valley, and over a steep, rugged pass of the Cumberland Mountains, a distance of sixty miles. By this time, heavy rains had set in, and the mountain streams, especially the Sequatchie, were swollen to such an extent as to impede the progress of the immense trains necessary to supply the army. Mules and artillery horses had been taken to the north side of the river, and sent into the different valleys, for sixty or seventy miles, in search of forage, while others had to die of starvation. The roads were getting impassable, trains were delayed, and the rations were becoming so reduced that the men were beginning to suffer from hunger. A single instance may be given by way of illustration. The Eleventh, as well as other regiments, went out one day on picket duty with empty haversacks. They had had no supper the previous evening; had no breakfast before going on duty; were on picket outside the intrenchments twenty-four hours, and came in again, and still nothing for breakfast. Under such circumstances, it was absolutely necessary to open the river as far down as possible, by driving the rebels from the north and west of Lookout.

There were two pontoon bridges thrown across the river, one at Chattanooga, the other a short distance below. The rebels attempted frequently to destroy these bridges by cutting logs and heavy timber, lashing them together, and setting them adrift from above, which, coming down on the swift current, would break the pontoons from their anchorage, and injure the bridges. Of course considerable timber, and even pontoons, would occasionally float down past the rebels at Lookout Point, the sight of which always gave them satisfaction. Frequently the rebels sent down in this manner very fine saw-logs, not many of which ever got further than Chattanooga. A short distance above the pontoons, a heavy boom was thrown across the river, and a detail from the pioneer corps was made to secure all the timber floated down, and which, of course, lodged against the boom. There were several saw-mills on the river bank, and they were kept busy at work sawing those very logs into planks suitable for boat-building purposes.

Under cover of the steep banks and bluffs, so as to be concealed from the rebel signal-corps, were soldier-mechanics, industriously at work building pontoons, making oars and boat-hooks, and fitting planks and string-pieces for bridges. Some houses were dismantled, the boards, rafters, and joists taken to the river bank, and, in a short time, a large number of pontoon-boats and barges, built from timber so conveniently furnished by the rebels themselves, were launched into the Tennessee River. One moonlight night, just hazy enough on the river to render objects at a distance somewhat indistinct, troops from Baird's and Reynolds's divisions were embarked in the pontoons, and, at a given signal, the whole were silently floated down the river. The oars, which were used just enough to make steerage-way, were muffled with pieces of tents and blankets. The men crouched as closely together as possible in the bottom of the pontoons, and carefully covered their muskets, lest they might be seen gleaming in the moonbeams. Orders were given that the utmost quietness must be maintained; no speaking above a whisper was to be allowed, and every man was to be ready for any emergency.

As it was necessary to run the fleet of pontoons, as much as possible, in the shadow of the woods and bluffs, they had to be floated close by the south bank, and, of course, under the very noses of Bragg's pickets.

As they floated past Lookout Point, our men could hear the rebel pickets talking to each other, and taking considerable comfort from the evidences they saw, indistinctly, on the river, of another break in the Yankee pontoon bridges.

"Why, Tom, look ye thar! Blamed ef that aint a pontoon!"

"Whar, Bill? Whar?"

"Why, don't yer see? Thar, in that streak o' dark under the bluff thar."

"Wall, now, so it is, by thunder! Come har, you 'uns back thar, and see another break. Har goes another Yankee pontoon bridge."

"Wall, now, ef it aint so, Bill! Reckon it'll take the Yanks a right smart chance o' work ter keep thar bridges goin' at that ar rate."

"Look ye! Look ye thar, Bill—ef it aint so arter all. Thar goes another—an' another!"

"Reckon we have 'em now, Jim; the Yanks can't git out of that ar pen up thar. Whew! look ye thar, boys—thar goes another. Golly! What's up with our'uns above? They've smashed Rosecrans's bridges this time, sartain." And so on.

On reaching Brown's Ferry, which is about eight miles below Chattanooga, the pontoons glided close to the southern bank—out sprang our soldiers and made for the pickets, when a scene occurred at once ludicrous and exciting. As the boats landed, and our soldiers leaped out, amid the dark shadows of the hills and woods, the rebel pickets, who had been jesting about the broken bridge, were heard, if not seen, laughing from the other side of their faces.

"Golly! Jim, them's Yanks! Look ye thar—right thar!"

"Whar, Tom? Whar?"

"Why, don't yer see? Thar's another lot of 'em landed down thar. The Yanks have played us a trick, by thunder!"

"Don't get skeered, Jim, them aint Yanks."

"Them is Yanks. Can't I see?"

"Who goes thar? Halt!"

Bang, whiz.

"Sergeant of the guard!"

Bang, bang, whiz.

"The Yanks are on us, Bill, sartin!"

"Surrender!" yelled our men, as they closed in on them, and abruptly stopped their dispute.

The rebel pickets were captured or killed. A strong skirmish-line was instantly thrown out; a detail made to throw up temporary breastworks; the pontoons were taken to the north side of the river to bring over another force that had marched down from Chattanooga across the peninsula on that side; and, in a short time, the rebels were driven back into the valley and up the spurs of Lookout. Meanwhile, a strong pioneer force was at work constructing a pontoon bridge some nine hundred feet long—a feat which was accomplished in six hours. Next day, Hooker, with a large force, crossed to the south side of the river, at Bridgeport, marched up as speedily as possible, and, on the afternoon of the second day, united with the force at Brown's Ferry.

By this adroit movement, the details of which had been executed so brilliantly and successfully, the roads were opened on both sides of the river. The rebels still held the point of Lookout, but could accomplish nothing after our forces had gained a foothold on the south side of the river. Not only were the roads secured, but the river, also, was cleared from Bridgeport to Brown's Ferry, and communications with the base of supplies fully established. A steamboat had been loaded with supplies at Bridgeport, in anticipation of this movement, and, in the course of a day or two, her whistle awoke the echoes of Lookout, as she steamed up to Brown's Ferry, with two hundred thousand rations for the hungry heroes of Chattanooga.

This movement was not only one of great importance, so far as establishing communications with Bridgeport were concerned, but it took the rebels so much by surprise that they had neither time nor opportunity to destroy any portion of the railroad before being driven back. In order to make the position as secure as possible, earthworks were thrown up by our forces, and the woods cleared off in front of the lines for a considerable distance. The rebel army was in such a peculiar position that Bragg could not extend or strengthen this part of his line without exposing his center, and he had to yield to the necessity of the case, and let our forces have undisturbed possession. It was the first step, however, in that brilliant strategy that resulted in hurling Bragg from his intrenched positions on Lookout and Mission Ridge, and sent him reeling and demoralized to the fastnesses beyond Taylor's Ridge, and, finally, to—it is hard now to tell where.

CHAPTER XXVII.

SECRETS OF THE DOMESTIC INSTITUTION—WHITE SLAVES—AN INCIDENT ON LOOKOUT MOUNTAIN—NEW APPLICATION OF SCRIPTURE.

If, in the providence of God, war is absolutely necessary for the purification and redemption of a people, how fearfully foul and degraded must that people be! And if only the stern rebukes of the sword can reach the hearts and consciences of those whose civilization and religion have been set forth as being of the highest order and purest character, and whose claims to be considered as the truest and fullest exponents and examples of intelligence, refinement, and piety, have been openly and continually insisted upon in Church and State, how false must have been their professions, and how arrogant and absurd their claims! And yet, every day in which this war has been carried on has only been making new and additional discoveries of the fearfully low state of morals and religion in the slaveholding Confederacy, and has been proving how hollow and pretentious have been the claims of lordly men-stealers to be considered as the only true embodiments of intelligence and refinement in the country. A few years ago, and but a few, the masses of Northern people were led to believe that Southern society was of the highest possible type; that, as was to be expected among a high-sprung, chivalrous people, whose keen sense of honor had become proverbial, there might be, occasionally, an unhappy quarrel, resulting, perhaps, in the use of the knife or revolver; that there might be even a Legree found, once in a great while, whose rough, angular exterior neither godly bishops, nor learned divinity doctors, nor the whole brotherhood of saintly pro-slavery preachers could smooth down sufficiently to retain the gilding of Gospel sanctity with which they labored hard to adorn him; but that these were mere exceptions to a general rule—only rough specimens of common clay accidentally found among the precious ingots of pure gold. But who, to-day, has temerity enough to stand forth and boldly reiterate such falsehoods? Who, among all the apologists of slavery in former days, would dare risk any little reputation for honesty or truth they may ever have possessed, by trying to shield the vile institution? Were they to escape the charge of falsehood and corruption, it would only be because they were looked upon as candidates for a lunatic asylum. Even now, one of the greatest curiosities in theological and ethical literature is Bishop Hopkins's voluminous and shamelessly wicked argument in defense of slavery and slaveholding rebels. In future years, his bitterest enemies will not find a surer method of sending down his character to posterity, blasted and blackened sufficiently to satisfy the deepest hate, than by simply engraving on his tombstone his own defense of human bondage.

Perhaps the reader will hardly accuse me of departing from an anti-slavery faith, when I say that the whites have suffered more, proportionately, at the hands of slavery than the blacks. They have suffered more, inasmuch as they had greater privileges and powers, and if they did fall, their fall was all the deeper, and their degradation all the greater.

The poor whites of the South—"the white trash," as they are generally called—a poor, degraded, ignorant, thriftless people, who are at once the objects of the slaveholder's hate, and the ready tools with which to work his schemes of villainy—bear unmistakable evidence of the crushing, grinding effects of slavery on the poor non-slaveholding whites, while the every-day evidences of the bleaching process on the colored race testify to the fearful immoralities of slaveholders themselves. The unbridled lust; the open, unblushing profligacy; the utter "confusion" wrought in all domestic sanctities, duties, and relationships, and all the nameless crimes incident to the rearing of human cattle for the slave shambles—all of which are the inevitable and necessary outgrowths of the horrid system—have covered Southern society with the foulest of moral ulcers—ulcers so foul and festering that, if allowed to vitiate and corrupt another generation, Nature herself would have taken revenge and spewed the adulterous brood out of the land. To converse with a Southerner on the subject of slavery—not by way of discussion, but to gain information—is to have one's self-respect violated, and feelings of manly modesty shocked and outraged. No wonder that every effort has been made by slaveholders in the South, and their abject apologists at the North, to cover up the loathsome secrets of the vile system, and conceal from the world its dark and diabolical history. It is well known that interested merchants drugged their consciences with moral opiates, while blood-stained gold found its way to their coffers. Corrupt politicians shamelessly sold themselves to slaveholding interests—and to the devil, too, for that matter—while gifts and bribes and political honors were showered upon them in return. Time-serving ministers threw away the keen-edged sword of Divine Truth, and, lest they might disturb the ease and comfort of their pro-slavery supporters, they wielded instead only contemptible pewter weapons, or they so garlanded God's sword with the flowers of rhetoric and poetry, or turned its keen edge with the rough ethics of organic wrong, that it would not cut. They covered up or explained away the handwritings of God himself, and brought into their pulpits smooth, dreary essays, through which they driveled and plodded, while those whose gains of oppression were increasing day by day, listened with easy self-complacency and comfort. Faithful ministers of the Gospel, who dared rebuke the evil spirit that had entered the high places of the Sanctuary, and spread desolation and woe, were mobbed, imprisoned, scourged, banished, tarred and feathered, hanged or shot, while reproaches and curses were heaped upon their names and characters. All this, and much more, to prevent agitation, and conceal from the gaze of the world the loathsome, secret workings of the SUM OF ALL VILLAINIES. But what hath God wrought since slaveholders raised their bloody hands to strike down Liberty, and make her dwelling-place a desolation! How wondrously He has thwarted their wisest plans, and defeated their deepest schemes! He hath truly caused the wrath of man to praise Him, while the remainder—the excess—of wrath he hath restrained. The very plans of the rebels have resulted in the ruin of their pet institution; for while the plowshare of war has been crashing through and tearing up the very foundations of Southern society, it has also been exposing to the gaze of an astonished world the dark chambers in which have rioted the foulest passions and the most atrocious vices. Those who have been in the army know these things; and they know, furthermore, that such a baptism of hate against slavery has descended upon the army, that every soldier is another Phinehas, to strike to the very heart the vile system—strike it till it dies, that "the plague may be stayed."

Even the women of the South, who, above all others, must necessarily have felt the keen, burning disgrace attaching to the vile institution, and whose womanly delicacy and refinement have been continually and systematically outraged, seem to have sunk under the debasing influences of the system, and to have become either inured or indifferent to its foulest and most repulsive features. I have known of instances where they even seemed to glory in the shame of their own social system.

In Nashville, there was a young staff officer, who, on seeing a beautiful little girl standing on the sidewalk in front of a house occupied by well-known feminine rebels, was so struck with her childish beauty and gracefulness, that he stooped down and kissed her. She was very fair, had bright blue eyes, ruby lips, her hair was in pretty wavy ringlets, and she was neatly dressed. A young lady, who noticed him kissing the child, sneeringly remarked:

"You seem to be very fond of kissing niggers."

"Good gracious! You don't call that child a nigger, do you?"

"Yes, I do. She is only a nigger—nothing else."

The little girl was absolutely prettier than the proud, shameless beauty that gloried in thus calling attention to her as only a "nigger, nothing more," and who, unwittingly perhaps, exposed one of the terribly foul and nameless crimes growing out of, and incident to, the vile system of slavery. Indeed, it is one of the marked features of this "domestic institution," that there are many "white niggers," as they are facetiously called, and who, like the little girl just mentioned, were it not for the practiced eye of the connoisseur of human merchandise, might pass for white men or white women. Why there should be so many fair girls, with rich, wavy tresses, or brunettes, with dark, sparkling eyes, or blondes, a little too pale, perhaps, with blue eyes and thin ruby lips, let those answer whose delicacy and moral sensibilities are so frequently shocked at the possibility of the negro being placed on a level with the white man. Perhaps they will inform us whether all these are evidences of elevation or degradation, and to which race the honor of being elevated, or the disgrace of being debased, really belongs. And, perhaps, too, they will explain the reason why a Southerner, from whom was gleaned considerable information, exclaimed, when speaking of these very matters—"Thunder! a man don't know now who he is marrying!"

As a further illustration of the purity of morals, high state of civilization, and general piety of slaveholding society, the following is inserted, being one of a number of similar advertisements taken from the *Atlanta Intelligencer:*

RUN AWAY—$250 REWARD—From my house in Forsyth Street, on night before last, a negro girl, about seventeen years old, about medium hight, stout made, weighs 140 pounds; *color, white;* hazel eyes, rather stoop-shouldered; was raised in Clarke County, Georgia. Any person returning the girl to me, or giving me such information as I may find her, will obtain the above reward. J. K. HEGAN.

A Woman's Idea of Poor White Children.

When passing through Trenton Valley, a little incident occurred which shows how the poor whites are regarded by the lordly slaveholders of rebeldom. By way of explanation, it may just be remarked that the valley is one of the best for raising fruit—especially peaches. The finest specimens I ever saw were gathered in the few orchards to be found in the valley. Peaches weighing from six to eight ounces, sound and well-flavored, were quite common.

"You have a very beautiful country, madam," said one of our party to a fair daughter of the "sunny South."

"Yes; good enough, I reckon," she replied, somewhat snappishly, as she eyed the Yankee invaders closely.

"It seems to be a fine fruit country. Why don't you have more orchards?" was the next question, put as politely as possible.

"Orchards!" she exclaimed, disdainfully. "Who would plant orchards, when all the fruit is stolen by the white trash young 'uns?"

"Send the children to school, and educate them as you ought to do," said our quarter-master. "If you would establish Sunday-schools, and teach the 'white trash young 'uns,' as you call them, your fruit would be safe enough."

"Do you 'uns think we 'uns are fools?" she answered quickly, while the flashing of her eye, and the hightening color of her cheeks showed that the Southern heart was being fired.

"Educate the white trash!" she continued; "you can't do it—they're worse than niggers!"—saying which, she nervously shook, not her feet, but her drapery, as a testimony against the Northern vandals who had dared to insinuate that children, though poor, might be educated.

It was not long after this incident occurred, that we had a very graphic illustration, and a very painful one, too, of the condition of the poor "white trash young 'uns," as this lady called them.

While crossing Lookout Mountain, the troops were employed in getting the artillery and supply-trains up the steep ascent. While waiting for this to be accomplished, our attention was called to a miserable log-cabin, in which were some half a dozen frowzy, tow-headed children—half naked, dirty, and hungry-looking. Now, be it remembered, our army was in this part of Georgia for the first time; that the country had not, as yet, been gleaned by our troops; that wealthy planters were all around, and yet here were a woman and several children huddled together in a ruinous hut, and in a starving condition. There was neither chair, table, nor bedstead—not a single article of furniture, nor sign of clothing or bedding, except a heap of rags—a miserable pallet—in one corner. Several officers on General Reynolds's staff, as well as the General himself, looked into this miserable abode, and were appalled at such a scene of wretchedness. Quite a number of the private soldiers did the same; and, all honor to their brave and generous hearts, many of them emptied their haversacks for the benefit of the hungry mother and children

The eldest of the family was a girl, perhaps eleven or twelve years of age, and who, had she been tidy and well-dressed, would have been really good-looking. One of the officers tried to draw her into conversation, with the following result:

"How old are you, sis?"

"Dunno," she replied, without raising her head—"ax mother, thar; 'spects she knows."

"Have you attended school?" he asked. "I suppose you can read?"

"No! I've never been to school," she replied, her eyes still bent downward, and her fingers twisting the fringed rents in the single coarse garment that was held together by sundry strings and suspender-buttons.

"Can you read?"

"No, I can't read—reckon I might larn—know some letters."

"Did you ever attend Sunday-school or go to church?" she was asked.

She looked as if she thought these were very preposterous questions, and answered:

"Wall, I heern tell something 'bout Sunday-schools over Big Sand, thar 'bouts, but dunno nothin' 'bout 'em."

"Do you know who made you?"

"Dunno who made me. Reckon mother, thar, made me. Ax her; she knows, I 'spect."

"What! Do you not know about God, who made you and me and all things? Did no one ever tell you about God?"

"Heern tell something 'bout some 'un they called the Lord; but, laws! we never saw him. Old Uncle Bill sometimes came to whar we lived over Sand, and used to talk 'bout sech things. Did yer ever see the Lord?"

Now, reader, remember, this conversation was held with a white girl in the State of Georgia—a part of that land where the "peculiar institution"—so long and so persistently defended by savage Legrees, polished, business-like Halcys, blustering Tom Lokers, and sanctimonious, smooth-faced ministers, elders, and deacons—has exercised its benign and Christianizing spirit; and where they have boasted of having so many powerful revivals that they were nearly as regular and plentiful as their "barbacues" and "breakdowns," and, it might be added, equally as valuable. Was not this incident a graphic illustration and proof of the position occupied by the poor in slaveholding society? And was it not a telling comment on the heartless words of the proud Southern lady—"Educate the white trash! you can't do it—they're worse than niggers?"

A New Application of Scripture.

For the special benefit of my clerical brethren, I am tempted to finish this chapter of odds and ends with a paragraph or two on exegetical theology. The exegesis being of African descent, and not copy-righted, any pulpit aspirant may use it, if he choose, except the *practical application*.

Reuben—"Uncle Reub," as he was familiarly called by our camp contrabands—was quite a genius in his way. According to his own account, he had been a faithful and laborious preacher among his "culled bredren," and was a strictly orthodox Baptist of the Hard-shell persuasion.

His contempt for any thing outside of immersion, in the religious world, was quite edifying, while his gravity and earnestness in quoting Scripture, usually wrong end foremost, would have graced the gravest of theological chairs. In addition to his onerous and self-imposed duties as a spiritual guide to his fellow-contrabands, he had charge of the major's horse. The major, it may be remarked, in passing, was a quiet old wag, and frequently remarked, rather dryly, that "Harry would thrive better if treated to less theology and more curry-comb."

It might also be stated that the major was not a firm believer in *total* abstinence, although I never saw him drink any thing except from a canteen, which is always supposed to contain water. Moreover, although holding ministers in all due respect, he was very fond of a joke at their expense.

One day, the major had a friend from a neighboring

regiment pay him a visit, and, having "something," invited him to partake. Having something to do in the tent, Reub was present long enough, during the visitor's stay, to see that a bottle was not far off. After the visitor left, Uncle Reub was noticed looking very much as a gentleman might be supposed to do who felt himself somewhat slighted. Suspecting, from the lengthy appearance of Reub's face, as well as the furtive glances he directed toward the bottle, what was wrong, the major said:

"You never drink any, I suppose, Reuben?"

"Wall, no, not 'xactly—dat is, major—I dun nebber drink when 'mong de gals an' boys. Yer see, major, wouldn't nebber do, nohow. I allers like to be 'sistent wid my perfession, as de good book says. But de fac' is, major, I dun nebber like 'fuse any thing from any gen'lman."

The major took the hint, and acted accordingly, by passing the nearly-empty bottle to Reub.

Taking it into his hand, with a pleasant, self-satisfied smile, he showed his affection for spiritual comforts by taking a vigorous pull at its contents. Then he returned the bottle, with an air of conscious dignity, saying.

"Dat's good liquor, major. Yes, sah, dat ar liquor's de ginuine stuff."

"Why, Reub, I never thought you would drink—you a preacher! Preachers don't drink, do they?"

"Wall, now, major," said Reuben—elevating his eyebrows, and placing his fore-fingers together, as if about to discuss a profound problem in theology—"yer see, as de good book says, we must be 'sistent to our sure calling and 'lection, and as Paul says in de 'pistle Revelations, dat it is not what passes into de mouth dat defiles a man, but it is what passes out. Now, does yer see de pint, major—does yer see it?"

"Yes," said the major, dryly, "I see it. Put the saddle on Harry."

Who will say that, with proper culture and polish, Uncle Reub might not shine alongside those eminent divines who have written such learned treatises to prove that slavery is in strict accordance with the Golden Rule—"Whatsoever ye would that men should do to you, do ye even so to them?"

CHAPTER XXVIII.

THE DYING SOLDIER'S DREAM OF HOME AND CHILDHOOD—THE SENTINEL—LIFE A BATTLE—THE SPIRITUAL VICTORY.

"Our friends may fill an early grave,
Our every hope in life be lost,
And 'midst the storm the rising wave
May see our bark 'midst breakers toss'd;
But Faith can gild the dreary tomb,
Where early friends in silence sleep;
And her bright arch can re-illume
That shore beyond the swelling deep.

"Faith speaks of myriads round the throne,
Who once were suff'rers here below;
And shows the path which led them on
To glory from a scene of woe.
She speaks of One whom hosts adore,—
Whom angels worship in the sky;
'Tis to the Lamb for evermore
Who once for guilty man did die."

If "the undevout astronomer is mad," then the irreverent or unfeeling visitor of a military hospital is more than mad. No one can pass through the wards of a hospital, and mingle with the sufferers there, by engaging in conversation with them, ministering to their wants, and entering, as it were, into their feelings, without becoming either a better or a worse man.

I do not mean that he will become more easily excited or overcome by the terrible scenes of human suffering that he must necessarily witness, neither do I mean that he will become less resolute in his efforts to do something toward alleviating distress, even amid all that is truly revolting to every tender and humane feeling. To become so used to scenes of suffering as to be perfectly calm and collected is by no means incompatible with tender feelings; hence, because a man does not exhibit a certain amount of nervousness, or give expression to every tender emotion, we are not to conclude that he has become so inured to scenes of the tragic and horrible as to have all the finer feelings blunted, or the more humane sensibilities destroyed. But we are not to forget, at the same time, that constant familiarity with scenes of suffering have a tendency either to harden or soften the heart. It will make a person either more callous and unfeeling, or more susceptible of kindly emotions and more keenly alive to the necessities, both physical and moral, of the sick and wounded. Any one who can look with cold indifference on the carnage of a battle-field, or the sad and terribly revolting scenes of a hospital, with all their accompaniments of the tragic and pathetic, must be possessed of a very bad heart. On the other hand, there is no man, of any pretension to true Christian character, who will not be all the better for any experiences he may have had in the almost every-day scenes of military life. If ever a single doubt or fear concerning the divine authority and saving power of the religion of Jesus Christ has disturbed his peace of mind, or threatened to unsettle his faith and darken his hope; if ever he has felt to murmur at the dispensations of Providence, or to complain at what he has thought to be his hard lot; if ever he has been tempted to look upon his brother man through the colored glasses of mere conventionalism, and value him just in proportion to his wealth, rank, or social standing; or if ever he is threatened with the foul spirit of cold, calculating selfishness, or the distrustful, cynical demon of misanthropy, let him go to those scenes of suffering where every look is agony, and every word a groan or a prayer, and he will depart a wiser and a better man.

If it were only for the benefit of my youthful readers—God's rich blessing rest upon each of them!—I would like to describe one of the many sad but impressive and interesting scenes I have witnessed among the wounded on the battlefield and in the hospital. At one time, I was called to witness the following, which I will call "The Dying Soldier's Dream of Childhood."

He was brought into the hospital mortally wounded, by the accidental discharge of a musket, although, by a false feeling of kindness, one or two of the surgeons told him his wound was severe but not dangerous. I thought it my duty to undeceive him; and so, sitting down beside him, and taking his hand in mine, while I brushed back the dark curls from his high, open brow, I tried to lead him easily into such a channel of conversation as I desired. I had not conversed long with him, till he suddenly inquired what I thought of his prospects of recovery? Rather avoiding, for the time being, giving a direct answer, I inquired how he felt himself in regard to that matter? He answered, with considerable hesitation, that the surgeons told him he would get along very well, but that he himself felt afraid that he would never recover. I noticed, too, that his lips quivered, and he drew a long, deep sigh. Then he turned his youthful, open face full upon me, and sighed again. There was a choking, fluttering sensation, which told the intensity of his feelings, and he said, "If I was only at home!"

Poor boy! Many a hill and valley and mountain gorge and broad river lay between him and his home! And the loving ones there were all unconscious of his deep distress; and, even before his name would appear in the columns of some daily paper as having been severely wounded, he would already be "where the wicked cease from troubling, and the weary are at rest." I spoke to him of the tender sympathy of the infinite Father, of the all-sufficient Savior, who was wounded for our transgressions, and bruised for our iniquities, and how that a full and free salvation was offered to all through the death and sufferings of the Lord Jesus. I could not get him to say much; so, after praying with him, I left him for a time. In a few hours, I called to see him again, and, in the course of conversation, endeavored to press home the momentous truths of salvation. At last, he opened his mind freely, and told me he thought he was once a Christian; that he sought an interest in Christ when a boy, and felt happy in the belief that he loved the Savior, that his happiest hours were spent in the Sunday-school, and that he used to take delight in prayer and reading the Scriptures.

"I remember, too," said he, "how my father prayed. O, chaplain, I had a good father—he 's in heaven now. How he prayed for *me*, that I might always be good! I remember the night that he died—and how happy he was, and how he sung, 'On Jordan's stormy banks I stand,' and how he put his hand on my head, and told me to serve God and meet him in heaven! O, if I was as good as my father was, it would be better with me now! I have forgotten all my promises—I have turned my back on Christ—what shall I do! what shall I do! I'm dying—I know I'm dying, and I am afraid to die! O, Jesus, have mercy on me, a sinner!"

I did not interrupt him till he had given full and free vent to his feelings, and then tried to point him to the all-sufficient Savior.

"Do you think God will have mercy on my poor soul?" he exclaimed, in such a piteous tone of voice, and with such genuine earnestness, that my own feelings overcame me, and I could barely say, "Yes, dear brother, God is ready *now* to bless you, to forgive you all your sins, and make you happy in the enjoyment of his love."

"But I have neglected prayer, and backslidden from God—I have sinned against light and knowledge. I knew better, chaplain, I knew better; for my conscience troubled me; it was God's Spirit striving with me. Yes, I knew better, for I once loved Jesus. O, Jesus, have mercy on a poor sinner!"

"Hear God's own answer to your question," said I. "'If any man sin we have an advocate with the Father—Jesus Christ, the righteous; and he is the propitiation for our sins; and not for ours only, but also for the sins of the whole world. God so loved the world that he gave his only-begotten Son, that whosoever believeth in him might not perish, but have everlasting life.' Now, these words are as much addressed to you as if there were not another sinner upon earth. Take them, as God's own words, to yourself, and remember that that dear Savior, whom you say you once served, loves you yet, loves you now, and is yearning over you with the deepest sympathy. He waits to take away the heavy burden from your heart, and give you joy and peace in believing. Just come back as a poor wanderer, weary and helpless, and remember you are coming to your own God and Savior, who knows just what you need, and how you feel, and is more willing to receive you and forgive you than you are to return to him."

"O, if I was just as happy as I once was; but now I'm here, wounded and dying; and I am suffering so I can not think—I try to think about the Savior and about salvation—and I try to pray! But, O, this awful pain! What will I do! what will I do! Jesus! Jesus! what will I do!" he exclaimed, in the deepest agony of body and mind.

"Believe on the Lord Jesus Christ—cast your poor troubled soul upon the Savior—just place yourself, as a poor, helpless sinner, in his hands, and you will be saved," said I, trying to lead his mind to the one only source of comfort.

The agony of this poor sufferer was terrible. His pitiful groans sunk into my very heart, and made me feel as if I was entirely powerless to do him good.

Sometimes it was difficult to tell whether his bodily or mental anguish were greatest. Frequently the deep, agonizing groan of bodily pain would end in a most pathetic cry for mercy, or a childlike petition to be received into the favor of his Heavenly Father. Sometimes he turned upon me such a pitiful, helpless look—such a look as a drowning child might cast toward its mother—a look of unutterable meaning, but which plainly said, "I'm dying—won't you help me?" Seeing that, to all appearance, he was rapidly sinking, I urged him to accept the free offer of reconciliation to God through the atonement of Christ, and after again praying with him, I left him for a little time. An hour, perhaps, had elapsed, when I was again beside him. The first words he uttered were:

"I'm trying to come back to God, and I think that he will not cast me off, but I'm afraid."

"I'm going to ask you one question," said I, "but you must not answer it till you think over it. It is this—Do you think that God loves you?"

He seemed to ponder the question a little, and then answered:

"I think—I think he does love me."

"Yes," I said, "God loves you dearly, and sympathizes with you in your great distress, and is so very anxious for your soul's salvation, that he is waiting even now, this moment, to forgive you all your sins, and make you happy in his love. You would believe the word of an earthly friend—why can you not believe the promise of your own Heavenly Father, who says, That whosoever believeth on the Lord Jesus Christ shall be saved? Just trust in him, just throw yourself as you are, a poor helpless sinner, into his hands, and you will be saved."

"Is that all I'm to do?" said he, musingly; "and yet what else can I do? Yes, yes, I think I see it all. I have been afraid to trust in the promises of God; I feel myself to be so unworthy—and I am unworthy, too, a poor, miserable sinner—but now, Jesus, dear Savior, I come to thee, a poor, helpless sinner—

'Here, Lord, I give myself to thee,
'Tis all that I can do.'

Yes, Lord, it is all that I can do!"

Then followed a scene I will never forget to my dying day. It was night. The temporary hospital was an old, dark, dingy house. The candle burned dimly, and seemed, by its flickering, uncertain light, to make the gloomy surroundings all the more gloomy. The poor, mangled soldier-boy lay rolling uneasily from side to side. Large drops of cold sweat stood like beads on his open brow. Quivering sensations seemed to pass through every nerve and fiber of his body, and there were long, deep, shivering sighs which told of the very extremity of mortal anguish. His large, bright eye grew dim, and seemed as if looking up from a great depth, while that mysterious change of color and feature took place, which tells that the wheels of life are about to stand still. Suddenly he threw out his arms, and clasped me tightly round the neck, as I stooped over him, and exclaimed:

"What shall I do! O, chaplain, what shall I do?"

"Put your trust in Christ, your own Savior, who died for you," I replied.

"I do believe in Jesus," he said, "and I think he will save me—yes, he will save me; but, O! what is this?—am I dying now?—tell me, am I dying?"

"Yes, you are dying, dear brother," I answered. "You will soon be in the spirit world. Is Jesus near you? Have you peace of mind?"

"It's all over now," he whispered. "God has, for Christ's sake, forgiven me, a poor sinner, and he will take me to himself. Good-by, chaplain, good-by—a little closer"—he drew me down, and put his cold lips to mine—"good-by; I hope to meet—you in—heaven—good-by."

He fell into a kind of stupor, or what might be called an uneasy slumber, and I sat by his side, waiting and watching.

He dreamed.

He seemed to be again at home, mingling with loved ones, for I heard him murmur, slowly and feebly:

"Mother!"

Then he seemed to be praying. He tried to clasp his hands, as if, a child again, he knelt at a parent's knee, and was repeating his evening prayer. I stooped over him, and listened attentively to every whisper. At last I caught a few disjointed sentences, as follows:

"Our Father—who art—this night—I lay me—down—O, Jesus—my Savior—take me—to heaven. Hallowed be—thy name."

There was then a pause, and a deep sigh. The angel of death had come! The golden bowl was broken, and the wheel stood still at the cistern! Poor, mangled sufferer, he had found Christ, and his dream of childhood's devotions gave place, we trust, to the brighter visions of glory, and the songs of salvation!*

THE SENTINEL.

Amid the general routine of camp life, as well as amid the exciting and perilous scenes of the battle-field, there is much to interest and instruct. There is no scene, however dark, no duty, however perilous, no circumstances, however doubtful or ominous, and no movement, however complicated or mysterious, but to the reflecting mind is significant and impressive. I have often thought how appropriate and instructive are the frequent allusions in Scripture to the habits

---

* While these pages were passing through the press, the author was invited to address a missionary meeting of the Trinity M. E. Sunday-school, Cincinnati. Thinking the above narrative would be interesting, I repeated it, stating that the young soldier had been a scholar in the Sunday-school, and referred to it when dying, that I did not know what Sunday-school he had belonged to, only that it was one in Cincinnati. At the conclusion of the remarks, Rev. Mr. Chalfant, the pastor, said:

"What was that soldier's name?"

"Thomas K. Mitchell," I replied. "He was sergeant-major of our regiment.

"You don't know what Sunday-school he belonged to?" said Mr. Chalfant.

"I do not. He was a member of a Methodist Church and Sunday-school in the city—that is all I know."

Mr. Chalfant rose, and, with great emotion, said:

"The soldier we have just heard of, and who died so peacefully, although in great suffering, was a member *of this very Sunday-school. His sister and mother are, perhaps, not present, but are members of this Church.*"

His statement had a thrilling effect.

and customs of the camp, and the duties and responsibilities of the soldier, especially when viewed in connection with those promises which refer to the blessed results of unswerving fidelity to the cause of Christ.

I had occasion once to be outside our lines, and, before it was possible for me to return, night and darkness had set in. The road was new to me; it led through dark, heavy woodland and rough, rocky hills, around deserted plantations and through swamps, covered with dark, jungle-like underbrush, peculiar to Tennessee and Georgia. The night was intensely dark and disagreeable, and only added to my feelings of anxiety and no little fear. In the language of soldiers, "it was no time to be fooling round among the pickets." As I came nearer our chain of sentinels, I rode more cautiously, and strained my ear for every sound; for careless travelers, and nervous or careless sentinels sometimes make mutual and fatal blunders. Presently a loud and clear voice sang out, sharply:

"Halt!"

To move a step further is to hear the click of the musket coming to a "ready."

"Who goes there?"

"A friend with the countersign," is the answer.

"Advance, friend, and give the countersign," is the next demand. The countersign is given in a low tone, with the point of the bayonet within a few inches of one's breast.

"All right!" and we pass on. This is repeated three or four times before reaching camp, and once there, all is safe. Now, at that very time, there was every possibility that some of these sentinels belonged to my own regiment, and knew my voice perfectly well, and were even expecting me to pass through that night; but they were not bound to know me or any one else but through the countersign.

For the time being the private soldier, on his post as sentinel, is superior to any one else. All must bow to his authority. He is not bound to know any one, whatever may be the rank or position occupied. The Commanding General, or the President himself, may ride up, but he is superior to either of them, and neither General nor President can pass without the countersign. The darkness which envelops the lonely sentinel, and causes him to strain his eyes to see every object that is suspicious, throws a vail, also, over rank and position, and obliterates all distinctions. He is clothed with absolute power, and has life and death in his hands. With his gun loaded and capped, he walks his solitary beat, and is as absolute, independent, and rigid in his exactions as the greatest monarch that wears a crown. For the time being his authority is supreme, and from his demands there is no appeal. Absolute, rigorous, inexorable, he places all persons of all ranks on the same common level; and he causes the Major-General, who commands the entire force in the field, to dismount from his horse, and give the countersign precisely in the same manner as the humblest private or smallest drummer-boy in the army. And not only so, but there is a deference and respect paid to the sentinel, which, without any particular law or order, seems, by habit and common consent, to be considered both necessary and becoming. No one can stand by and witness the forms and ceremonies of "guard-mounting" without being impressed with the idea that those who, for the time being, are on "guard duty" are considered as occupying an honorable and responsible position. It seems as if every part of the routine tended to impress on the mind of each one of the guard that he was honored by being detailed for that important duty; that he was considered as worthy of all respect; that the lives of his comrades, the safety of the army, and even the honor and welfare of his country were in his hands, and that the utmost confidence was placed in his fidelity and courage. I never visited a picket-post, nor passed a sentinel on duty, but I felt solemn; and as I returned his salute, I have felt to say to him, "You have preached to me a better sermon than ever I preached to others."

He holds conversation with no one; he can neither whistle nor sing to pass away the time which drags heavily along; he dare not sit down, nor relinquish the grasp of his gun. No lights are allowed on the picket-line, and on the coldest night he has no fire to warm his chilled and weary limbs. Away from his comrades, standing at his post alone, perhaps in some dark and shadowy ravine, or in some thick woods, the enemy in front, watchful, cunning, and ready to take any advantage, his position is at once dangerous, harrassing, and honorable. With a firm grasp on the lock of his musket, he watches closely every object, peers anxiously into the dark shadows in the distance, listens attentively to every sound, and is distrustful of all beneath and around him. Only in one direction can he look without suspicion, and that is upward to the cold, gray sky, where the stars shine forth, in calm and sublime majesty, like holy watchers in the City of God. The rustling among the leaves close by, or the quivering of the twigs in the nearest tree, may only be the antics of some restless squirrel, or the moving of some homeless little bird, as it cowers closer under the lee of a sheltering branch, or it may be the stealthy tread of an enemy, who even now has taken deadly aim at the sentinel's bosom. Always cool, calm, and collected, yet with every faculty of body and mind strained to its utmost tension, and keenly alive to the dangers and responsibilities of his position, thus he watches with sleepless vigilance, while his comrades, in the camp behind him, repose in comparative comfort and security. And thus the weary hours of the sentinel's watch pass away, his duty being lightened by the welcome "relief" of comrades on duty with himself. And, at last, with what a thrill of gladness does he hail the first faint flush of the eastern sky, which tells him that "The night is far spent, and the day is at hand!" How happy and thankful he is when he sees the "morning star," that bright, beautiful herald of the coming day, rising from behind the eastern hills, and shedding forth a mild, peaceful radiance amid the departing shadows of the night! And as the sky gradually brightens, and the streamers dance upward from the rising sun, tinging the rolling clouds with their rosy hue, and fringing them with crimson and gold, he hears the bugle sounding the *reveillé* in the distant camps, and he rejoices in the thought that, ere long, he will be relieved from duty, and rest from his weary watchings.

And is this not a picture of the Christian's life? Is he not a spiritual soldier, engaged in a spiritual conflict, and contending for a prize in comparison with which all earth's crowns and kingdoms and glories and honors are but as the vapors of the summer's morn, or as the airy bubbles which float on the troubled stream? Yes, the Christian is indeed a soldier—a soldier for Christ; and though his foes are many and powerful, yet he can say, "We are more than conquerors through Him that loved us."

Some of the most impressive and instructive lessons of the Bible are conveyed to us in the language of the camp and field. Sometimes the language is direct, and has the ring of the actual conflict, as in the Psalms of David. At other times, there is merely an allusion to military habits and customs, as in some of the Epistles of Paul. The great apostle himself concludes what might be called his testimony, with the words of a war-worn veteran:

"I have fought a good fight; I have finished my course; I have kept the faith."

But there is no military duty referred to so frequently in the inspired volume as that of the sentinel:

"Watch ye, stand fast in the faith, quit you like men, be strong!"

"Let us not sleep as do others, but let us watch and be sober." "Be ye, therefore, sober, and watch unto prayer." "Watch and pray that ye enter not into temptation." "Take ye heed, watch and pray." "And what I say unto you, I say unto all, WATCH."

Such are a few of the many passages to which the sentinel or watcher's duty is referred; and when these and kindred passages are studied as they ought to be, what a flood of light is thrown upon the Christian's character, his duties and responsibilities! How intensely anxious to be faithful in all things must the apostle have been when he uttered these thrilling words: "I, therefore, so run, not as uncertainly; so fight I, not as one that beateth the air; but I keep under my body and bring it in subjection; lest that by any means, when I have preached to others, I myself should be a castaway!" And how tender, yet earnest and emphatic, was his injunction to Timothy: "Fight the good fight of faith, lay hold on eternal life whereunto thou art also called, and hast professed a good profession before many witnesses!"

When we consider the circumstances which surround the Christian, the spiritual foes which war against the soul, the temptations which must be overcome, the evil inclinations which must be subdued, the sins which so easily beset us in our onward and upward march to glory, and the absolute necessity of a constant, vigorous, earnest reaching forth toward the prize of full Christian attainments—holy happiness in living, and happy holiness in dying—how appropriate are the allusions to military customs, and how impressive are the lessons which those allusions teach.

Dear reader, are you a soldier for Christ? Have you gone forth to the great battle of life with him as your Leader, your Almighty Protector, and ever-loving Friend? If you have, then go forward fearlessly and faithfully, for the victory is certain and the reward is sure. Remember that life is a struggle, a daily conflict, and not a time of repose. Remember that on your head rests not as yet the crown of glory, but the helmet of salvation; that as yet you do not wave the palm of victory in the home of the redeemed, but you wield the sword of the spirit on the battlefield of life; that as yet you are not clothed with the radiant robes of the conquerors in heaven, but with the armor of God upon earth. This, then, is the battle and the weary march, and the "watchings oft;" but yonder are the final victory, and the gladsome rest, and the joyful entrance into the City of God. O, there are, beyond all the fierce conflicts, and the anxious watchings, and the long, dark nights of sorrow, and the weary hours of anxious care, other and brighter scenes!

Yonder, yet in the distance, but seen by the eye of faith, is the bright, beautiful morning of joy; and yonder are the immortal crowns, and the garments shining as the sun, and the harps of gold which roll the melodies of salvation as a mighty, swelling tide-wave of joy and praise through the bowers of Paradise! And yonder are the evergreen shores of the better land, where the pure in heart shall meet again, amid scenes of ravishing beauty and fadeless splendor! Yonder is the great White Throne, before which are the innumerable company of angels and the spirits of just men made perfect, who serve God day and night in his temple! Yonder are the fountains of glory which play perpetually, and the streams of joy that flow forever, and to which the blessed Redeemer will lead his white-robed followers, that they may drink and rejoice for evermore! And last, but not least—no, no! but better, more glorious, more welcome than all—is JESUS, our dear, blessed Savior, for whose presence we have had such mysterious heart-longings, and without whom heaven would be deprived of all its beauty and joy! When He places the crown upon the spiritual warrior's head, then the warfare is accomplished, the weary pilgrimage is ended, and the tears are forever wiped away.

Be faithful, dear reader, in the spiritual conflict, for victory is certain, and the glorious prize is sure. And when thou hast fought thy last battle and thou art gone to be with thy Savior, of thee it shall be said:

"SERVANT of God! well done;
Rest from thy loved employ;
The battle fought, the victory won,
Enter thy Master's joy.

. . . .

The pains of death are past,
Labor and sorrow cease,
And life's long warfare closed at last,
His soul is found in peace.
Soldier of Christ! well done;
Praise be thy new employ;
And, while eternal ages run,
Rest in thy Savior's joy."

CHAPTER XXIX.

REBEL BARBARITIES.

FROM the first shot which the rebels fired at Fort Sumter till the present hour, the slaveholders' rebellion, in all its phases, has been but one continuous and fearful history of cowardly brutality and barbarism. War, at any time, in any country, and under any circumstances, is fearful, cruel, and unnatural. But fearful, cruel, and unnatural as it undoubtedly is, even when conducted with some little regard to the claims of common humanity, how terrible must it be when vindictive cruelty, that should cause the cheeks of savages to blush with shame, is permitted to glut itself with insults, injuries, and even death, on a fallen and helpless foe! When the atrocities perpetrated during the Sepoy rebellion in India were made known, all Christendom stood aghast at the fearful tale of wholesale butchery and fiendish cruelty. It was supposed that such scenes had never been enacted in the history of the world, and, possibly, never would be again. But, horrible as the cruelties perpetrated by the frenzied Sepoys were, they have been completely eclipsed a thousand times by the conduct of the rebels since they began their causeless and wicked rebellion.

With but few exceptions, they have never evinced the least feeling of honor or mercy—even of common humanity—toward those of the Union army that have fallen into their hands.

After our army, under Thomas and Sherman and Hooker, had driven Bragg from Lookout and Mission Ridge, and sent him reeling and discomfited beyond the mountain fastnesses of northern Georgia, the Chickamauga battlefield was then seen as a terrible record of worse than savage brutality. No full description of the revolting scenes which our soldiers then beheld has ever been given, and probably never will. There are various reasons for this, one of which is, that there would be needless pain inflicted on the relatives of those noble heroes who fell in battle. Long after we had driven the rebels back, and our men had been burying their dead comrades, who had been denied the common boon of humanity—a grave—the visitor would be startled by sights that would make the blood chill. Ghastly skeletons, lying exposed to the winds of heaven, bare and bleached, could be seen as fearful witnesses of rebel inhumanity. Shallow graves were found, from which protruded perhaps a bare, bald skull, or perhaps the bleached bones of hands and feet. A few handfuls of earth, thrown up carelessly, and partly washed away by the rains, was all that hid many of the dead from the light of day. There lay members of my regiment, the joy and pride of dear domestic circles, concerning whom I have had to maintain silence when dear parents or loving sisters spoke of them, because of the manner in which they were found on that horrid field. They were recognized by their comrades, and what was left of their mutilated remains decently buried; but they were recognized only from marks on their clothing, and the locality in which they fell. In several places we found bodies, or rather remains, lying between burned logs, part of which—an arm or leg, for instance—was calcined, as if subjected to intense heat, while other parts of the body were crisp and dry. It is firmly believed by all who saw those revolting scenes, that many of our wounded were burned alive, horrible as it may seem, for bodies were found partly consumed, where the contraction of the muscles, and the clenched fingers, seemed to indicate an attempt to grasp something, while the general appearance gave evidence of a violent struggle of some kind. In one place, the body of a Union soldier was found, with both ears cut off, and in another, several bodies from which the heads had been removed. These had been set up on stakes and rails of the fences, or fastened on limbs of trees. A few, and but a few, graves of Union soldiers were marked. One, in which twelve had been buried—a long trench—had a board inscribed "Twelve Union soldiers," and another, probably an officer's, was honored with a flat stone, on which was marked, "A damned Yankee nigger-thief lies here to rot and pollute our soil."

But I forbear. The details are sickening. But one thing is certain, the wretches who could descend to such a depth of brutality, and be guilty of such aimless, wanton treatment of the helpless wounded or the harmless dead, can never escape a fearful retribution even in this world; and it is a matter of serious doubt whether they will ever find a place of repentance.

Chickamauga! Chickamauga! the horrid Golgotha of Tennessee, where an accursed slaveholders' treason slew the flower of the country, and refused the harmless dead the poor but common boon of humanity, will be remembered—yes, with a bitter and terrible remembrance! And when, at any time, wicked compromisers with wrong will even dare to whisper of the rights of slaveholders, the veterans of Chickamauga and Mission Ridge, and all who are worthy their friendship, will fling in their teeth that terrible word, CHICKAMAUGA, and point to the mutilated remains and the ghastly skeletons there, which the burning sun and the drenching rain had bleached—"Unknelled, uncoffined, and unknown."

Our children's children will reverently walk over the hallowed field of Chickamauga. They will note with interest its historic associations, and listen with thrilling interest to the tales of heroic bravery which, perhaps, some gray-haired sire may tell; they will read, too, about the Fort Pillow butchery, and the brutalities at Plymouth; they will listen to the horrid tales of Andersonville and Libby, where our noble patriot soldiers were systematically and deliberately tortured and starved to death; they will read and study the long, fearful narratives of wanton cruelty, and unpitying, unrelenting hate, in comparison with which the blind, frenzied rage of the Indian Sepoys can scarcely be named. And, as they read or hear such tales, they will not only learn to love their country, but they will learn, too, to hate, with deepest hate, the iniquitous system of slavery, in the interest and spirit of which those scenes were enacted.

THE NATIONAL CEMETERY.

Not far from Chattanooga are the beautiful grounds of the National Military Cemetery. The location and general outlines are all that could be desired for such a purpose, while the facilities for improving and adorning what will be truly a necropolis of patriot soldiers are abundant. Seventy acres have been set apart for this sacred purpose. The work of improvement has been in progress since January, 1864, and stumps, stones, dead timber, and other *debris*, have been mostly removed. Drives and walks have been laid out, and the grounds have been divided off so that soldiers from the various states are buried in allotted sections. Large numbers of the bodies of those who were killed in battle, or who died of wounds or disease, and who were buried in the various temporary graveyards around Chattanooga and on the field of Chickamauga, have been taken up and buried carefully, while preparations for erecting a grand National Monument have already been made.

The surrounding scenery is of the most beautiful and varied description. On the east and south is Mission Ridge, while on the west rise the dark and romantic outlines of Lookout Mountain. A beautiful undulating valley, stretching from far away in the north-east, sweeps nearly around the gentle slopes of the cemetery grounds, and stretches away toward the south and west, till it is bounded by the blue, hazy mountains in the far distance, behind which the setting sun goes down in such splendors as are seen only in a southern sky. Many a time I have gazed with rapture on those scenes of surpassing loveliness; and, while standing in deep meditation on the hallowed ground where sleep the thousands of our patriot soldiers, I have caught myself soaring away in imagination to that land of fadeless splendor, where war's fierce tumult shall never be heard, and where death shall be unknown. And as I looked upon the varied scenery of towering mountains, reflecting back the glories of the setting sun—the lesser hills enveloped in a soft blue haze which gave one an idea of dreaminess, together with the peaceful valley lying in repose and beauty, and lighted up with the various tints and mild splendors of evening—I have felt to pray, with passionate earnestness, "O God, rebuke the wild waves of human passion which are surging to and fro in our land, and make man's heart as loving and peaceful as thou hast made his earthly home beautiful and pleasant!" But as I looked at the dread enginery of war at my feet and all around me—the frowning embrasures and the deep-throated cannon, the huge piles of grape and solid shot, the gleaming of the sentinel's bayonet in the distance, the various picket-posts, and all that pertained to military life—I felt as if we were far from that day spoken of by the old prophetic bards, and longed for by all of God's children.

And yet, faith in the visions of those holy men of old, faith in the promises of God, faith in the transforming and purifying influences of the Gospel, points with "radiant finger" toward a brighter and happier day for our beloved country and for the world at large. Even now the dark clouds are measurably driven away, and the glad sunshine of happier days yet in store for us, is already streaming forth from our hitherto troubled sky. Let us rest assured that sin will not always triumph; wrong will not always prosper; oppression will not always unfurl its grim and defiant banner, and flaunt it shamelessly in the face of God and man. Cold, calculating selfishness will not always grind the faces of the poor, nor take advantage of the sufferings and necessities of the afflicted. War's fearful shock will not always be felt, nor its fearful scenes always be enacted. Woman, as wife or mother, will not always weep in sadness and loneliness for loved ones who will return no more. No; for that God, who rolled back the surging waters of the Deluge, and spanned the dark and stormy sky with the rainbow arch, will roll back the waves of strife, and span our troubled heavens with a brighter bow than that of old. Christ's banner of Love and Purity and Peace will yet be unfurled on every shore, and float on every breeze, while the songs of Zion will be heard in every land, and shoutings of sacred joy will burst from every lip. O, to be found at work with Christ in hastening on the blessed day of the world's restoration to God! Talk of honor and position and riches! What honor so great, what position so honorable, and what riches so enduring and satisfying as those that can be gained in working for Christ and humanity! When the brightest earthly crown has faded, and the most honorable of earth's names have been forgotten, the crown of the poorest and weakest of Christ's followers will be shining with resplendent glory in heaven, and his name will be recorded in the Lamb's Book of Life. May the reader of these lines be found among those who have labored for Christ and humanity, and who shall be accounted worthy to receive that crown and dwell forever in the presence of God!

COURAGE AND GENEROSITY.

In the foregoing pages, a few, and but a few, of the many interesting scenes I have witnessed in the army have been depicted. Some of the scenes witnessed, and of which, perhaps, but imperfect outlines have been given, were very touching and tender. Others were more moving and sublimely grand, as exhibitions of heroic endurance and bravery. Some again were perhaps humorous and amusing; but, prominent among all the moving, panoramic scenery of army life during my experiences on the battlefields, East and South, in the camp or the hospital, there is one scene, one picture of mingled bravery and generosity, that rises before me every day. There are some things we never forget; there are some pictures of life so deeply engraven on our hearts that they will never be effaced; and there are some, too, that we never wish to forget; but we rather cherish them as precious memories of scenes and thoughts and deeds, the remembrance of which may have faded from all hearts save our own. What is about to be related is one of those incidents which seldom occur without impressing our hearts with more exalted opinions concerning our fellow-men, and it might form a fitting close to these Lights and Shadows of Army Life, because it is a picture that has no shadows at all—it is all sunshine. The background may be a little dark, but it will only serve the better to reveal, in all their brilliancy and beauty, the sunlight of generous sympathy which falls upon it.

While proceeding from the center to the left, where our division was hotly engaged with the enemy, among the many wounded that were being assisted to the rear was a little group—three soldiers—all of whom were severely wounded, and who were slowly wending their way from the front. They were linked arm in arm, the center one being supported by the other two. The soldier thus supported by his comrades was in a sad state. His face was covered with blood, and it seemed, at first sight, as if part of his head had been torn away. On coming nearer I noticed that he must be blind; for, if his eyes were not shot out, his forehead seemed to be so broken and torn that it was lying in a livid mass over his face, exposing, at the same time, his brain. One of the two soldiers who were assisting him had his left arm rudely tied up with a handkerchief, while with his right he supported his wounded comrade in the center. The man on the right was wounded in his right hand, and was evidently suffering very much. With his left hand under his comrade's right, he was rendering what assistance he could to get him along. And thus those two noble men, faint with the loss of blood—one with a rifle-ball in his arm, and the other with part of his hand shot away—were assisting a third, whose head had been partially laid open by a piece of shell, and who was thereby rendered helpless.

"I wish you would dress this man's wounds," said one of them, as I came up; "he can't go much further unless something is done for him."

We got him into a fence-corner, and laid him down

on the grass. I washed the blood and dust from his face, replaced the fragment of skull that was still attached by a small piece of flesh, and bandaged the whole. While having his wound dressed he uttered not a single complaint—hardly a groan. Giving him a little wine, I told him he must remain where he was, and I would have an ambulance sent to convey him from the field.

"Now, John, you get your wound dressed," said the one whose fingers were shot away.

"No; I can wait," said his comrade. "You get your hand seen to—guess you 're suffering more than I am."

"No, I aint. I can wait better than you," said the other; but he had to clench his teeth as he spoke, nevertheless.

"Let me look at your hand," said I; for I noticed he was suffering like a martyr.

Two fingers were gone, a third was cut nearly in two, the fourth was barely touched. One rifle-ball had done the whole work.

"You need more done for you, my brave fellow, than I can do for you here. However, we can try to make you a little more comfortable."

Having put a temporary dressing upon his mutilated hand, and spoken an encouraging word to him, I turned to his comrade in bravery and generosity.

"O, it's only a flesh wound, that's all!" said he. "I'll soon be all right again; but then I'd better take care of it, I suppose."

It was only a flesh wound, but it had bled profusely, and, poor fellow, he was quite faint. I noticed he grew deathly pale as he laid his head against a fence-rail for support. I got some water for him, and he revived considerably; and, in a short time, I got his arm dressed temporarily. The truth was, that those men had nerved themselves with the determination to assist their helpless and apparently mortally wounded comrade, and had exerted themselves to the utmost verge of human endurance in their generous work, and they both sank utterly exhausted with the efforts they had put forth, and with their own pain and loss of blood. In a short time I succeeded in getting two of them into an ambulance, the third walked on without any assistance.

I never met with those men again, probably never will; but they preached to me the noblest and most eloquent sermon on true manliness and Christian effort and true self-sacrificing generosity I ever heard; and if all the professing soldiers of Christ engaged on the great field of spiritual strife would exhibit the same generous feeling, the same heroic endurance, in behalf of the unfortunate and suffering, what a worldful of unselfish, Christ-like love and effort would there be! Whatever may be our circumstances in life, we can all do something for Christ and humanity. If we have nothing to give for temporal relief, we can at least speak a kind word, and manifest a sympathizing spirit. If we can not go forth in the front ranks of the conflict for righteousness and truth, we can at least encourage those who do, and we will find it frequently the case that words of sympathy and encouragement do more good than gold or silver.

Encouragement.

In the midst of all that is fair and promising in our country, there are not a few good people who are disposed to look upon the dark side of things, and, even now, when the rebellion may be said to be crushed, see only handwritings of wrath against us as a people. In the midst of rejoicing, they are sad, and they spread sackcloth over all the bright and unmistakable tokens of God's favor. They say, and they say truly, that the entire nation has sinned most woefully; but the inferences drawn from this are as incorrect as they are gloomy. May not a people repent? Have there not been practical manifestations on the part of the people, and of the Government, to establish righteousness and truth in the land? Has not our starry banner been washed of the last and the least foul spot of oppression? And is there not in sentiment and action an infinite gulf between the slave oligarchy of the South and the nation—yes, the nation at large? If the great heart of the North has not already been touched by God's finger, and caused to pulsate, more or less, in harmony with the great and good principles of Jehovah's own government, then the country is gone beyond hope of redemption. For, grant that the North has been corrupt, and, in many instances, has connived with wrong, the South has for long years been festering with the foulest of moral abominations—abominations deliberately and systematically pursued, and which entered into and influenced all phases of social life. If the North has not yet reached the broad and elevated platform of a Christian civilization, then the

South has been sunk in the very depths of practical heathenism, and has been guilty of the crimes of deliberate and persistent barbarism—crimes rendered all the more wicked and inexcusable from their being committed in this enlightened age of the world. If a requisite number of righteous men can not be found in the North to save the country from the fate of Sodom and Gomorrah—a fate that all the crowned despots and aristocrats of Europe have desired to befall us—the South assuredly can not produce them, for social life in the South has been Sodom itself. And, wicked as the North is—and wicked we have been, and, alas! still are—yet, in our efforts for truth and freedom, if God can not in mercy smile upon us, then we may rest assured that the perfections of his character, the principles of his moral government, his providential dealings with the children of men in all past ages, and the declarations of his own Word, forbid the thought that he can smile upon the South in her insane and God-dishonoring effort to establish human bondage on this continent; and therefore, in either case, the fate of the nation is sealed.

But, far from taking any such dark views of this matter, we ought to feel the rather encouraged and hopeful. The truth is, that the nation, as such, is now in a more healthful, hopeful state, in all respects—in political purity, ardent patriotism, Christian beneficence, financial soundness, and in all that pertains to national greatness—than at any time since the first stone of Freedom's temple was laid by our Revolutionary fathers. True, a few years ago, there were no tumults nor wars in our midst. No armed battalions were seen going forth to engage in deadly strife, with those born under, and protected by, the same dear old flag. All was order and peace; but it was the peace of moral death. It was like the order, decorum, and stillness which reigned among the dry bones which lay bleaching in Ezekiel's Valley of Vision. There was little to disturb the harmony and peace which prevailed while moral and political death was holding high carnival, and feeding on the very heart of the nation. But as the ancient Seer of Israel was commanded to prophesy, and say, "O, ye dry bones, hear the word of the Lord," so likewise has the awakening, quickening voice of God been sounding through the nation, and a strange, fearful shaking has been the result. The nation has been aroused as no nation has ever been aroused before, and the noise we have heard, and the tumults we have seen, have been the noise and tumult of our country's resurrection. From one end of the land to the other, from the Atlantic to the Pacific, we have heard the din and tumult of an exceeding great army aroused from inglorious and fatal slumber by the reveillé of Jehovah; and that army, under his protection and leadership, has been rolling back the proud and defiant hosts of robbery and oppression. True, the confusion has been great, and the sky overhead has been dark, and the lurid flash of the thunderbolts of war has been seen athwart the gloom, and men's hearts have often been failing them for fear. And there are many stricken hearts, too, in the land, that will never be healed till they drink of the crystal streams of glory; and there are many eyes dim with tears, that will never be bright till they look upon the face of Jesus, and the fadeless beauties of the better land; but, notwithstanding all these, God has been working in a most signal manner for the honor of his name, and the glory of his power in the redemption of our country, and for freedom throughout the world. What we are in special need of just now is faith in God—faith in his wisdom to guide and govern the world; faith in his power to overturn every opposing institution that retards the progress of his kingdom upon earth; faith in his unwavering love for the children of men, and his benevolent designs in their behalf; and faith in his declarations concerning the purposes and plans of the wicked, that they shall all be defeated, and it shall be seen that verily God reigneth.

> "Deep in unfathomable mines,
> Of never failing skill,
> He treasures up his bright designs
> And works his sovereign will."

But this is not all. It is refreshing to know that there are, in our country, thousands and tens of thousands of noble, generous souls who feel, more than ever, that the greatest wealth is the wealth of good deeds, kind words, and noble and ennobling effort in behalf of righteousness and truth; and that, while sordid selfishness has been looking at every political change or public calamity with a view to extortion and self-aggrandizement, there has been seen, among the masses of the people, the development of a purer and nobler spirit. This is one of the most hopeful signs of the times—one of the most beautiful tints in the rainbow of hope and promise which has been, and still is, spanning the moral and political horizon in our days of gloom and peril. And may it not be that God has been working out a great problem that has often baffled and perplexed the earnest men and women of our land; namely, how the people were to be educated for, and brought to stand upon, the broad platform of Christian generosity and beneficence! How the all-devouring lust of gain, which, for years, had been threatening our religious and benevolent enterprises, could be subdued, and a healthy, high-toned spirit of Christian liberality be infused into the masses of the people! Our God is a wonder-working God, and it will be seen, by the present generation, that he does cause the wrath of man to praise him—not only by confounding the plans of the wicked, and bringing their devices to naught, defeating them in their efforts to protect and perpetuate wrong and outrage—but also by bringing out the latent principles of Christ-like love and Christ-like beneficence on the part of his own Church and people. Since this war commenced there has been more genuine liberality, more hearty, earnest charity exhibited by the people at large, than ever has been known in the history of the nation. The truth is, that the world has never furnished such instances of patient, persevering labor—such perfect outgushings of genuine sympathy—in behalf of a nation's soldiers, as the loyal states of our nation have exhibited during these years of war and bloodshed. Hundreds of thousands of the noble women of our land have been plying the busy needle, rolling bandages, making lint, preparing fruits, wines, and other delicacies and comforts, for the sick and wounded in the field and hospital; and, although the calls upon their labors and charities have been incessant, they have met every demand with a cheerfulness and zeal which tell how deeply they have been interested in the nation's great struggle. All honor to them for their noble and persevering efforts! Perhaps my position and experience in the army enable me to speak more decidedly as to the good the various aid societies have accomplished, and are accomplishing, through the Sanitary and Christian Commissions; for, in numberless instances, I have been witness to the fact that the sick and wounded would have been entirely destitute but for the timely aid of those blessed institutions.

May the fountains of practical benevolence, so fully and gloriously opened up during the days of tumult and war, not be like the rain-season wells of the desert, which furnish refreshment to the weary traveler only for a short time, but may they be like the perennial fountains whose sources are deep in the mountain's bosom, which flow on and flow ever, as well in summer as in winter, and around which are the green verdure, the blooming flowers, and the cooling shade of the stately palm. Let us cherish, then, faith in God, and work with him and for him earnestly, lovingly, perseveringly. LET US WORK "UNTIL THE SPIRIT BE POURED UPON US FROM ON HIGH, AND THE WILDERNESS BE A FRUITFUL FIELD, AND THE FRUITFUL FIELD BE COUNTED FOR A FOREST. THEN JUDGMENT WILL DWELL IN THE WILDERNESS, AND RIGHTEOUSNESS REMAIN IN THE FRUITFUL FIELD; AND THE WORK OF RIGHTEOUSNESS WILL BE PEACE; AND THE EFFECT OF RIGHTEOUSNESS, QUIETNESS AND ASSURANCE FOREVER."

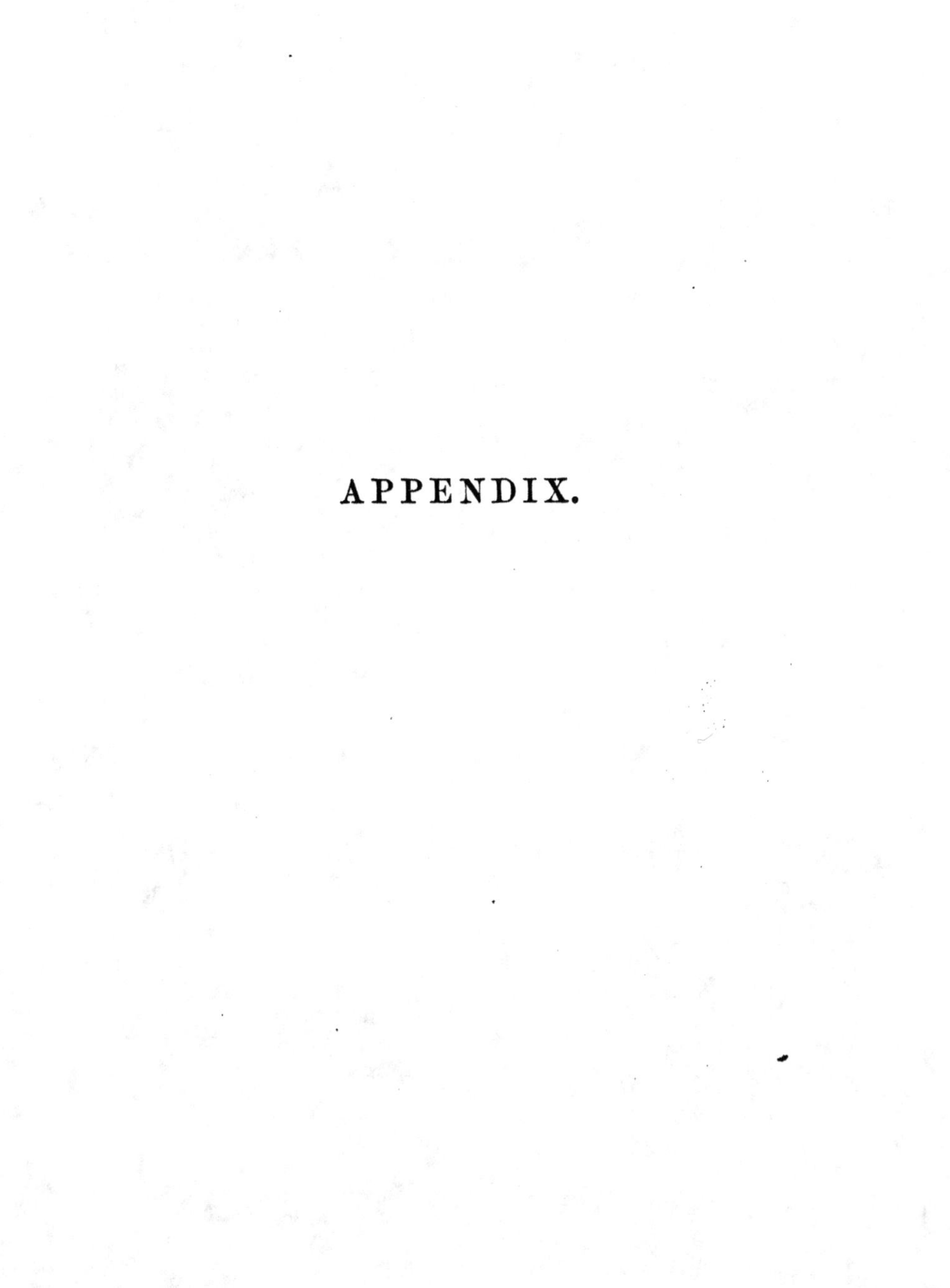

APPENDIX.

APPENDIX.

THERE are some matters of a more limited, or, perhaps, local interest, with which it has been considered not best to burden the main body of this work, but which might be thrown into an appendix. There are many points of historic interest connected with the Eleventh Ohio Regiment which its members, and those who had friends in any way connected with it, would be glad to see placed on record. Neither to avoid these, nor yet unduly obtrude them on the attention of the general reader, has been the aim of the author. Nevertheless, he has too much respect for his comrades in arms, with whom he was associated in the camp and on the battlefield, and he has too many endearing remembrances of their valor and patriotism, as well as of their respect and kindness, to exclude from this little work a tribute of praise, or, if nothing more, an expression of kind remembrance.

When this part of the work was first projected, the intention was to have a list of all who belonged to the regiment so arranged that the military history of each man would be given, but this plan had, finally, to be abandoned, as it would have swelled the work far beyond any reasonable size. A list of all the commissioned officers and non-commissioned staff is given, as also a list of those killed in action or who died of disease.

Field and Staff, Eleventh Regiment O. V. I.

C. A. De Villiers, Colonel. Commissioned July 6, 1861. Dishonorably dismissed the service, in accordance with the sentence of a general court-martial, approved by General Frémont in General Order No. 16, April 4, 1862.

Augustus H. Coleman, Colonel. Promoted from Captain of Co. D to Major, on original organization of regiment. Promoted to Lieutenant-Colonel January 9, 1862. Promoted to Colonel April, 1862. Killed in action at Antietam, September 17, 1862.

P. P. Lane, Colonel. Promoted from Captain of Company K. Date of commission as Colonel, September 17, 1862. Resigned and relieved from duty November 3, 1863.

Joseph W. Frizell, Lieutenant-Colonel. Commissioned July 6, 1861. Resigned and relieved from duty December 21, 1861.

Ogden Street, Lieutenant-Colonel. Promoted from Captain of Co. C September 17, 1862. Was in command of regiment from November 3, 1863, till regiment was mustered out at the expiration of term of service, June 21, 1864.

Lyman J. Jackson, Major. Promoted from Captain of Co. —, Thirty-first Regiment O. V. I., to Major Eleventh Reg. O. V. I., January 9, 1862. Resigned and relieved from duty November 4, 1862.

Asa Higgins, Major. Promoted from Captain of Co. G October 1, 1862. Was mustered out with regiment, June 21, 1864.

J. F. Gabriel, Surgeon. Commissioned July 7, 1861. Resigned and relieved from duty September 21, 1862.

J. McCurdy, Surgeon. Promoted from Assistant Surgeon of Twenty-third Regiment O. V. I. to Surgeon Eleventh Regiment, October 15, 1862. Appointed Medical Director, June, 1864.

H. Z. Gill, Assistant Surgeon. Commissioned July 7, 1861. Resigned and relieved from duty July 29, 1862.

S. Hudson, Assistant Surgeon. Commissioned July 9, 1862. Resigned September 26, 1862.

A. C. McNutt, Assistant Surgeon. Commissioned July 11, 1862. Resigned February 8, 1863.

N. H. SIDWELL, Assistant Surgeon. Commissioned December 1, 1862. Mustered out with regiment, June 21, 1864.

GEORGE W. DUBOIS, Chaplain. Commissioned July 10, 1861. Resigned and relieved from duty January 31, 1862.

W. W. LYLE, Chaplain. Commissioned January 31, 1862. Mustered out with regiment, June 21, 1864.

J. H. HORTON, Adjutant. Commissioned June 14, 1861. Resigned and relieved from duty June 16, 1862.

J. E. ALEXANDER, Adjutant, *vice* Horton, resigned. Promoted from First Lieutenant, Co. B, June 12, 1862. Mortally wounded at the battle of Bull Run, Va., August 27, 1862. Subsequently died in United States Hospital, Alexandria, Va., October 20, 1862.

ROBERT C. MORRIS, Adjutant, *vice* Alexander, died of wounds. Promoted from Second Lieutenant of Co. K June 16, 1863. Promoted to Captain September 9, 1863. Assigned to Co. I December 3, 1863. Mustered out with regiment, June 21, 1864.

MILTON H. WILSON, Adjutant, *vice* Morris, promoted. Promoted from Sergeant-Major September 9, 1863. Mustered out with regiment, June 21, 1864.

J. D. SHANNON, R. Q. M. Appointed Regimental Quarter-master July 7, 1861. Resigned August 16, 1861.

E. H. PRICE, R. Q. M., *vice* Shannon, resigned. Appointed from First Lieutenant of Co. C August 5, 1861. Relieved from duty as Regimental Quarter-master December 18, 1861.

J. W. MCABEE, R. Q. M. Commissioned November 29, 1861. Entered on duty as Regimental Quarter-master December 18, 1861. Appointed as Topographical Engineer on General Turchin's Staff, ——, 1864. Mustered out with regiment, June 21, 1864.

Non-commissioned Staff.

T. K. MITCHELL, Sergeant-Major. Appointed July 20, 1861. Relieved from duty January 3, 1862. Reappointed May 23, 1862. Died of wounds, received by accidental discharge of rifle, January 9, 1863.

P. R. WAY, Sergeant-Major. Appointed January 3, 1862. Relieved from duty May 23, 1862.

M. H. WILSON, Sergeant-Major, *vice* Mitchell, died of wounds. Promoted from Quarter-master Sergeant January 11, 1863. Promoted to Adjutant September 9, 1862.

D. C. Stubbs, Sergeant-Major, *vice* Wilson, promoted. Appointed from Sergeant Co. I January 1, 1864.

O. Crissinger, Quarter-master Sergeant, *vice* Wilson, promoted. Appointed from Co. C January 11, 1863.

T. L. Winslow, Commissary Sergeant. Appointed March 1, 1862. Promoted to Second Lieutenant —— —, 1864. Mustered out with regiment, June 21, 1864.

Joshua Harden, Hospital Steward. Appointed —— —, 1861 Mustered out with regiment, June 21, 1864.

Henry Hart, Drum-Major. Appointed July 20, 1861. Discharged, on account of disability, January 25, 1864.

Company Officers.

C. J. Childs, Captain Company A. Appointed June 14, 1861. Resigned May 5, 1862.

T. L. P. De Frees, Captain Co. B. Appointed June 20, 1861. Resigned August 26, 1861.

O. Street, Captain Co. C. Appointed July 1, 1861. Promoted to Lieutenant-Colonel September 17, 1862.

J. V. Curtis, Captain Co. D. Appointed June 19, 1861. Resigned April 25, 1862.

W. L. Douglass, Captain Co. E. Appointed December 19, 1861. Resigned September —, 1862.

S. Johnson, Captain Co. F. Appointed June 14, 1861. Resigned September 17, 1861.

R. B. Harlan, Captain Co. G. Appointed July 9, 1861. Resigned July 19, 1861.

Asa Higgins, Captain Co. G. Appointed July 23, 1861. Promoted to Major October 1, 1862.

John C. Drury, Captain Co. H. Appointed June 17, 1861. Resigned December 19, 1861. Subsequently reëntered the service in the Ninety-fourth Regiment O. V. I., and was killed in action at Perryville, Ky.

J. P. Staley, Captain Co. I. Appointed August 9, 1862. Resigned June 16, 1863.

P. P. Lane, Captain Co. K. Appointed July 7, 1861. Promoted to Colonel September 17, 1862.

G. W. Hatfield, Captain Co. A. Appointed January 9, 1862. Promoted from First Lieutenant. Resigned —— —, 1863.

A. Duncan, Captain Co. B. Appointed August 26, 1861. Promoted from First Sergeant. Mustered out with regiment, June 21, 1864.

E. H. Price, Captain Co. C. Appointed September 17, 1862. Promoted from First Lieutenant. Mustered out with regiment, June 21, 1864.

H. L. Seymour, Captain Co. D. Appointed April 18, 1862. Resigned ——, 1862.

L. G. Brown, Captain Co. E. Appointed August 2, 1862. Mustered out with regiment, June 21, 1864.

S. Teverbaugh, Captain Co. F. Appointed November 12, 1861. Promoted from First Lieutenant. Mustered out with regiment, June 21, 1864.

A. H. Chapman, Captain Co. G. Appointed October 1, 1862. Promoted from First Lieutenant. Resigned ——, 1864.

J. B. Weller, Captain Co. H. Appointed May 1, 1862. Promoted from First Lieutenant. Resigned April 18, 1863, on account of disability from wounds received at Antietam.

R. C. Morris, Captain Co. I. Appointed September 9, 1863. Promoted from First Lieutenant and Adjutant. Mustered out with regiment, June 21, 1864.

G. Johnson, Captain Co. K. Appointed September 16, 1862. Promoted from First Lieutenant. Resigned, on account of disability from wounds, December 20, 1863.

E. C. Jordan, Captain Co. A. Appointed October 3, 1863. Promoted from First Lieutenant. Mustered out with regiment, June 21, 1864.

D. L. Layman, Captain Co. D. Appointed November 20, 1862. Promoted from First Lieutenant. Mustered out with regiment, June 21, 1864.

D. K. Curtis, Captain Co. H. Appointed October 3, 1863. Killed in battle at Mission Ridge, Ga., November 25, 1863.

C. Longley, First Lieutenant Co. A. Appointed October 3, 1863. Mustered out with regiment, June 21, 1864.

J. D. Shannon, First Lieutenant Co. B. Appointed June 20, 1861. Resigned August 23, 1861.

W. K. Young, First Lieutenant Co. C. Appointed October 1, 1862. Resigned May 25, 1863.

Silas Roney, First Lieutenant Co. E. Appointed December 19, 1861. Resigned May 11, 1862.

N. S. McAbee, First Lieutenant Co. F. Appointed November 12, 1861. Resigned June 12, 1862.

C. B. Lindsey, First Lieutenant Co. G. Appointed July 23, 1861. Resigned April 19, 1862.

C. N. Hoagland, First Lieutenant Co. H. Appointed June 17 1861. Resigned November 12, 1861.

F. M. Anderton, First Lieutenant Co. I. Appointed August 9, 1862. Resigned March 22, 1863.

T. L. Steward, First Lieutenant Co. I. Appointed August 8, 1863. Promoted from Second Lieutenant. Mustered out with regiment, June 21, 1864.

G. P. Darrow, First Lieutenant Co. K. Appointed July 7, 1861. Resigned November 5, 1861.

C. J. Cottingham, First Lieutenant Co. K. Appointed December 26, 1861. Resigned —— —, 1862.

J. E. Alexander, First Lieutenant Co. B. Appointed August 26, 1861. Appointed Adjutant June 12, 1862. Died of wounds received in action, October 20, 1862.

J. H. Horton, First Lieutenant Co. —. Appointed June 14, 1861. Appointed Adjutant July 19, 1861.

C. J. McClure, First Lieutenant Co. K. Appointed June 5, 1862. Resigned March 15, 1864.

T. Cox, First Lieutenant Co. K. Appointed June 17, 1862.

M. L. Edwards, First Lieutenant Co. C. Appointed November 20, 1862. Mustered out with regiment, June 21, 1864.

J. C. Kiefaber, First Lieutenant Co. D. Appointed October 3, 1863. Mustered out with regiment, June 21, 1864.

G. E. Peck, First Lieutenant Co. E. Appointed August 20, 1862. Killed at Mission Ridge, November 25, 1863.

G. S. Swain, First Lieutenant Co. F. Appointed October 3, 1863. Promoted from Second Lieutenant. Mustered out with regiment, June 21, 1864.

P. A. Arthur, First Lieutenant Co. G. Appointed September 17, 1862. Mustered out with regiment, June 21, 1864.

C. P. Achuff, First Lieutenant Co. H. Appointed September 17, 1862. Resigned May 2, 1863.

A. L. Conklin, Second Lieutenant Co. K. Appointed June 16, 1862. Promoted from Sergeant. Mustered out with regiment, June 21, 1864.

J. W. La Rue, Second Lieutenant Co. A. Appointed June 14, 1861. Resigned September 1, 1861.

J. G. Buckingham, Second Lieutenant Co. B. Appointed November 29, 1862. Resigned June 1, 1863.

G. S. Hardenbrook, Second Lieutenant Co. B. Appointed June 23, 1863. Mustered out with regiment, June 21, 1864.

H. M. Wilson, Second Lieutenant Co. C. Appointed July 1, 1861. Resigned November 10, 1861.

W. Crubaugh, Second Lieutenant Co. C. Appointed December 26, 1861. Resigned —— —, 186–.

S. A. Collins, Second Lieutenant Co. E. Appointed June 3, 1862. Resigned —— —, 186–.

W. H. H. Gahagan, Second Lieutenant Co. D. Appointed June 19, 1861. Resigned October 28, 1861.

S. Williams, Second Lieutenant Co. D. Appointed December 26, 1861. Resigned April 19, 1862.

L. C. Holabird, Second Lieutenant Co. D. Appointed June 5, 1862. Transferred to another department May 5, 1863.

J. E. Elliott, Second Lieutenant Co. E. Appointed December 19, 1861. Resigned June 12, 1862.

W. M. Culbertson, Second Lieutenant Co. E. Appointed May 1, 1862.

John Roney, Second Lieutenant Co. G. Appointed November 1, 1862. Mustered out with regiment.

Joseph Pearson, Second Lieutenant Co. H. Appointed October 20, 1862. Mustered out with regiment.

List of Deceased Officers and Soldiers, Eleventh Regiment O. V. I.

Lieutenant-Colonel A. H. Coleman. Killed at Antietam, Md., September 17, 1862.

Adjutant John E. Alexander. Died of wounds received at Bull Run, Va., October 20, 1862.

First Lieutenant G. E. Peck. Killed at Mission Ridge, November 25, 1863.

Captain D. K. Curtis. Killed in action at Mission Ridge, November 25, 1863.

Charles Allen, Company A. Killed at Mountain Cove, Va., August 25, 1861. Buried at Hawk's Nest.

John Hammond, Co. A. Killed in action at Antietam, Md., September 17, 1862.

Aubrey Hatfield, Co. A. Died of disease, October 11, 1861. Remains sent to his home.

Adolphus L. Schwartz, Co. A. Died of disease, October 5, 1861. Buried at Gallipolis, O.,

John Wroe, Co. A. Killed at Cotton Hill, Va., November 10, 1861.

Daniel Banion, Co. B. Killed while on picket at Cotton Hill, Va., November 10, 1861.

Robert Batchelor, Co. B. Killed at Gauley Bridge, Va., November 10, 1861.

James Roach, Co. B. Killed in action at Mountain Cove, Va., August 20, 1861.

Stephen B. McDaniel, Co. C. Died of disease, October 19, 1861. Buried at Gallipolis, O.

Henry Brown, Co. C. Died of disease, August 9, 1861. Buried at Gallipolis, O.

John Johnson, Co. C. Died of disease, November 20, 1863. Buried at Summerville, Va.

James McCreary, Co. C. Killed in action at South Mountain, Md., September 14, 1862.

John Sinnings, Co. C. Died of disease, November 8, 1861. Buried at Gallipolis, O.

John C. Travis, Co. C. Died of disease, September 11, 1862. Buried at Washington, D. C.

John V. Wolverton, Co. D. Died of disease, September 20, 1861. Buried at Fayetteville, Va.

Archibald Darrow, Co. D. Died of disease, September 9, 1861. Buried at Troy, O.

John L. Palmerston, Co. D. Died of disease, September 15, 1862. Buried at Washington, D. C.

Roswel S. Wagner, Co. E. Died of disease at Raleigh, Va., June 7, 1862. Remains sent to his home, Troy, O.

John Baker, Co. E. Killed at South Mountain, Md., September 14, 1862.

Frederick Henry, Co. E. Died of disease, February 18, 1862. Buried at Point Pleasant, Va.

James Westfall, Co. E. Died of disease, February 7, 1863. Buried at Point Pleasant, Va.

Oliver S. Bolser, Co. F. Died of disease, January 21, 1862. Remains sent to his home.

George W. Kirk, Co. F. Died of disease, March 3, 1862. Remains sent to his home.

James Wolfe, Co. F. Died of wounds received at Antietam, Md., September 18, 1862. Buried at Frederick, Md.

James H. Channell, Co. G. Died of disease, November 7, 1861. Remains sent to his home.

John R. Henry, Co. G. Killed at South Mountain, Md., September 14, 1862.

Henry G. Keenan, Co. G. Killed by falling off railroad cars, August 26, 1862.

John G. Smithson, Co. G. Died of disease, August 9, 1861. Buried at Gauley Bridge, Va.

Solomon R. Byrkett, Co. H. Died of disease, February 14, 1862. Buried at Troy, O.

Ludwig Hartstein, Co. H. Killed at Rich Creek, Va., August 25, 1861.

Andrew F. Thompson, Co. H. Died of wounds received at South Mountain, Md., October 8, 1862.

Thomas Vandyne, Co. H. Died of wounds received at Tyler Mountain, Va., July 25, 1861.

Jacob M. Wentz, Co. H. Killed at South Mountain, Md., September 14, 1862.

John Boss, Co. K. Killed at South Mountain, Md., September 14, 1862.

William A. Fowler, Co. K. Died of disease at Point Pleasant, Va., January 24, 1862.

Benjamin Stearns, Co. K. Died of disease at Cincinnati, O., July 15, 1861.

John Schlosser, Co. K. Killed at South Mountain, Md., September 14, 1862.

John Werner, Co. K. Killed at Antietam, Md., September 17, 1862.

Corporal Charles W. Wright, Co. K. Killed at Antietam, Md., September 17, 1862.

Jacob Beck, Co. I Died of disease at Summerville, Va., December 27, 1862.

Sergeant-Major Thomas K. Mitchell. Killed, by accidental discharge of a rifle, January 9, 1863.

James Melaney, Co. D. Died of disease, March 12, 1863. Buried at Carthage, Tenn.

Perry Carter, Co. D. Died of disease, April 19, 1863. Buried at Carthage, Tenn.

John R. Dixon, Co. G. Died of disease, April 12, 1863. Remains sent to his home.

Jesse C. Bartholomew, Co. H. Died of disease, April 22, 1863. Buried at Carthage, Tenn.

Joseph P. Weller, Co. I. Died of disease, February 23, 1863. Buried at Nashville, Tenn.

Frederick Lucke, Co. B. Died of disease, May 22, 1863. Buried at Carthage, Tenn.

Charles Segar, Co. D. Died of disease, May 18, 1863. Buried at Carthage, Tenn.

George Anderson, Co. D. Died of disease, May 29, 1863. Buried at Carthage, Tenn.

Henry C. Day, Co. A. Died of disease, May 6, 1863. Buried at Nashville, Tenn.

Thomas H. Fall, Co. I. Died of disease, May 17, 1863. Buried at Carthage, Tenn.

Jacob Reif, Co. K. Died of disease, May 19, 1863. Buried at Columbus, O.

Rensselaer Carson, Co. K. Died of disease, May 25, 1863. Buried at Carthage, Tenn.

Henry Baudendistle, Co. A. Killed by accidental bursting of a shell, June 20, 1863.

J. F. Colther, Co. E. Died of disease, June 3, 1863. Buried at Carthage, Tenn.

Ephraim A. Morrow, Co. F. Died of disease, June 2, 1863. Buried at Carthage, Tenn.

J. Funk, Co. H. Died of disease, May 2, 1863. Buried at Louisville, Ky.

J. F. Kemper, Co. I. Died of disease, June 5, 1863. Buried at Carthage, Tenn.

Sergeant Thomas Shain, Co. I. Died of disease, June 25, 1863. Buried at Carthage, Tenn.

George Williams, Co. A. Died of wounds received by accidental bursting of a shell, July 21, 1863.

William Allen, Co. K. Died of disease, July 19, 1863. Buried at Murfreesboro, Tenn.

JOSEPH WYRICK, Co. A. Died of wounds received by accidental explosion, August 14, 1863. Remains sent to his home.

MARTIN SCHEELER, Co. B. Died of disease, August 15, 1863. Buried at University Place, Tenn.

Corporal DAVID L. BROSIUS, Co. C. Died of disease, August 8, 1863. Remains sent to Salem, O.

FREDERICK KUMMER, Co. B. Died of disease, September 20, 1863, and left on field at Chickamauga, Ga. Died in an ambulance during battle.

PATRICK MURPHY, Co. B. Killed on a reconnoissance, at Chattanooga, Tenn., September 24, 1863.

Sergeant GEORGE CART, Co. D. Killed at Chickamauga, Ga., September 20, 1863.

CHARLES GEHRCH, Co. E. Died of disease at Trenton, Ga., September 18, 1863.

Corporal WILLIAM B. CROWELL, Co. I. Killed in action at Chickamauga, Ga., September 20, 1863.

PETER KEWEN, Co. I. Killed in action at Church Mound, Ga., September 17, 1863.

JOSEPH BRINKE, Co. K. Taken prisoner at Chickamauga, Ga., and died at Andersonville, Ga., —— —, 1864.

MARION POWELL, Co. K. Killed in action at Chickamauga, Ga., September 20, 1863.

Sergeant JACOB R. STERRITT, Co. D. Died of wounds received in action at Chickamauga, Ga., October 22, 1863.

GEORGE S. TAPLEY, Co. B. Killed at South Mountain, Md., September 14, 1862.

MANVILLE HOGLE, Co. B. Killed at Mission Ridge, November 25, 1863.

JOHN H. PECK, Co. I. Died of disease at Chattanooga, Tenn., October 5, 1863.

JACOB H. BOON, Co. H. Died of wounds received in action at Mission Ridge, December 9, 1863.

E. DOLD, Co. K. Died of disease, October 18, 1863.

CONRAD SCHEELER, Co. B. Killed in action at Mission Ridge, November 25, 1863.

LOUIS BOON, Co. C. Died of disease at Louisville, Ky., April 19, 1864.

SEBASTIAN CALLAHAN, Co. C. Died of disease, February 12, 1864.

W. Brandon, Co. D. Drowned at Gallipolis, O., February 25, 1862.

Elias Bainey, Co. D. Killed in action at Mission Ridge, November 25, 1863.

John Vancamp, Co. D. Died of wounds received in action, October 22, 1863.

Samuel Lippincott Co. F. Died of disease, November 10, 1863.

John B. Roberts, Co. G. Died of disease at Nashville, Tenn., January 30, 1864.

Hiram Partlow, Co. H. Died of disease at Nashville, Tenn., April 4, 1864.

Michael Hoath, Co. K. Killed in action at Mission Ridge, November 25, 1863.

Marion B. Wolf, Co. I. Died of wounds received in action, December 6, 1863.

Simeon Shidler, Co. I. Died of wounds received in action, December 13, 1863.

G. L. Murphy, Co. I. Died of wounds received in action, November 26, 1863.

Noah Sams, Co. I. Died of disease, February 27, 1863.

George Smith, Co. K. Taken prisoner at Chickamauga, and died at Andersonville, Ga., —— —, 1864.

William Reamer, Co. H. Taken prisoner at Chickamauga, September 20, 1863. Died at Andersonville, Ga.

Charles Martin, Co. A. Taken prisoner at Chickamauga, September 20, 1863. Died at Danville, Ga.

Isaac Avery, Co. B. Taken prisoner at Chickamauga, September 20, 1863. Died at Danville, Ga.

William Cart, Co. D. Taken prisoner at Chickamauga, September 20, 1863. Died at Andersonville, Ga.

Martin Williams, Co. D. Taken prisoner at Chickamauga, September 20, 1863. Died at Danville, Ga.

W. H. H. Boyle, Co. E. Taken prisoner at Chickamauga, September 20, 1863. Died at Andersonville, Ga.

John Collier, Co. G. Taken prisoner at Chickamauga, September 20, 1863. Died at Andersonville, Ga.

Henry McKnight, Co. G. Taken prisoner at Chickamauga, September 20, 1863. Died at Andersonville, Ga.

John Hicks, Co. G. Taken prisoner at Chickamauga, September 20, 1863. Died at Andersonville, Ga.

John Carbondale, Co. H. Taken prisoner at Chickamauga, September 20, 1863. Died at Richmond, Va.

Charles Morris, Co. H. Taken prisoner at Chickamauga, September 20, 1863. Died at Andersonville, Ga.

THE END.

www.ingramcontent.com/pod-product-compliance
Lightning Source LLC
LaVergne TN
LVHW020059110826
845151LV00001B/27